FAIR PLAY

FAIR PLAY

The Ethics of Sport

FOURTH EDITION

Robert L. Simon
Hamilton College

Cesar R. Torres
The College at Brockport,
State University of New York

Peter F. Hager
The College at Brockport,
State University of New York

WESTVIEW PRESS

A MEMBER OF THE PERSEUS BOOKS GROUP

Westview Press was founded in 1975 in Boulder, Colorado, by notable publisher and intellectual Fred Praeger. Westview Press continues to publish scholarly titles and high-quality undergraduate- and graduate-level textbooks in core social science disciplines. With books developed, written, and edited with the needs of serious nonfiction readers, professors, and students in mind, Westview Press honors its long history of publishing books that matter.

Published by Westview Press,
A Member of the Perseus Books Group

Find us on the World Wide Web at www.westviewpress.com.

Every effort has been made to secure required permissions for all text, images, maps, and other art reprinted in this volume.

Westview Press books are available at special discounts for bulk purchases in the United States by corporations, institutions, and other organizations. For more information, please contact the Special Markets Department at the Perseus Books Group, 2300 Chestnut Street, Suite 200, Philadelphia, PA 19103, or call (800) 810-4145, ext. 5000, or e-mail special.markets@perseusbooks.com.

Typset in 10.5 point Minion Pro by the Perseus Books Group

Library of Congress Cataloging-in-Publication Data

Simon, Robert L., 1941–

  Fair play : the ethics of sport / Robert L. Simon, Cesar R. Torres, Peter F. Hager. — Fourth edition.

    pages cm

  Includes bibliographical references and index.

  ISBN 978-0-8133-4920-6 (paperback) — ISBN 978-0-8133-4921-3 (e-book)
1. Sports—Moral and ethical aspects. 2. Sports—Social aspects. I. Title.

  GV706.3.S56 2014

  796.01—dc23

                                                                    2014003077

10 9 8 7 6 5 4 3 2 1

To our families,
with thanks for their patience and support

Contents

Preface

Sport plays a significant role in the lives of millions of people throughout the world. Many men and women participate actively in sports, and still more are spectators, fans, and critics of sport. Even those who are uninvolved in sports, bored by them, or critical of athletic competition often will be significantly affected by them, either because of their relationships with enthusiasts or, more importantly, because of the impact of sport on our language, thought, and culture.

Because sports are a significant form of social activity that affects the educational system, the economy, and, perhaps, the values of citizens, they raise a wide range of issues, some of which are factual or empirical in character. Social scientists, historians, physicians, and writers have raised many such issues that concern sport. For example, sociologists may be concerned with whether participation in sports affects the participants' values, and psychologists might try to determine what personality features contribute to success or failure in competitive athletics.

In addition to factual and explanatory questions, sports also raise philosophical issues that are conceptual and ethical in nature. Conceptual questions concern how we are to understand the concepts and ideas that apply in the world of sports. What are sports, anyway? How are sports related to rules? Do those who intentionally break the rules of a game even play it, or are they doing something else? Are there different forms of competition in sports? Is it possible to compete against oneself?

Ethical questions raise the moral concerns many of us have about sports. Should sports be accorded the importance our society gives them? Is there too much emphasis on winning and competition? Are college sports getting out of hand? Why shouldn't we cheat in a game if it will bring us a championship? What, if anything, makes the use of steroids to enhance performance in sports unethical? How should men and women be treated in sports if they are to be treated equitably and fairly? Should we be aiming more for excellence in competition among highly skilled athletes, or should we place greater value on more participation? Does the commercialization of sports actually corrupt the game? *Fair Play* examines such questions and evaluates the principles to which thoughtful people might appeal in trying to formulate answers.

Not only are questions in the philosophy of sport important in their own right, but they can also serve as a useful introduction to broader philosophical issues. Most students come to philosophy courses with knowledge of sports, and many have a deep interest in ethical issues raised by sports. This initial interest can serve as a launching pad to introduce students to the nature and value of philosophical inquiry. For example, questions about whether the use of steroids to enhance athletic performance is fair can lead to broad inquiry into the nature of fairness and the just society.

Perhaps most importantly, issues in the philosophy of sport are of great intrinsic interest and are well worth our attention. Philosophical questions force us to stretch our analytical powers to the fullest and question basic presuppositions. Those that arise in the philosophical examination of sports, like any others, require us to test and evaluate fundamental justificatory principles and engage in rigorous critical inquiry.

Readers of earlier editions of this book will find significant changes in the current edition. Most significantly, this is the first edition of *Fair Play* to be a collaborative project. Robert L. Simon, the author of the earlier editions, introduces his coauthors as follows.

> I am extremely happy to have two stellar scholars in the philosophy of sport join me in this project. Cesar R. Torres and Peter F. Hager have written cogently on a great variety of topics bearing on the ethics of sport, ranging from moral issues in youth sports to developing the theories of broad internalism and the quest for excellence that ground much of this book's argument. They bring new perspectives to our discussion and improve the quality of the work immensely. I am proud to have worked with them on this project and am sure our readers will likewise welcome their contributions.

This new edition, although preserving the major approaches and lines of argument of earlier ones, contains significant changes as well. Perhaps what is most essential to this new text is that we have moved the theoretical framework on which we rely, broad internalism and mutualism in competitive athletics, earlier in the text to Chapter 2 so we can more easily apply it in later chapters to concrete issues that arise in sports. We also make clearer the relationship between broad internalism as an approach to justifying ethical claims in sports and mutualism as a theory of competition justifiable on broad internalist grounds. Broad internalism itself is expanded to include aesthetic as well as ethical criteria for evaluation applicable to sports.

Readers of earlier editions will find new examples of ethical disputes in sport, such as "Spygate," the New England Patriots' hacking into the electronic communications on strategy among opposing coaches during the 2007 NFL season, among others. We also preserved key examples discussed in earlier editions whenever doing so advanced our discussion. Among the most significant additions to our philosophical discussions are an examination of William J. Morgan's recent defense of "deep conventionalism" as well as discussions of ethical issues that arise in youth sports and of ethical issues relevant to the behavior of sports fans. Another significant change is the inclusion of study questions at the end of each chapter.

We hope this edition provides a deeper insight into major issues in the philosophy of sport while remaining accessible to students and others new to the philosophical investigation of sport.

Fair Play never would have been written had it not been for the challenges to our own views of sport put forth by friends, colleagues, and, especially, our students, all of whom have been critical of many of our views but always in a way that has been helpful and insightful. We have also benefited from the tough questions and helpful suggestions posed by colleagues in the International Association for the Philosophy of Sport, including Scott Kretchmar, William J. Morgan, Jan Boxill, and others far too numerous to mention. We are grateful to all of you.

Robert L. Simon would like to thank the original editors of the first edition of this book, Ray O'Connell and Doris Michaels of Prentice-Hall, for their initial encouragement, and Spencer Carr, Sarah Warner, and Karl Yambert of Westview for their support during work on earlier editions of *Fair Play*.

All three of us would especially like to thank Ada Fung, our initial editor for this edition, not only for her work on this edition but also for encouraging us to take this project on in the first place, without which this book would not exist, and her suggestion that collaboration among us would be a terrific way to go. She was right, as we hope our readers will agree. We also want to thank the whole team at Westview, especially editor Elizabeth Hansen, whose good advice helped bring the manuscript to completion, the production and publicity staff, including Victoria Hensen (sales and marketing) and Carolyn Sobczak (project editor), and our copy editor, Josephine Mariea, for their extraordinary efforts on our behalf.

Finally, but of special importance, we want to thank our families for their support and for putting up with the inevitable distractions that kept us in our studies or preoccupied us as times when our attentions should have been focused closer to home. This book could never have been written without their love and encouragement.

We hope our readers enjoy this book as well as learn from it and that we have contributed to continuing critical dialogue on the role of ethics in sport.

≡ 1 ≡

Introduction

THE ETHICS OF SPORT

Robert Simon reports that the following incident not only stimulated his interest in the philosophy of sport but also suggests the kind of issues philosophical inquiry in sport raises:

> I would like to think this book began on an unfortunately not atypical cold and rainy late October day in upstate New York. I had been discussing some of my generally unsuccessful efforts in local golf tournaments with colleagues in the philosophy department and let drop what I thought was an innocuous remark to the effect that although winning isn't everything, it sure beats losing. Much to my surprise my colleagues objected vehemently, asserting that winning means nothing. In their view the recreational aspects of sport, such as having fun and trying to improve—not defeating an opponent—are all that should matter. I soon found myself backed into a corner by this usually unthreatening but now fully aroused assortment of philosophers. Fortunately for me, another colleague entered the office just at the right moment. Struck by the vehemence of the argument, although he had no idea what it was about, he looked at my opponents and remarked, "You folks sure are trying to *win* this argument."[1]

This incident illustrates two important aspects of a philosophical examination of sports. First, issues arise in sports that are not simply empirical questions of psychology, sociology, or some other discipline. Empirical surveys can tell us whether people think winning is important, but they cannot tell us whether that is what people ought to think or whether winning really ought to be regarded as a primary goal of athletics. Second, the incident illustrated that logic could be applied to issues in the philosophy of sport. Thus, at least on the surface it appeared my colleagues were in the logically embarrassing position of trying hard to win an argument to the effect that winning is unimportant. Of course, they might reply that their goal was not winning but the pursuit of truth, but athletes might similarly argue that winning is important because it is a sign of achieving their true goal, excellence.

We will return to the issue of whether winning is important in Chapter 2. For now let us consider further what philosophical inquiry might contribute to our understanding of sport.

Ethical Issues in Sport

Sports play a major, if sometimes unappreciated, role in the lives of Americans. Most of us are exposed to them as children. As a result of our childhood experiences, many of us become participants and retain some affiliation with sports for life, even if only as spectators.[2] Athletes and fans devote a great deal of time and effort to sports at all levels, so much so that their involvement is surely one of their most personally significant activities. The situation is not unique to the United States. Intense interest in sports is virtually a global phenomenon. Whether it is ice hockey in Canada, Scandinavia, or Russia; baseball in Latin America and Japan; or soccer in Europe, South America, and Africa, sports play a major role worldwide. The ancient Greeks, Romans, and Native Americans all valued sport. Indeed, participation in sports and the related activity of play is characteristic of most, if not all, human societies.

Although there is a tendency to regard sports as trivial, it is not clear that such a view is justified. Those critical of sport or bored by athletic competition must admit sport plays a significant role in our lives, even if they believe that dominance is misguided or even harmful. At the very least it is surely worth discovering what it is about sport that calls forth a favorable response among so many people from so many different cultures.

Reflection upon sport raises issues that go beyond the bounds of sport itself. For example, reflection on the value of competition in athletics and the emphasis on winning in much of organized sports may shed light on the ethics of competition in other areas, such as the marketplace. Inquiry into the nature of fair play in sport can also help our understanding of justice in a wider social setting. Indeed, because many of our basic values, such as fairness and honesty, are often absorbed through involvement in athletic competition, inquiry into values in sport may have important general implications in addition to the intrinsic interest it invokes from participants and fans.

Sport raises many kinds of philosophical issues. For example, what is a sport? Football, baseball, and soccer clearly are sports. But some have doubts about golf. What about chess and auto racing? How are sports related to games? Is participation in sport always a form of play? Questions such as these raise issues that go well beyond looking up words in a dictionary. To settle them we will need to rely on a theory of what makes something a game, a sport, or an instance of play. Dictionary definitions often presuppose such theories. But the theories a definition presupposes may be unclear, may leave open how borderline cases are to be thought of, or may just be wrong. For example, one dictionary account of games classifies them as competitive activities. But must all games be competitive? "Playing house" arguably is a game, but is it competitive? What about playing catch?

Some of the most important kinds of philosophical issues that arise in sport are ethical or moral ones; these are the kinds of issues about which this book will be primarily concerned. Some moral issues in sport concern specific actions, often of athletes. For example, the strategic acts referred to as "diving" in soccer and "flopping" in basketball have caused considerable concern for many involved with these sports. These acts call for a player to attempt to deceive officials and others by falling to the ground after an opponent has nearly or negligibly made contact with her in hopes of drawing a foul call and receiving an undeserved compensatory advantage. In soccer, dives are often executed within the opposing team's penalty area so the diver's team will be awarded a penalty kick, a free shot at the goal with only the goalie, who cannot move directionally until the ball is contacted, between her and the goal. In basketball, defenders tend to flop when they believe they can draw a charging foul that will result in a change of possession and nullify the results of a shot in progress. Players on offense will flop on field goal attempts in order to secure an additional free throw if they make the shot or two free throws if they miss it.

To some the above tactics may seem fair enough because both are conventional strategic moves players on either side can employ. But in each of these situations the flopper or diver is using a questionable form of deception to neutralize an opponent's fairly earned advantage and/or gain a high-percentage scoring opportunity. Many in soccer and basketball sporting communities have spoken out against these acts, contending they are not consistent with the spirit of the respective sports and their rules. Their arguments have influenced governing bodies to institute rules and regulations against flopping and diving and to define sanctions for those who continue to use them. Still, questions remain regarding whether such rules and penalties are warranted due to the use of a particular kind of deception. Is the type of deception used in flopping and diving unethical? What makes it different from the legal, creative forms of deception we applaud in sport?

Other ethical issues in sport involve the assessment of rules or policies—for example, many sports organizations' prohibition of competitive athletes' use of performance-enhancing drugs. What justifies this prohibition? Is it because performance-enhancing drugs such as steroids often have harmful side effects? But why shouldn't athletes, especially competent adult athletes, be free to take risks with their bodies? After all, many of us would reject the kind of paternalism that constantly interferes with the pursuit of our goals whenever risky behavior is involved. Think of the dangers inherent in a typical American diet, which contains a high proportion of unhealthy fats and sugars.

Or should performance-enhancing drugs be prohibited because they provide unfair advantages to some of the competitors? Are the advantages any different from those conferred by the legal use of technologically advanced equipment? Moreover, would the advantages still be unfair if all competitors had access to the drug? Defenders of baseball slugger Barry Bonds, who is alleged to have achieved his home run records in part with the assistance of performance-enhancing drugs, claim that some opposing pitchers undoubtedly also used performance enhancers, thus equalizing the competition.

Questions of marketing, sports administration, and the formulation of rules also involve moral issues, although the moral character of the questions raised may not always be obvious. For example, consider whether a rule change ought to be instituted that might make a sport more attractive to fans at the professional or college levels yet diminish the skill or strategy needed to play the game. Some would argue that the designated-hitter rule in American League baseball, which allows teams to replace their usually weak-hitting pitcher with a designated hitter in the batting order, is such a case. The rule may make the game more exciting to the casual fan, who values an explosive offense; however, it may also remove various subtleties from the game, such as the decision about when to remove the pitcher from the game for a pinch hitter or the value of the sacrifice bunt, which weak-hitting pitchers might be capable of executing.

The use of the shootout tiebreaker to force outcomes in National Hockey League (NHL) regular-season games presents a second example of how formal structural changes can have moral effects. Shootouts are essentially one-on-one skills competitions between individual shooters and goalkeepers. Although such tiebreakers may please fans and bring further excitement to NHL ice hockey, they do not require players and teams to utilize other primary offensive and defensive skills that make ice hockey the unique sport it is. The NHL does not use shootouts to decide the outcomes of playoff games, presumably because the league recognizes that the flaws of the practice make it inferior to "sudden death" overtimes, in which ties are broken in actual play. Given the acknowledged flaws of the shootout, why doesn't the NHL accept the ties that naturally occur in regulation time as valid results of regular-season contests, as it once did, rather than padding the standings' point totals of teams who thrive in crowd-pleasing shootouts? Wouldn't a decision to accept ties lead to a more honest assessment of excellence over a full season and a more accurate and fair ranking of playoff contenders for the postseason?

Although the previous two examples are not as obvious moral issues as some of the other examples cited, they do have moral or, at least, evaluative components. They raise questions about the purposes or goals of sport, what social functions it ought to serve, and whether sport has an integrity that ought to be preserved. Similar issues may arise when we consider when technological innovations ought to be permitted in sport and when they ought to be prohibited for making a sport too easy.

At a more abstract level other ethical issues concern the values central to competitive sport itself. Is competition in sport ethically permissible or even desirable, or does it create a kind of selfishness, perhaps an analog of a narrow form of nationalism that says, "My team, right or wrong"? Does the single-minded pursuit of winning, which is apparently central to competition in sport, help promote violent behavior in fans? Does it teach competitors to regard opponents as mere obstacles to be overcome and not as fellow human beings? Is it related to the anger many participants' parents show in youth sports, which culminated in 2001 when an enraged parent killed a hockey coach? What kind of competition in sport can be defended morally, and how great an emphasis on winning is too much?

Questions such as these raise basic issues about the kinds of moral values involved in sport. They are not only about what people think about sport or about what values they hold; rather, these questions are about what people *ought* to think. They require the identification of defensible ethical standards and their application to sport. Critical inquiry into the philosophy of sport consists in formulating and rationally evaluating such standards as well as testing them by seeing how they apply to concrete issues in sport and athletics.

Sport, Philosophy, and Moral Values

Just what does philosophy have to contribute to reflection about sport and moral values? It is evident even to a casual observer of our society that sport in the United States is undergoing intense moral scrutiny. How can philosophy contribute to this endeavor?

Philosophy of Sport

Misconceptions about the nature of philosophy are widespread. According to one story, a philosopher on a domestic flight was asked by his seatmate what he did for a living. He replied, perhaps foolishly, "I'm a philosopher," a statement that is one of the greatest conversation stoppers known to the human race. The seatmate, apparently stupefied by the reply, was silent for several minutes. Finally he turned to the philosopher and remarked, "Oh, and what are some of your sayings?"[3]

The image of the philosopher as the author of wise sayings can perhaps be forgiven, for the word "philosophy" has its roots in the Greek expression meaning "love of wisdom." But wisdom is not necessarily encapsulated in brief sayings that we might memorize before breakfast. The ancient Greek philosopher Socrates provides a different model of philosophic inquiry.

Socrates, who lived in the fifth century BC, did not leave a body of written works behind him; however, we know a great deal about his life and thought primarily through the works of his most influential pupil, Plato. As a young man, Socrates, seeking a mentor from whom to learn, set out to find the wisest man in Greece. According to the story he decided to ask a religious figure, the oracle at Delphi, the identity of the man he was seeking. Much to Socrates's surprise, the oracle informed him that he, Socrates, was the wisest man in Greece. "How can that be?" Socrates must have wondered; after all, he was searching for a wise teacher precisely because he considered himself ignorant.

However, looking at the oracle's answer in light of Plato's presentation of Socrates, we can discern what the oracle meant. In the early Platonic dialogues, such as the *Euthyphro*, Socrates questioned important figures of the day about the nature of piety or the essence of knowledge. Those questioned purported to be experts in the subject under investigation, but Socrates's logical analysis discredited their claim to expertise. These experts not only failed in what they claimed to know but also seemed to have accepted views they had never exposed to critical examination.

Perhaps in calling Socrates the wisest man in Greece the oracle was suggesting that Socrates alone was willing to expose beliefs and principles to critical examination. He did not claim to know what he did not know, but he was willing to learn. He was also not willing to take popular opinion for granted but was prepared to question it.

This Socratic model suggests that the role of philosophy is to examine our beliefs, clarify the principles on which they rest, and subject them to critical examination. For example, in science the role of philosophy is not to compete in formulating and testing empirical hypotheses in biology, chemistry, and physics; rather, philosophers might try to understand in what sense science provides objective knowledge and then examine claims that all knowledge must be scientific. If we adopt such a view of philosophy, the task of the philosophy of sport would be to clarify, systematize, and evaluate the principles that we believe should govern the world of sport. This task might involve a conceptual analysis of such terms as "sport" and "game," an inquiry into the nature of excellence in sport, an ethical evaluation of such principles as "winning should be the only concern of the serious athlete," and an application of ethical analysis to concrete issues, such as disagreement over whether athletes should be permitted to take performance-enhancing drugs.

This book is concerned primarily with ethically evaluating principles that many people associate with sport and employing that analysis to examine specific issues. Its major focus is the nature of principles and values that should apply to sport. Thus, its concern is predominantly normative rather than descriptive—assessing what ought to be rather than describing what is. Perhaps only a few people think of sports as activities that raise serious moral issues. They see sport either as a mere instrument for gaining fame and fortune or as play, something relatively trivial that we do for fun and recreation. However, as the headlines of our daily newspapers show all too frequently, serious moral issues do arise in sports.

But can moral issues be critically examined? Is rational argument even possible in ethics? Aren't moral views just matters of opinion? Can moral principles be rationally evaluated and defended, or are they mere expressions of personal feelings that are not even the sorts of things that can be rationally evaluated or examined?

Ethics and Moral Reasoning

If reasoned ethical discourse is impossible, rational inquiry into ethical issues in sport is impossible. Although we cannot consider all possible reasons for skepticism about whether rationally justifiable moral positions can be developed, one widely cited reason for doubting the objectivity of ethics is relativism. Because relativism is so widely suggested as a basis for skepticism about the role of reason in ethics, a brief discussion of it will prove helpful. The remainder of this book attempts to consider moral issues in sport rationally. Clearly, if this attempt succeeds, it counts as an example of reasoned inquiry in ethics.

Relativism

Perhaps the most widely cited position that rejects the rationality and objectivity of ethical discourse is relativism. In his best-selling book, *The Closing of the American Mind*, Allen Bloom blamed relativism for much of what he saw as the moral and educational decay infecting American universities in the 1980s. According to Bloom "There is one thing a professor can be absolutely certain of: Almost every student entering the university believes, or says he believes, that truth is relative."[4] At the time relativism was so widely supported, according to Bloom, because its opposite was—incorrectly, as we will see—identified with a kind of dogmatic absolutism. This misidentification continues to haunt higher education today, as a positive emphasis on values such as diversity, pluralism, and respect for others and their ideas has influenced many to adopt relativist moral positions so as to avoid appearing intolerant. The price we pay for this misidentification is our inability to formulate, articulate, and defend standards we think are correct. But just what is relativism in ethics?

Actually, no one position has a unique claim to the title of relativism;[5] rather, relativism is more like a family of related positions that share such features as the rejection of a universal outlook or perspective and the suspicion of principles that claim to be true or justifiable for all. According to *descriptive* relativism the moral judgments people make and the values they hold arise from or are relative to their culture, socioeconomic state, or ethnic and religious background. For example, secular culture in the West tends to be permissive of sexual contact between consenting adults, but such contacts have been much more strictly regulated at other times and in other places. In the world of sport some cultures may place more value than others do on winning and less on, say, the aesthetic appeal of play. Different sports communities may recognize different conceptions of fair play. In golf, for example, players are expected to call penalties on themselves and are open to criticism if they do not, whereas in basketball, players defer to the calls of officials. This form of relativism is descriptive in that it is making a factual claim about the origin or empirical basis of our values. It claims to tell us where *in fact* our values originate or describes the practices to which they are thought to apply rather than what we *ought* to think about them.

What does descriptive relativism have to do with whether our moral beliefs and judgments are or can be rationally justified? Some argue that if descriptive relativism is true, there cannot be objectivity or rationality in ethics: no one's ethical judgments would be any more justifiable or correct than anyone else's; rather, people's ethical judgments would be mere subjective claims based on their distinct and different backgrounds. In this view, our moral values are the prejudices we absorbed as children. Perhaps they were presented to us as self-evident truths, but in reality they are only the blinders of our particular culture or group.

Accordingly, some claim that skepticism about the rationality and objectivity of ethics follows from descriptive relativism. Skepticism denies that we can know whether ethical beliefs or claims are justified or whether some are more reasonable and more defensible than others.

This kind of philosophical skepticism needs to be distinguished from an ordinary and perhaps healthy kind of skepticism in ordinary life that cautions us not to accept the opinions of others at face value but rather to examine whether they are well supported. Philosophical skepticism of the kind at issue here denies that our ethical or moral views ever can be well supported or that we can know which moral views are rationally warranted and which are not. Ordinary skepticism cautions us to look for evidence for our views, but philosophical skepticism questions whether it is even possible, even in principle, to provide evidence or rational support for our ethical views.

Others have suggested that descriptive relativism implies not skepticism but rather ethical (value) relativism. Ethical relativism is the view that each culture's moral code is right for that culture. For example, according to ethical relativism repressive sexual practices are morally right for cultures that have such practices embedded in their moral codes but not for more liberal cultures or groups. Applied to sport, such ethical relativism might assert that we ought to follow the values of our own sports communities: if we are golfers, we should call the penalties on ourselves, but if we are basketball players, we should leave it to the referees, even if they make a terrible call in our favor that enables us to win a game.

Ethical relativism differs from skepticism in that skepticism denies that any ethical perspective is more justifiable or reasonable than any other—or denies that we can *know* which perspectives are more justifiable than others. Whereas ethical relativism endorses an ethical view; namely, what is right for you to do is what your culture or community says is right.

What is the significance of these views for the ethical analysis of sport? If skepticism is correct, it follows that we cannot justify any position on questions of ethics that arise in sport, as skepticism denies that any ethical perspective is more justified than any other. For example, we could not justify either the claim that the use of anabolic steroids to enhance performance is warranted or the claim that it is unwarranted. However, if ethical relativism is correct, what is morally justifiable depends on the group to which one belongs. Perhaps the use of performance-enhancing drugs is permissible for cultures that find it permissible but not for those that find it impermissible. Perhaps fighting is ethically acceptable when NHL players are participating in league contests but not when those same players are competing for nations and/or countries during the Olympic Games, where fighting is expressly impermissible.

Does descriptive relativism really have the skeptical implications examined above? Is relativism acceptable in the forms discussed above?

A Critique of Relativism

First, consider the argument that the truth of moral skepticism follows from the truth of descriptive relativism, because if the thesis of descriptive relativism—that moral codes of different cultures and groups conflict—is true, then moral skepticism is true. To evaluate this argument, we need to consider what general conditions an argument must meet to be acceptable. If the premises of an argument are to justify a conclusion, two fundamental requirements must be satisfied: (1) The premises must be true. False statements cannot be acceptable evidence for the truth of a conclusion. (2) The premises must be logically relevant to the conclusion; otherwise, the conclusion could not follow from the premises because they would be irrelevant to it. For example, we would not accept the conclusion that "the major goal of competitive sports is winning" on the basis of the claim that "Washington, DC, is the capital of the United States." Even though the latter claim is true, it has nothing to do with the former claim and, therefore, cannot support it.

Consider again the argument that because the moral codes of different cultures and groups conflict, no set of moral judgments or principles can be correct, reasonable, or justified. First, the argument assumes that descriptive relativism is true, but is it? If descriptive relativism claims no more than that the moral codes, principles, and judgments accepted in different societies sometimes conflict, it may well be true. But it leaves open the possibility that behind the apparent disagreement there is deeper agreement on some morally fundamental values. The area of agreement might constitute the basis of cross-cultural universal values that some investigators have claimed to detect. For example, people from a wide variety of cultural, ethnic, socioeconomic, and religious backgrounds condemn incest, torture, and the random killing of members of one's community. Protests against Communist regimes in China and the old Soviet Union and, more recently, against rigid forms of Islamic fundamentalism that deny women fundamental rights; against the murder and rape of non-Arabs, thus amounting to genocide in the view of many observers, in Darfur; or against recent government military attacks on civilians in Egypt and Syria are evidence for the broad appeal of values such as liberty and human rights.

This point can be taken further. Apparent surface disagreement can disguise deeper agreement in values. For instance, consider a dispute between a basketball coach and her assistant before a big game. The head coach wants to use a pressure defense to take advantage of her team's agility and the opponent's lack of speed. The assistant argues against this strategy because it may cause overanxious and inexperienced defensive players to commit too many fouls. In this example there is disagreement over which tactics to follow. But behind the disagreement is a common value or principle both coaches share. Each is trying to select the strategy that will be in their team's best interest and will allow the team to best accentuate its strengths and minimize the effects of its weaknesses.

A parallel situation is possible in ethics. Suppose culture A believes that old people should be separated from the group and left to die when they can no longer contribute to the general welfare, but culture B disagrees. Clearly, there is a disagreement here, but both cultures might share deeper fundamental values as well. For one thing, the circumstances of each culture might differ. Culture A may barely be surviving at the subsistence level; culture B may be affluent and, therefore, able to care for its older members. Perhaps culture A consists of nomadic bands that must move quickly to keep up with game. Arguably, each culture may accept the same basic principle of promoting the greater good for the group, but the principle might apply differently in the different circumstances in which each group finds itself. Similarly, in sport those who espouse values like justice and inclusion may still debate how, for example, gender equity should be measured in relation to high school or intercollegiate athletics. Accordingly, although the descriptive relativist is undoubtedly correct in pointing to moral disagreement among groups, it remains controversial whether there is fundamental disagreement about all values or whether underneath the surface disagreement most societies have a deeper acceptance of fundamental core values.

Suppose, however, that we concede for the sake of argument that there are no universally accepted values or moral principles. The greatest weakness of the relativist argument is that, even if this point is conceded, moral skepticism does not follow. The premise of descriptive relativism is logically irrelevant to supporting moral skepticism. If cultures or groups disagree about moral problems, this does not mean there are no correct or justifiable resolutions to the dispute. That certain values are not accepted does not mean they are not acceptable or justifiable. Similarly, some cultures believe the world is flat and others believe it is round, but this does not by itself establish that there is no correct answer concerning the shape of the earth.[6] Whether a justifiable resolution of a dispute is possible depends on whether justifiable modes of ethical (or scientific) inquiry can be applied to it. Moral disagreement can arise just as much from ignorance of such modes of inquiry, misapplication of them, or factual disagreement (as when one group of athletes denies and one asserts that steroids cause harmful side effects) as it can from the impossibility of distinguishing reasonable moral claims from those that are less reasonable.

Disagreement alone is not sufficient to show that no rational modes of inquiry exist, let alone that they are insufficient to resolve the issue at hand.

Whether moral claims can be justifiable depends on the reasons or evidence that might support them. The mere fact of disagreement on an ethical issue between two sides does not show that both have equally good reasons for their view. Similarly, moral agreement that some values are justified does not establish by itself that they are justifiable; that too depends on the reasons that can be provided in their support. In disagreement or agreement, justification depends on the kinds of *reasons* that can be provided to support our moral views, not simply on whether others share our values.

Of course, the failure of descriptive relativism to establish moral skepticism doesn't show that there is a correct resolution to moral controversies, only that the presence of cultural or group diversity does not rule out such a resolution in advance of inquiry.

Does descriptive relativism do any better in establishing ethical relativism, the thesis that what your group or culture says is right or wrong for you is really right or wrong for you? For example, is it morally right to take anabolic steroids to enhance your performance in sports just because your peer group or even your culture says it is right?

Once again no such implication follows. For reasons similar to those outlined above, just because groups may disagree on ethical issues does not show that each group's moral views are right for its members. One might just as well argue that if your culture believes the earth is flat, you ought to believe the earth is flat as well. If such an absurd view were correct, we would never be justified in trying to correct or change the view of our culture or peer group even if we had strong reasons for thinking their views were unfounded. Historically this would mean the views of those who protested against the discrimination women and African Americans experienced in sport throughout the 1950s and 1960s were wrongheaded because they sought to challenge the status quo in an American society that, at best, permitted and, at worst, endorsed such social injustices.

The previous example illustrates that ethical relativism has the unacceptable implication that the views of our culture or of other groups to which we belong are acceptable just as they are. But surely even if our peers do, for instance, advocate the use of performance-enhancing drugs in sports or fighting in ice hockey, they are not automatically correct to do so. We need to engage in ethical inquiry and argument to see whether the best reasons that can be given to support a view actually do support it rather than accepting it merely because it is the view of the group to which we belong.[7]

Therefore, moral disagreement among cultures or other kinds of groups should not deter us from engaging in a moral inquiry designed to subject moral claims in sports or elsewhere to rational criticism and evaluation. Moreover, such a view does not make us dogmatic or intolerant of the views of others. Indeed, tolerance and the avoidance of dogmatism are themselves values, and many think they have objective support. If moral skepticism were justified, there would be no rational basis for tolerance itself if cultures disagreed about its value. Accordingly, commitment to rational inquiry in ethics does not make us arrogant dogmatists; if anything, it makes us open to the insights of those who may be different from us so long as we are willing to subject their views as well as our own to the test of reasoned inquiry in ethics. Thus, commitment to moral inquiry can help free us from insular prejudices and allow us to test our views by seeing whether they can stand up to the reasoned criticism of others.

Absolutophobia: The Seductive Appeal of Crude Relativism

In spite of such serious intellectual weaknesses, crude forms of relativism and skepticism appeal to many, especially to some college students. This subgroup of students seems unwilling to make moral judgments, and it views those who do as opinionated or "judgmental."[8] Why do so many people, particularly students, believe that some of the greatest crimes in human history, including genocide and slavery, should not be morally condemned or, perhaps more understandably, that there are no rational grounds for such condemnation? We doubt there is one root cause of such attitudes, but we do suggest that certain intellectual errors contribute to such an attitude.

First, moral language is sometimes misused to bully or intimidate people into accepting the speaker's position. Moreover, moral positions that are held fanatically and asserted dogmatically leave no room for reasonable response. Morality may then be seen as a refuge for dogmatists who assert but never question their own absolutes and use the fear of being labeled "immoral" or "unfair" to force people to adopt favored views. Part of the reaction against "political correctness" on college campuses perhaps reflects resentment against ardent activists trying to impose their views on others. Religious zealots and extreme right-wing politicians as well as those on the extreme left sometimes use moral language as a weapon to stifle dissent.

However, such misuse of moral language does not imply that moral judgments cannot be justified. Indeed, to favor tolerance, judiciousness, and appeal to reason over dogmatism and zealotry is to favor one set of values over another, and, therefore, to make a moral judgment. Respect for the views of others and willingness to reason with them about values is as much a moral outlook as dogmatism and fanaticism are.

Second, many people reject "absolutes." But moral judgments about what is right or wrong, fair or unfair, or just or unjust seem to presuppose the very absolutes we are told do not exist. The first thing to note about rejecting absolutes is that it is unclear what an "absolute" is supposed to be. If an absolute is a simple rule that is self-evident and immune from rational scrutiny, it is far from clear that moral judgments can be absolutes. But if an absolute is a reasonable claim well supported by evidence, surely we are all committed to absolutes. In fact, the denial that absolutes exist in this sense seems itself to be one, as presumably it purports to be reasonable, well supported, and true. Whether critical rational inquiry can support moral claims can best be seen by exploring moral issues and not by dismissing moral claims through fear of committing an absolute (absolutophobia), no matter how murky that concept may be. In any case, the key point is that even if no moral judgments can be self-evident or immune from critical scrutiny, some moral judgments may still be reasonable, well supported, and justifiable.

Perhaps another reason for reluctance to make moral judgments is an interpretation (or misinterpretation) of multiculturalism. Although "multiculturalism" stands for a family of related positions rather than just one central doctrine, most multiculturalists hold that we should learn to understand and respect cultures other than our own. But sophisticated multiculturalists ought not to blur this claim by asserting that we should not criticize others' moral views. This second claim would prohibit them from criticizing opponents' views of multiculturalism or from objecting to intolerance of others. Because multiculturalists want to assert that their approaches are morally more acceptable than those they reject, they would undermine themselves by embracing extreme forms of moral relativism and skepticism.

We suggest that many who express skepticism about morality are not true skeptics or relativists but instead hold a disguised morality that tolerates and respects diversity. But by denying the moral basis to condemn evils such as the Holocaust, slavery, and racial oppression, such people are unable to condemn any wrongdoing; they cannot even defend the values that lead them to tolerate and respect diversity to begin with. If the legitimate desire to avoid moral fanaticism drives us to see the condemnation of any evil, however great, as an unwarranted intellectual arrogance, then the truly arrogant and the truly fanatical will never fear moral censure, no matter what evil they choose to inflict.

Moral Reasoning

Dogmatism and fanaticism can be avoided if we base our moral views on reasoning and encourage critical examination of them. But how are we to distinguish cogent from weak or incorrect moral reasoning? Philosophers and ethicists have not agreed that any one theory of moral reasoning is the correct one or even whether theories of moral reasoning are morally neutral or are themselves part of a substantive code of ethics. Some philosophers have serious doubts about the objectivity of moral judgments, although not on the crude grounds criticized in earlier sections. Perhaps the best way to determine whether moral judgments can be rationally assessed is to examine moral issues in detail. We will do that, in connection with sport, in subsequent chapters. The following comments may be helpful in assessing moral judgment and argument.

At a minimum it is doubtful whether one can evaluate moral arguments with the precision and rigor appropriate to mathematics. This does not mean we cannot recognize the difference between well-supported and poorly supported positions. As Aristotle suggested, we should "look for precision in each class of things just so far as the nature of the subject admits; it is evidently equally foolish to accept probable reasoning from a mathematician and to demand from a rhetorician scientific proofs."[9] This does not mean that ethical reasoning must be imprecise; it may resemble a sound case made by a skilled judicial scholar rather than strict mathematical proof.

Although good moral reasoning cannot be totally uncontroversial, the following three criteria will prove especially helpful. First, moral reasoning must be impartial. In evaluating a moral issue we are not asking, "What's in it for me?" We want to see what position is supported by the best reasons when impartially considered. This is an important point for individuals and groups in sporting contexts, where strategic forms of instrumental reasoning are often mistaken for moral reasoning. Moral deliberation has a broader perspective than simply self-interest. Thus, we cannot justify the claim that "the use of steroids by Olympic athletes to enhance their performance is morally legitimate" simply by claiming that "the use of steroids will help me gain a gold medal in the Olympics." The latter claim may show that the use of steroids is in the speaker's interest, but it does nothing to show that personal interest is the only relevant moral factor.

Philosophers have proposed various models or theories of impartial reasoning. For example, R. M. Hare has suggested that impartial moral reasoning requires us to imagine ourselves in the place of all those affected by the action or policy being evaluated, giving no special weight to any one perspective.[10] John Rawls, author of the important book *A Theory of Justice*, has suggested that in thinking of social justice we must reason as if we were behind a veil of ignorance that hides from us the knowledge of our individual characteristics or social circumstances.[11] Thus, impartiality prohibits us from arbitrarily assigning special privileges to our own gender, race, social class, or ethnic group because it would be irrational to do so if we had to consider such a policy impartially from the perspective of all affected, as Hare requires, or in ignorance of our own group membership, as Rawls suggests.

Some theorists regard some theories of impartiality, such as those of Rawls and Hare, as too abstract to apply or to work with. Can we truly reason as if we did not know our place in society, as Rawls suggested, or fully grasp the perspective of others, as Hare's approach seemingly requires? Don't such theories commit us to taking what Thomas Nagel refers to as "the view from nowhere"?[12] Shouldn't we therefore abandon the notion of impartiality rather than commit ourselves to such an impossible viewpoint?

These criticisms may overstate the difficulties. After all, in ordinary disputes we may say to the other party, "You wouldn't hold such a view if you didn't benefit from it." And we often do try to understand things from the point of view of others and encourage others to do the same. Thus, in evaluating whether the women's athletic program at a university is being treated fairly when compared to the men's program, we may ask ourselves whether we would find both programs equally acceptable regardless of the one in which we participated.

The core idea of impartiality, which is what the theories of philosophers such as Hare and Rawls try to capture, is that we are prohibited from arbitrarily assigning special weight to our own position or interests. Thus, a referee in a basketball game, to be impartial, must make calls in accord with the rules, not in accord with the team he or she likes better. Whatever the best theory of impartiality, impartiality plays an important and justifiable role in our ordinary moral thinking. Why otherwise insist that rules, officials, judges, and professors grading papers be impartial? The core idea is not that they necessarily must adopt a view from nowhere (or any particular theory of impartiality) but rather that they must apply appropriate standards fairly, reasonably, and equally.

Second, in addition to satisfying the requirement of impartiality, the positions we take must be systematically consistent. For example, if one holds that it is wrong to assault another person but that it is permissible for a professional hockey player to assault another player during a game, one's position appears inconsistent. Unless one can show that the two situations are relevantly dissimilar, one or the other position must be given up. If the two situations are similar in the relevant moral respects, assault in one cannot be permissible and assault in the other impermissible because there would be no difference between them to justify the difference in judgment made about them. If, however, one were to present contextual evidence demonstrating that, for example, fighting in professional ice hockey keeps players from committing more brutal acts of violence out of frustration or anger, it may be possible to morally justify fighting under certain circumstances.

Third, the principles one uses in making moral decisions must account for reflective judgments about clear moral examples. For example, in golf we start with a firm conviction that competitors in a tournament should not lie about their scores. But let's say a particular golfer believed it was permissible to turn in a wrong score merely to benefit himself. Reflective judgment about this example would reveal that turning in the wrong score was a case of lying about the score. The principle that competitors should not lie can be applied to the example of this particular golfer and would normally be grounds for rejecting or, at least, questioning the individual golfer's belief. After all, if golfers could lie about their scores, the whole point of a golf tournament, to find out who played best, would be undermined.

Of course—and this is what makes our third criterion controversial—we must be sure our reactions to situations are critical and reflective, not merely unanalyzed, culturally conditioned responses. It is all too easy to be influenced by cultural, social, and even biologically based presuppositions. For example, our initial reaction that it is permissible for hometown fans to boo and wave while an opposing basketball player shoots a crucial foul shot may simply be a prejudice we share with other hometown fans. However, some of our judgments about particular situations may be reflective and unbiased and, therefore, allow us to check our principles. Fans' antics at a game in which we have no vested interests, for example, might lead us to reflect on the distinction between sportsmanlike and unsportsmanlike fan conduct in sport.

Thus, our reflective reaction to actual and hypothetical examples may be a useful guide for moral inquiry; without such consideration our principles would be empty abstractions. Conversely, we can criticize an abstract principle by showing that its application would lead to unacceptable consequences for concrete action.

The more an ethical theory survives counterexample and criticism, the more confidence we would seem to be entitled to place in it. Just as we expose our scientific theories to testing, so we should test our moral perspectives by exposing them to others' criticism. Although clinging to our entrenched moral views by never exposing them to opposing views may feel good, the price we pay for such a policy is to prevent ourselves from discovering errors that others may recognize. We also lose opportunities for confirming our views when we refute our critics' objections. Just as a scientific theory gains credibility by surviving tests, so may a moral view gain credibility by surviving criticism in the crucible of moral debate.

From a critical perspective at least three strategies can undermine a moral view. We can argue that such a view would not be held if impartially considered, that its various parts are inconsistent or inharmonious, or that the view has unacceptable implications for action. Nothing said so far implies that only one moral perspective, code of ethics, or set of principles will survive moral criticism. It is possible that all who go through an extended process of moral inquiry will hold the same moral view; it is equally possible that a kind of moral pluralism will flourish. However, it is unlikely that serious and extended moral inquiry will rate all moral perspectives as equally justified. Many will be rejected as inconsistent, biased, vulnerable to counterexample, or deficient on some other appropriate ground. Thus, although there is no guarantee our criteria of moral reasoning are the only defensible ones or that they will yield strictly determinate results for all investigators, they at least provide guidance in the rational evaluation of moral issues. By applying them, we employ reason in ethics.

Let us turn now to moral issues in sports. The discussion will ask us to make and evaluate moral judgments about controversial cases—hence, the importance of the discussion about the justifiability of moral judgment. The challenge will be to develop positions that we can impartially affirm, are consistent with our views in related areas, and rely on principles whose consequences for action are acceptable. We will begin by examining possible theoretical frameworks for ethical analysis in sporting contexts and studying a fundamental issue for sport, the importance that should be assigned to competition and winning.

QUESTIONS FOR REVIEW

1. Describe a variety of ethical issues that arise within sporting contexts. What specific moral questions do these issues raise?
2. What is relativism? Explain this general philosophic stance and the specific forms of it discussed in the chapter. What criticisms of these views did the authors present? Do you agree with their critique? Why?
3. What is skepticism? Explain why skeptics believe people cannot rationally support their ethical beliefs and opinions. Do you agree with the authors' critique of skepticism? Why?
4. Why are many people today accepting relativist viewpoints, and why are they hesitant to critique the moral beliefs of others? Explain why the authors believe ethical debate is important in today's world and how it helps to counter dogmatic absolutism.
5. Identify the three criteria of good moral reasoning presented by the authors, and explain how each is important in the process of developing sound moral positions.

Notes

1. Robert L. Simon, *Fair Play* (Boulder, CO: Westview Press, 1991), 1.

2. According to one of the most extensive studies done on this topic, the *Miller Lite Report on American Attitudes Towards Sports*, completed in the 1980s, 96.3 percent of the American population frequently played, watched, or read articles about sports or identified with particular teams and players at that time. Moreover, nearly 70 percent followed sports every day, and 42 percent participated daily. *Miller Lite Report on American Attitudes Towards Sports* (Milwaukee, WI: Miller Brewing Company, 1983). Although comparisons over decades are difficult to make because different studies focus on different aspects of behavior, there is no evidence that interest in sports has declined to any significant extent in recent years. For a more recent assessment of sport participation trends, see Ronald B. Woods, *Social Issues in Sport*, 2nd ed. (Champaign, IL: Human Kinetics, 2011), 38–42. Data on attendance for many professional sports also show continued widespread interest by the general population. See, for example, the data on attendance collected by University of Michigan economist Rodney Fort, available at https://sites.google.com/site/rodswebpages/codes.

3. Edmund Pincoffs of the University of Texas told Robert L. Simon this story some time ago. He was the philosopher in the story, and the remark was addressed to him.

4. Allen Bloom, *The Closing of the American Mind* (New York: Simon and Schuster, 1987), 25.

5. Our discussion of relativism draws heavily on distinctions made by James Rachels in *The Elements of Moral Philosophy* (New York: McGraw-Hill, 1993), 17–25, particularly the distinctions between various forms of relativism. Errors in their use or in our criticism of crude forms of relativism are entirely our own.

6. There may be a temptation to reply that because science is different from ethics, the example in the text is irrelevant. Disagreement in science doesn't show the impossibility of a rational resolution of a dispute, but disagreement in ethics does. But what entitles the skeptic to assume that science is rational but ethics isn't? The skeptic needs to show just how science and ethics differ in ways that are relevant to supporting skepticism and not simply assume the difference to be self-evident when that very assumption is being challenged. In any event, the logical point still stands: disagreement on an issue by itself does not establish that we can never tell whether one side has better reasons for its views or is more justified than the other.

7. There are other difficulties with ethical relativism as well. For example, what counts as a culture? Is the sporting community a culture? Is there such an entity as Western culture, or are there only loosely related cultural subgroups within the West? What should we do if we belong to different cultures, each of which makes conflicting moral recommendations? What if our religious culture tells us that abortion is wrong, but the secular culture of our peer group says it is permissible? Ethical relativism, which tells us to follow the dictates of our culture, would seem to be useless when the dictates of the cultures to which we belong clash.

Finally, cultures rarely speak with one voice. Thus, the genital mutilation of females as practiced in some African cultures is not only criticized by many Western observers but also by those within the culture itself who oppose the practice. Ethical relativism, by assuming that cultures speak with one voice, obscures the ethical diversity and moral disagreement that exists within them. The important issue concerns not just what a culture asserts but also whether critical rational inquiry supports or can support the assertion.

8. Robert L. Simon discusses the issues this comment raises, particularly some students' reluctance to make moral judgments, in "The Paralysis of Absolutophobia," *Chronicle of Higher Education*, June 27, 1997, B5–B7, http://chronicle.com/article/The-Paralysis/74721/.

9. *Nichomachean Ethics*, bk. 1, chap. 2, sec. 25, trans. W. D. Ross, in *The Basic Works of Aristotle*, ed. Richard McKeon (New York: Random House, 1941), 936.

10. See, for example, R. M. Hare, *Freedom and Reason* (New York: Oxford University Press, 1965), and his *Moral Thinking* (Oxford: Clarendon Press, 1981).

11. John Rawls, *A Theory of Justice* (Cambridge, MA: Harvard University Press, 1971).

12. Thomas Nagel, *The View from Nowhere* (New York: Oxford University Press, 1986).

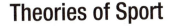

Theories of Sport

FRAMEWORKS FOR EVALUATION

The victory of the US women's team in the 1999 World Cup Soccer matches was one of the most exciting events in sports in the last decade of the twentieth century. Not only were the contests leading to this triumph hotly contested, with the final game decided in a shootout, but many saw the team as symbolizing the emergence of women into the center of attention in athletic competition. The team's stars, popular and highly skilled players such as Mia Hamm and Brandy Chastain, were heroes to many young girls who played in soccer leagues across the country as well as to adults throughout the United States.

However, the final plays of the world championship game, in which the Americans defeated China, became the center of an important ethical controversy. Regular and overtime play had ended in a tie, and the game was to be decided by a shootout in which players from each team would go one-on-one against the opposing goalie. The team that scored the most goals after a set number of attempts would win the game. Under the rules, which prevented the goalkeeper from moving forward to cut off the shooter's angle until a shot was launched, the offensive player had a major advantage.

So the world championship was on the line while the offensive players matched each other goal for goal as the shootout progressed. The American goalkeeper, Briana Scurry, decided that one of the remaining Chinese players, Liu Ying, seemed to lack confidence. When Liu made her move against Scurry, the American goalie decided on a controversial tactic to stop the shot. As the

Chinese player made her move, Scurry, by stepping forward in violation of the applicable rule limiting the movement of goalies, attempted to deprive Liu of the angle she would need to score. The tactic worked: Scurry blocked the shot and the Americans won. But did they win fairly?

As one view has it, "It's only cheating if you get caught." A more sophisticated and surely more defensible modification of that view is that it is the referee's job to call the game, and as long as the player is willing to accept the penalty if detected, no unethical behavior is involved. As another prominent goalkeeper put it, "What Briana did was perfectly normal. She took a step and the referee didn't call it. I don't call that cheating."[1]

Is it cheating to commit what we will call a strategic foul, an intentional violation of the rules designed to secure a tactical advantage? What if it is done openly and with willingness to accept the penalty if the referee calls the foul? What if it is a common practice, one the players know about and accept, as is fouling at the end of a basketball game to stop the clock? Scurry's move in the World Cup has been defended on exactly such grounds: all goalkeepers do it, players know that goalkeepers do it, and a penalty is prescribed under the rules if the violation is detected. After all, it is not as if Scurry was trying to hide her move from the referee or claim an advantage for herself that she would not accord to other goalies as well. But what happens to sports as rule-governed activities if players decide for themselves when to obey the rules and are encouraged to test referees to see what they can get away with? Do we have a true sports contest if each team plays only by the rules it feels are useful to obey at a given moment?

Consider a second example. During the 2007 National Football League (NFL) season the New England Patriots, the best team in the league, in violation of league rules, were found to have been tapping into the electronic communications of New York Jets defensive coaches during a contest. This enabled the Patriots to identify the plays the Jets would run in advance so the strategies the Jets employed could be countered not simply by better play but by prior knowledge of the Jets' tactics. Was this ethical? It violated league rules, and for that reason alone it was morally suspect. As a result of what has come to be called "Spygate," the Patriots' head coach Bill Belichick was fined $500,000 in addition to other penalties the league imposed on the Patriots. But does the rule make moral sense? Why is it unethical to use technology to discover what tactics and strategies the other team will employ? After all, if a pitcher in baseball telegraphs what pitch is coming next, perhaps by the way he grips the baseball, alert opposing coaches will pass on the information to the batter. Is what goes on in baseball an acceptable way to seek as advantage, but is what happened in Spygate cheating?

Consider a third example that also raises issues of ethics in competition. In early October 1990 the highly regarded University of Colorado Buffaloes played a home football contest against the University of Missouri. Top national ranking was at stake. The final seconds saw Colorado trailing 31–27 but driving toward the Missouri goal line. Somehow, in the confusion on the field, the seven officials on the field, the "chain gang" working the sideline markers, and the scoreboard operator all lost track of the downs. On what should have been the fourth and deciding down Colorado failed to score, in part because the Colorado quarterback, mistakenly thinking he had another play left, intentionally grounded a pass. In fact, the officials signaled that Colorado had another chance, unaware that the Buffaloes already had used the four chances to score the rules allowed. Colorado scored on the illegal but unnoticed fifth down to eke out a 33–31 "victory."

Did Colorado really win? Should the final score have been allowed to stand? It was decided that the officials' mistake was not the sort of error that can be overruled. But should the University of Colorado have accepted the victory? Is such a "win" meaningful in an important ethical sense?

These examples raise questions about how to conduct competition in athletics ethically. They raise issues of sportsmanship and fair play. By examining them we can better understand the values that may be used in assessing competitors' behavior within the athletic contest itself.

Theories of Sport

Many of us will have intuitive reactions to cases such as those described above. For example, some of us might think that because Scurry broke the rules of soccer, her behavior was unethical and that the American victory was tainted. Others, however, might respond that rules are often not strictly observed and that if goalies generally follow the convention of moving early to get the best position to block a shot on goal, the behavior is allowable because it is a common practice in the sport of soccer. (Similarly, in baseball, umpires do not insist that the shortstop or second baseman actually be touching second base when pivoting to make a double play.) But which intuitive reaction is most justifiable?

In part because our immediate reaction to moral issues in sport can conflict, not just with the opinions of others but often also internally, as when we are of two minds about an issue, *theories of sport* will prove useful in our inquiry into the values that should apply in athletic competition. But what is a theory of sport?[2]

One way of approaching that question is to ask what theories of sport are good for. Thus, one important function of a theory of sport is to help us make distinctions between activities that are sports from those that aren't, even if the distinction is not always a sharp one. Is chess, often called "the sport of kings," a sport? What about fishing? Must a sport be a game like baseball, or can an activity like hiking also be a sport? Distinguishing sports from other related activities is important not only because of the intellectual issue of whether we can even make such a distinction—perhaps the concept of *sport* is too vague to admit of useful analysis, or perhaps sports have nothing in common that defines all of them—but also for theoretical and normative reasons as well. For example, if we are to explain why sports are so fascinating to millions of people around the globe, we need to distinguish them from other activities, such as walking for exercise, that also may be important for reasons of health but differ from sports in very significant respects.

Thus, theories of sport serve a normative or evaluative function. To the extent that they help us identify salient features of sport, they provide material we can use to assess sport morally as well. For example, the importance we assign to winning in athletic contests may be at least in part a function of what we believe are the values sport should promote. By identifying key values that should apply in competitive sport, a justifiable theory of sport may help us to analyze more cogently problematic cases such as Spygate and Colorado University's victory on the fifth down.

We can think of a theory of sport, then, as a body of statements, some of which may be quite abstract, that helps us not only identify sports and distinguish them from other activities but also provide an assessment of the value of sport and a normative framework for examining ethical issues that may arise in sport, especially in athletic competition.

Theories of sport, then, should serve at least the following three functions. First, they should offer a characterization of sport that helps us to distinguish sports from other activities, even if we cannot always do so due to complex borderline cases. Second, they should explain the features of sport that make it of significant interest to people around the globe, not only for participants but for spectators and fans as well. Third, they should explain the value (or disvalue, if they are critical of sport and sporting practices) of sport and provide the resources for the moral evaluation of sport, perhaps especially competitive athletics, and the ethical issues that arise in particular sporting contexts.

Sports and Games: The Analysis of Bernard Suits

Perhaps the best way to begin our discussion is by considering the nature of sport itself. One plausible approach is to suggest that all sports are games of physical skill. This suggestion would cover clear cases of sports such as baseball, golf, soccer, and football. But whereas running marathons is a demanding physical activity, are marathons games? Is gymnastics a game? Let us consider further.

If the thesis we are examining is that sports are games of physical skill, we may need to clarify the notion of "game." The great twentieth-century philosopher Ludwig Wittgenstein suggested that while we can clarify such concepts as "game," we cannot strictly define them.[3] In particular Wittgenstein called into question that the concepts we use always have an essence or set of necessary and sufficient defining characteristics. In raising this issue, he questioned the Platonic search for the form that lies behind our conceptual scheme—the form we search for when we ask such questions as "What is beauty?" "What is truth?" and "What is justice?" Thus, in a passage about games Wittgenstein wrote,

> Consider for example the proceedings we call "games." . . . What is common to them all?—Don't say: "There *must* be something common or they would not be called 'games'"—but *look and see* whether there is anything common to all.—For if you look at them you will not see something common to *all*, but similarities, relationships, and a whole series of them at that. To repeat: don't think but look![4]

Wittgenstein suggested that games resemble each other as family members do: in a plurality of overlapping ways but without any one characteristic or set of characteristics that each and every family member has. For this reason many theorists influenced by Wittgenstein have regarded "game" as a "family resemblance concept" and denied that any precise definition of "game" can be provided.

Was Wittgenstein right about games? In a series of influential works another philosopher, Bernard Suits, raised doubts about Wittgenstein's challenge and proposed another important account of games. Suits's book *The Grasshopper: Games, Life and Utopia* is an analytically acute but humorous analysis of the nature and point of games.[5] If Suits is correct, we can define "game" and then go on to understand sports as games of physical skill.

Games, Suits pointed out, are governed by constitutive rules that define what counts as winning and losing and that distinguish moves that are permissible within a game from those that are impermissible. Thus, dribbling is a permissible way of advancing the ball in basketball, but running with the ball is not, precisely because the constitutive rules allow the former but not the latter. Dribbling too much can be bad strategy and violate what might be called strategic rules for playing well, but still, dribbling is allowed in a way that running with the ball is not.

However, constitutive rules govern many activities, such as taking an examination in a course, that are not games. Suits, therefore, introduced additional criteria to distinguish games from other practices defined by constitutive rules. In particular, the rules of games create challenges by setting up what Suits called unnecessary obstacles to achieving the goals the players must pursue. Thus, it is a simple matter to put a ball into a hole, but it becomes exceedingly difficult to put a ball into a hole when, in golf, it must be done with what former British Prime Minister Winston Churchill called "implements ill-designed for the purpose." In other words, the constitutive rules of games create unnecessary challenges that make accomplishing an ordinary task (putting a ball into a hole), which Suits called the *pre-lusory goal*, into a challenging game (golf) that requires a legitimate golf score, the *lusory goal*.

In a game, moreover, we accept the constitutive rules simply in order to try to meet the challenge of the game. Suits called this the "lusory attitude." Thus, to return to our earlier example, although taking an examination in a college course may have constitutive rules (for example, that students may not refer to notes or texts during the examination period), taking a test is not a game because tests normally are constructed not simply to create interesting challenges but rather to assess student learning and provide a basis for certification that enables participants to get jobs or secure entrance to graduate and professional school.

Consider, then, the suggestion, based on this rough summary of Suits's account, that a game is defined by (1) constitutive rules that set up unnecessary obstacles to achieving a particular goal by defining permissible and impermissible ways of achieving it, and (2) the rules are accepted just to allow participants to attempt to meet the challenges so created. As Suits aptly said when summarizing his view, a game is "a voluntary attempt to meet unnecessary obstacles." Sports, then, would be, as already suggested, games of physical skill.

Should we accept Suits's account? Of course, there are difficulties with it. First, it may be objected, participants may accept the rules for a variety of reasons other than the lusory attitude—for example, to get exercise, to socialize and make friends, or, in the case of professionals, to make money. However, a proponent of Suits's definition might reply, with a good deal of plausibility, that although these may be participants' motives, they still get exercise or make friends or make money by trying to meet the obstacles set by the rules. In fact, professional athletes achieve fame and fortune precisely by overcoming the challenges of the game. Tiger Woods has been considered the best golfer because he does better than anyone else at shooting low scores within the rules of the game.

Philosophers of sport debate whether Suits's definition is completely successful. Many questions remain to be examined. Thus, a marathon seems to be a sporting event, but we do not commonly call marathons "games." A "game of marathon" might be something children may play in imitation of a genuine marathon. Suits might reply, however, that this is just a fault of ordinary language; a marathon has the structure of a game regardless of whether it is *called* one. Suits himself at one time raised questions about whether sports like gymnastics or synchronized swimming are more like performances than games, and his account of games continues to be interpreted, debated, and evaluated within the professional literature.

Regardless of whether Suits has identified the essence of games, his account can illuminate the following discussion of the ethics of sport in two ways. First, his account certainly seems to fit paradigmatic instances of sports such as baseball, lacrosse, football, soccer, golf, and many other clear instances of sporting activity. Second, his emphasis on the role constitutive rules play in setting up unnecessary obstacles calls attention to the notion of games as activities undertaken and valued fundamentally because of the challenge the rules create. Indeed, in *The Grasshopper* Suits suggested that meeting the challenges of games is an intrinsically valuable human activity and that a life of game playing might be what constitutes utopia. Even if we don't fully accept this last point, we can acknowledge the intrinsic interest athletes have in meeting challenges for their own sake.

Keeping Suits's account in mind, let us see whether it can help us develop a theoretical account of sports that we can apply to better analyze issues of sportsmanship and fair play within competitive athletics.

Internalism and the Ethics of Sport

In this section we will examine the view that sport has a kind of internal morality that is tightly (perhaps conceptually) connected with the structural features of athletic competition. We will apply the results in Chapter 3 to the examples cited at the beginning of this chapter. We'll begin by considering two approaches to the connection between competitive sports and moral values.

Externalism denies that sport is an independent source or basis of ethical principles or values, although sophisticated externalists acknowledge and even emphasize that sports play a significant role in reinforcing values already extant in the culture and in socializing participants and spectators to accept those values as their own. On this view the values that sport promotes either express or simply mirror, reflect, or reinforce the values dominant in the wider society. Thus, to take one example, in a predominantly capitalist society sport may emphasize such capitalist values as intense competition and rivalry, whereas in more communal and less individualistic societies more emphasis may be given to teamwork and the role of opposing players as facilitators who help make good competition possible.

Internalism, in contrast, holds that sport is itself a significant source of or basis for ethical principles and values, can have a significant degree of autonomy from the wider society, and can support, stand for, and express sets of values of its own that may conflict with the values dominant in the broader society. Thus, in his important work entitled *Leftist Theories of Sport*, William J. Morgan defended the idea of a "gratuitous logic" of sport, positing that sport does not merely mirror or reinforce the values dominant elsewhere.[6]

Internalism should not be taken to mean the internal values of sport are unique or have no basis in broader ethical principles such as respect for persons and fairness. Rather, it claims, first, that key values in sport are not mere reflections of values popular or dominant in the society, and, second, these values are related to and can at least in part be supported by ethically defensible conceptions or interpretations of competition in sports.[7]

Why is this distinction between externalism and internalism important for the concrete problems we raised earlier, such as the ethics of rule breaking for strategic purposes? Perhaps it is this: if internalism is correct, then the ethical principles embedded in or implied by central features of athletic competition may provide a morally relevant framework for adjudicating difficult moral issues that arise in athletic competition. Of course, just because some values or moral principles are internal to sport does not mean they are justifiable or well supported by reasons. Nevertheless, they may provide a useful starting point for analysis. Let us begin by considering one form of internalism and the critical response to it.

Formalism

Formalism is the name given to a family of positions that characterizes games, such central elements of games as winning and losing, and allowable moves within the activity, primarily in their formal structures and particularly in their constitutive rules. Formalism reflects Suits's emphasis on the constitutive rules of sports as the formal structure of sport. Thus, in a narrow sense formalism has been characterized as the view that such reference to the constitutive rules of the game can define game derivative notions as "a move or play within a game" and "winning a game."

In a broader sense formalism is the view that games (and sports to the extent that sports are games of physical skill) can be defined primarily by reference to constitutive rules. The goals or obstacles of the sport are defined by those rules and are unintelligible outside the context of the rules. A move within a game is what the constitutive rules permit or require, and such rules also define what counts as winning a game. For example, using a tank during a football game to run over the opposing team's defensive players is not a move within the sport, as such moves may be made only in accord with the constitutive rules. There are different versions of formalism, so "formalism" might best be regarded as an umbrella term covering a family of positions that, although closely related, sometimes differ on points of varying degrees of significance.

Formalism not only is a theory about the nature of games but also has normative implications. Perhaps the best known is the incompatibility thesis: cheaters violate the rules by failing to make moves within the sport and, therefore, fail to play it. One can win the game only by playing it, and because cheaters do not play, cheaters can't win.

The emphasis of formalists on the constitutive rules of the game has helped us understand the nature of games. However, formalism as characterized so far lacks the normative resources to address many of the moral problems that arise in connection with sports. (To be fair, many versions of formalism were developed to define the notions of "game" and "sport" rather than to resolve ethical issues arising in games and sports.)

Issues of sportsmanship, for example, often go beyond conformity to the formal rules of a sport. Thus, consider the case of clubless Josie, a top amateur golfer who arrives at a national amateur golf championship without her clubs. Clubless Josie has lost her clubs not because she is clueless but because her airline was careless. Josie's chief rival, Annika, has a spare set of clubs virtually identical to those Josie has lost. Should Annika lend poor clubless but not clueless Josie the spare set of clubs so Josie can compete in the tournament? Because Josie's problem does not concern the application of rules, whether formalism addresses this question is unclear.[8]

Some formalists might reply that their view, sympathetically interpreted, supports lending the clubs to Josie. If we correctly understand the *spirit* or *point* of the rules, which is to promote competition, we should do what enhances competition. However, in appealing to the spirit of the rules or their underlying point, formalists go beyond a narrow version of formalism and ask *how* we are to understand the spirit of the rules or their underlying point. We will consider this expanded form of formalism, which we call broad internalism, below.

Formalism also has problems with the ethics of rule changes and rule formation. How are proposed changes in the rules or sets of rules for new sports and games to be assessed? Formalists might point out that the rules of many sports include what legal philosopher H. L. A. Hart called "rules of change." A rule of change for golf might state that a proposal becomes a rule of golf if and only if it is accepted through established procedures by the governing golf organizations of an area, such as the United States Golf Association (USGA) and the Royal and Ancient in Britain. But although such rules of change might establish when a rule change becomes official, they do not establish whether the change is good or bad for the game.

Consider, for example, the proposed rule that anyone who commits a strategic foul in the last four minutes of a basketball game is thrown out of the game and the opposing team is then awarded thirty straight foul shots. Because it is so penal, such a rule might eliminate strategic fouling. But is it a good rule? Is basketball a better or worse game if fouling late in the game to stop the clock is allowed as a legitimate tactic? Similar questions might be raised about the designated-hitter rule in baseball or proposals to give the goalkeeper more freedom of movement during shootouts in soccer. Although formalists are quite right to emphasize the formal structure of games, it is not clear how their theory might apply to ethical questions in sport that formal or structural features alone cannot necessarily resolve.

Conventionalism

Many theorists argue that in emphasizing the formal constitutive rules of given sports, the formalists have ignored the implicit conventions that apply to the sport in question. These conventions are sometimes referred to as the "ethos of the game."[9] For example, with respect to strategic fouling in basketball, conventionalists argue that a convention in basketball permits such fouls as a legitimate strategic move within the game. Because the players all accept the convention and each team knows the other team will strategically foul at appropriate points in a contest, no team has a special advantage over others. Therefore, strategic fouling is not cheating but rather is justified by practice and the widely accepted social conventions within that practice.

But can social conventions be a source of value in sports? Although conventionalists have made a contribution to our understanding of sporting practice by exploring the role of the ethos and cultural context of games, does the ethos have normative force? Do the conventions express what *ought* to take place as well as describe what *does* take place in sporting practice?

Consider clubless Josie. For one thing, if such a dilemma were highly unusual, there might be no applicable convention. Conventionalism, like formalism, would not tell us what should be done. But suppose there was an applicable convention under which players were not supposed to lend equipment to fellow competitors. Would that settle the issue, or would it simply raise the deeper issue of whether that convention was ethical or reflected appropriate standards of fair play? Thus, one major problem with conventionalism is the ethical status of the conventions themselves.

This is true even where conventionalism is plausible—namely, its analysis of strategic fouls in sports such as basketball. But even in basketball it is unclear whether the mere existence of conventions settles the issue of strategic fouling. The critics of strategic fouling acknowledge that they are opposing a widely accepted practice as well as the conventional understandings upon which that practice is based, but they argue that appeal to central values implicit in the logic of sports requires the reform of existing conventional behavior. Unless we are to immunize conventions from criticism and, in effect, always choose to preserve the existing understandings of sport, challenges to existing conventions cannot be dismissed simply because they counter our present conventional understandings of sporting practice.

It also is unclear whether conventionalism can respond any better than strict formalism can to the evaluation of proposed changes in the rules or conventions of a sport. When is a change for the better? How are we to evaluate a proposed change to the conventions of basketball, for example, to the effect that players on a losing basketball team should not foul simply to gain a strategic advantage? Just as appeal to the existing rules alone cannot settle the issue of whether a proposed rule change is or is not an improvement, so appeal to existing conventions cannot be the sole basis for evaluating proposals for reform. Arguments for and against the proposed changes, either in the rules or in the conventions, would have to come from elsewhere. But from where?

Although these criticisms are decisive against most forms of conventionalism, William J. Morgan has recently suggested that a different form of conventionalism, which we will call deep conventionalism, avoids them. We will consider his views after we develop an alternative to conventionalism we call broad internalism or interpretivism, as Morgan's views emerged in part as a reaction to the broad internalist position.

So far, then, the discussion suggests that narrow versions of both pure formalism and conventionalism lack the intellectual resources to deal with the important ethical issues that arise in sport. It is hard to see how emphasizing either existing formal rules or social conventions can resolve fundamental moral issues in sport or provide the moral and educational development many expect sport to provide. Perhaps a third position can do better.

Broad Internalism: Expanding the Formalist Approach

In a series of writings in jurisprudence noted legal scholar Ronald Dworkin has criticized legal positivists, particularly the highly influential legal philosopher H. L. A. Hart, for holding too narrow a view of the nature of law.[10] Because legal positivists, particularly Hart, tend to identify law with a formal structure of rules, their views resemble the formalist approach to the analysis of games and sport. According to Dworkin, the legal positivists have identified law with a model of formal rules. One of Hart's major contributions is to show the diverse rules that make up law, including criminal sanctions, rules of change and adjudication, and the Rule of Recognition, which identifies the rules of the legal system and distinguishes them from nonlegal rules, such as rules of etiquette, which normally have no juridical standing.

Dworkin has argued that in addition to rules there are legal principles that have normative force within the legal system. What makes these principles legal ones rather than simply moral principles imported from beyond the law and applied according to the particular political and ethical commitments of individual judges is that they are either presupposed by the legal system or provide a logical basis for some of its key elements. In other words the principles must be presupposed in order for us to arrive at the most comprehensive, coherent, and morally acceptable account of the law itself, the best interpretation of the legal system. In fact, a principle is not justified as a "legal principle" unless it meets this condition.

An analogous position in the philosophy of sport has been developing for some time.[11] Although many writers are sympathetic to various aspects of formalism or may even view themselves as formalists, they go beyond narrow versions of formalism in developing resources for the ethical assessment of behavior that can be distinguished from rules without being mere conventions. The considerations they point to seem to be presuppositions of sporting practice in the sense that they must be accepted if our sporting practice is to make sense or, perhaps, make the *best* sense. Before developing this view, which we will call broad internalism (some writers following Dworkin prefer to call it *interpretivism*), let us consider some examples.

In "Fair Play as Respect for the Game" Robert Butcher and Angela Schneider maintained that "if one honors or esteems one's sport, . . . one will have a coherent conceptual framework for arbitrating between competing claims regarding the fairness . . . of actions."[12] Where does this conceptual framework come from? Butcher and Schneider suggested that sports themselves have interests; athletes show respect for the game when they make its internal interests their own. Thus, they claimed that "the idea of the interests of the game provides a means for judging one's own action in relation to the sport. . . . Taking the interests of the game seriously means that we ask ourselves whether or not some action we are contemplating would be good for the game concerned, if everyone did that."[13]

Butcher and Schneider illustrated their position by applying it to poor clubless Josie (who in earlier versions of the example is a racquetless squash player rather than a clubless but not clueless golfer). "The notion of respect for the game provides ample reason for lending Josie the racquet. At the personal level . . . you would forgo a valuable experience and personal test if you decline to play Josie. At a more general level, the sport of squash is enhanced by people playing and competing at their best whenever possible. Squash at the institutional level would not be served by neglecting to play a . . . scheduled match. You should want to lend Josie your racquet."[14]

This is an example of broad internalism because appeal is being made to norms or principles internal to the idea of sport. These principles are not mere social conventions; rather, they might even provide a basis for criticizing existing social conventions if they supported requiring Josie to forfeit the match. Neither are they formal rules of the game. Although broad internalists might well want to avoid the metaphysical complications attached to the notion of games having interests—games may not even be the sort of entities that can have their own interests—perhaps all that internalists need to say is that the point of playing competitive golf would require the match be played.

A second and very instructive example of broad internalism was provided by J. S. Russell in an article entitled "Are Rules All an Umpire Has to Work With?"[15] Russell, appealing explicitly to Dworkin's views in jurisprudence, argues against the view that rules are all an umpire has to work with. He discusses plays from American baseball that call on umpires and officials to extend, change, or interpret rules that, by themselves, may be indeterminate when applied to hard cases.

For example, in an 1887 American Association game between Louisville and Brooklyn, a Louisville player named Reddy Mack, who had just scored, jostled the Brooklyn catcher, thereby interfering with him, and as a result allowed another Louisville player to score. At that time the rules of baseball stated that no base runner could interfere with a fielder, but the Louisville player might have reasoned that when he crossed home plate he was no longer a base runner. The umpire, Wesley Curry, called Mack out for interfering with the catcher. As the rule technically did not apply once Mack had crossed home plate and ceased to be a base runner, did Curry make the right decision?

Russell points out that Curry's decision "was not explicitly covered by the rules, but his actions seem irreproachable, were not overturned, and were the basis for a subsequent rule change. . . . Any other decision would have invited a nine-inning . . . wrestling match."[16]

Russell was going beyond explicit formal rules here and offering what might be called an interpretation of baseball. Thus, following Dworkin's suggestions in legal philosophy, Russell suggests that "we might try to understand and interpret the rules of a game, say, baseball, . . . to generate a coherent and principled account of the point and purposes that underlie the game, attempting to show the game in its best light."[17] Russell cited, as an example of a principle that might underlie such competitive sports as baseball, the injunction that "rules should be interpreted in such a manner that the excellences embodied in achieving the lusory goal of the game are not undermined but are maintained and fostered."[18]

Broad internalism, then, is the view that in addition to the constitutive rules of sport, there are other resources connected closely—perhaps conceptually—to sport that are neither social conventions nor moral principles that merely mirror the dominant morality in society. These resources, which include moral requirements and aesthetic demands such as the injunction to avoid ugly games such as those marred by excessive fouling, can be used to adjudicate normative issues in sports and athletics. In William J. Morgan's terms, sport has an independent "gratuitous logic" of its own that makes it more than a mirror reflecting the values of society.[19]

A particular interpretation is justified by how well it fits or explains the key features of the sport at issue and, more broadly, the purpose of the practice of sport itself. In other words, by providing a cogent account of the unnecessary obstacles established by the constitutive rules, the interpretation presents sport in its best moral and aesthetic light.[20] Thus, allowing Reddy Mack's action to stand in Russell's example would not do justice to the constitutive rules of baseball, which do not imply that wrestling is a fundamental skill of the sport. It also would make the game uglier by eliminating the beauty of long throws to the catcher to prevent a runner from scoring and would make fights among players who react angrily to opponents' aggressive physical moves much more likely, thereby lowering the moral standing of the game.

A Deep Conventionalist Response

Although sports philosopher William J. Morgan also takes an internalist and interpretivist perspective—hence his comment about the "gratuitous logic" of sport—he also suggests that many broad internalists (including Robert Simon) have been too quick to reject conventionalism. Even as Morgan agrees that the kind of objections we raised earlier against conventionalism are decisive against what might be called superficial conventionalism, another version of conventionalism, which we will call *deep conventionalism*, avoids them entirely.[21]

Our earlier discussion suggested that conventionalism lacked the resources to allow for a moral or aesthetic critique of sport: conventions might be morally acceptable, but they need not be. Similarly, they may or may not regulate sport in an aesthetically acceptable manner; for example, they may create incentives that make ugly games relatively rare.

Morgan, however, maintains that this objection to conventionalism fails to distinguish between surface (what he calls coordinating) conventions and deep conventions.[22] The former might include some commonly accepted maxims such as "Losing teams in basketball games may intentionally foul opponents so as to stop the clock and force the opponents to make free throws to hold their lead." As a number of writers have argued, this surface convention is not shown to be acceptable or justifiable just because it is accepted.

Perhaps Morgan's key contribution to an internalist defense of conventionalism is his argument that in addition to surface conventions there also are deep conventions that do have critical force. These conventions express the underlying theory of sport that critical reflection indicates makes the best sense of existing social practices.

According to Morgan, these social practices differ according to the historical social context in which they are embedded. Thus, strategic fouling in basketball may be morally acceptable in a deep reconstruction of the semiprofessional ethic dominating much of contemporary American sport but may be considered totally unethical in sporting contexts dominated by the ethic of gentlemanly generosity toward opponents prevalent in upper-class nineteenth- and early twentieth-century England, as captured in the award-winning movie *Chariots of Fire*.[23]

Note that Morgan's approach is quite compatible with and may even presuppose broad internalism in that it requires us to find the best overall interpretation of sporting practices within given social-cultural contexts. The dispute between Morgan and such writers as Russell, Nicholas Dixon, and ourselves, if this account of Morgan's view is accurate, is not between internalism and externalism or between broad internalism and noninterpretive approaches; rather, it is over whether interpretations can justifiably be claimed to transcend particular social contexts and at least make a claim to be justified across (all) social-cultural contexts. Indeed, on Morgan's view, different deep conventional paradigms of sport are incommensurable, so reasoned dialogue between their supporters is bound to fail.[24] Thus, according to Morgan, broad internalism as we have presented it requires us to transcend the social and cultural framework in which we are embedded and view sport from an ahistorical "view from nowhere" that in actuality is impossible for any of us to achieve.

Morgan's version of deep conventionalism is an important theoretical approach to sport. However, we do not share his pessimism either about the possibility of fruitful dialogue between advocates of different sociohistorical paradigms of sport or about the possibility of achieving rational resolution of such disputes through extended discussion.

In particular, broad internalism, as we understand it, need not be committed to an ahistorical or transcendent approach presupposing a view from nowhere. Instead, we can start from discourse in a particular historical context with the goal that continued discussion among interlocutors with diverse viewpoints might promote a consensus among advocates who were at one time in disagreement. Thus, discussion starts in a particular historical context but can transcend it and work toward universality. The discussion always takes place in a historical context. However, if a consensus reached through rational discourse survives extended criticism from significantly differing perspectives over an extended period of time, that surely gives us good (although not infallible) reason to believe the theory of sport in question is truly warranted or justified. Robert Simon has called this position "justificatory realism," as it holds that in such circumstances we have good grounds for thinking we agree on a theory because there truly is compelling evidence in its favor rather than thinking there is compelling evidence it its favor only because we already accept it.[25]

This suggests that debate between proponents of different paradigms of sport need not be incommensurable in the way Morgan suggests. Although the point needs further development than can be given here, it surely is plausible to think that proponents of the amateur or gentlemanly paradigm dominant in nineteenth- and early twentieth-century England can understand the importance of the pursuit of excellence and learning about oneself and others through the crucible of competition. Conversely, proponents of the modern or professional model surely can understand the idea that competitors are not enemies or mere obstacles to success but rather are persons to be treated fairly and with respect. Professional golfer Tim Clark, after losing the 2013 PGA Sony Open in spite of firing a wonderful sixty-three in the last round, said in his postround interview that "if you play well and someone plays better and beats you, then hats off to him—you have to feel good for him." Indeed, elite tournament golf is a wonderful example of a rational consensus that might be reached through dialogue between proponents of highly competitive sport and advocates of the gentlemanly model, as it blends a high degree of competitive intensity with an ethic of courtesy toward opponents and respect for the rules of the game. For example, golfers are expected to call penalties on themselves, and this is a common, virtually universal practice at elite levels of competition.

In any case, broad internalists and deep conventionalists agree that to understand and evaluate sporting practices we need to engage in an interpretive process that requires us to go beyond formal rules and develop a framework based on either principles (broad internalism) or deep conventions (deep conventionalism). Both approaches allow for the critique of existing sporting practice, either on the grounds that they violate important principles of sport or that they violate the deep social conventions underlying our present historically situated sporting practices. Although the issues between these two positions will be the subject of continued debate, we maintain that if a set of principles (an interpretive theory of sport) survives extended rigorous criticism from a broad set of perspectives leading to widespread or even universal acceptance by thoughtful people, we have good reason to believe it is really justified and not a mere historically limited social consensus. Of course, all such judgments are fallible and subject to revision in the face of criticism, but that should no more discourage us from the pursuit of justification and truth in sport than in other fields such as science itself, where theories are also subject to revision if the results of inquiry and discussion warrant it.

Although further debate about the best theoretical approach to evaluating sporting practices surely will continue, the approaches we have considered so far in this chapter can be useful in examining ethical issues in sport. We will begin this examination by considering competition in athletics that has been the subject of considerable criticism, both from some scholars as well as from segments of the general public.

Competition in Athletics

Is It Morally Defensible?

"Winning is not the most important thing; it's the only thing." This widely cited claim, often attributed (perhaps falsely) to the late Vince Lombardi, famous former coach of the Green Bay Packers, raises a host of issues that are central to the moral evaluation of sports. What importance should be assigned to winning in athletic competition? Consider sportswriter Grantland Rice's declaration: "For when the One Great Scorer comes to mark against your name, He writes—not that you won or lost—but how you played the Game," and the rejoinder by coach Forest Evashevski that one might as well say of a surgeon that it matters not whether his patient lives or dies but only how he makes the cut.[26]

Questions about the importance of winning are closely tied to but not identical with questions about the value of competition. Should we be concerned primarily with winning or with competing well? Is competition in sport a good thing, or can it be harmful or even immoral? Should winning be an athlete's most important goal? What degree of emphasis should we place on competitive success and winning in athletics?

At first glance competition seems to be the very nature of sport. We speak of sporting events as competitions or contests, evaluate athletes as good or bad competitors, and refer to other teams as opponents. But perhaps the connection between sports and competition is far looser than these habits suggest. Thus, someone can play golf or run a marathon just for the enjoyment of the activity. Indeed, all sports can be played noncompetitively. Men and women may participate for exercise, to forget about work, to enjoy the company of friends, and to enjoy the outdoors. Another goal of participation might be improvement. Such players, often described as competing with themselves, aim not at defeating opponents but at improving their own performances. Still others may have the aesthetic goal of performing the movements of their sport with skill and grace. For example, playground basketball players may value outstanding moves more than defeating their opponents. A leading amateur golfer of her generation, after years of hard practice, remarked that she wanted "to make a swing that you know is as close to perfection as you can get. And you say, 'Boy, look at what I did.' That's all it is."[27]

But even though not every player aims for or is motivated by competitive success, it doesn't follow that competition isn't part of the sport. A group of people may play softball just to interact with friends, but the point of the game, as defined by the rules, is to score more runs than the opponent. Even if participants' principal desire is to get exercise, they are doing so by trying to achieve the goals of the game as prescribed by the rules. An outfielder who is playing softball primarily to escape from the pressures of work still tries to catch a fly ball rather than just letting it drop, because a successful catch may prevent the opponent from scoring.

Critics of competition in sports do not object so much to games that have an internal competitive element as defined by the constitutive rules; rather, as we will see, they object to participants holding the defeat of an opponent as their main desire or goal. That is, the constitutive rules of games define what it takes to win, but it does not follow that the players themselves should aim primarily or even largely at winning rather than, say, improving, getting exercise, or interacting with friends on the playing field. Competition in sports in the fullest sense can be thought of as participation in sport contests with the intent or major goal of defeating an opponent. In such clear cases competition seems to be a zero-sum game. Because not all competitors can defeat an opponent, defeat by one precludes a like attainment by the other in the same contest.

Thus, according to the critics, athletic competition teaches or embodies a "me first" or "my team, right or wrong" attitude that promotes selfishness or, at best, a kind of narrow loyalty to one's team. This leads to regarding opponents not as persons but, at worst, as enemies and, at best, mere obstacles to be overcome rather than persons in their own right. Finally, because virtually all value is placed on winning, the value of the process of playing the game is overlooked or minimized. Losers are failures, and the value of practice, preparation, and competition are erased or forgotten as a result of losing the game.

Can a morally acceptable defense of competitive sports be developed? If such an ideal of competitive sports can be defended, we will be able to separate instances of competition in sports that are ethically defensible from those that are not. This knowledge can then be applied in later chapters to concrete issues in sport.

The Critique of Competition in Sport

Why is it even necessary to make a moral evaluation of competition in sport? Isn't it enough to say simply that participants and spectators alike enjoy such competition? To critics of competition in sport, that is not enough. They argue that such competition is either inherently immoral or that it reinforces other social values that are undesirable. Many persons, including some professional athletes, who have criticized competition and overemphasis on winning have proposed a more relaxed attitude toward sport, at least at most levels of amateur play, than the one the competitive creed sanctions. Proponents of competition in sports, in contrast, have argued for its moral value. General Douglas MacArthur, an American World War II hero, may have overstated the case when he maintained that participation in competitive sports was "a vital character builder" that "molds the youth of our country for their roles as custodians of the republic."[28] Overstated or not, that view is widely shared.

A moral evaluation of competition in sports is necessary if we are to make a rational assessment of such conflicting views. It will be useful to divide the arguments about the morality of competition in sports into two kinds. The first is concerned with the good or bad consequences of competitive practices, either to competitors themselves or society at large. The second is concerned not with the effects of competition but with its intrinsic character.

The Consequences of Competition

One way of evaluating competition in sports is to assess its consequences. Surely, whether a practice has good or bad effects on other people is relevant to moral evaluation. The important ethical theory known as utilitarianism holds that an action or practice is morally justified only if it has better consequences for all affected than the alternatives do.[29]

Utilitarianism sounds like a relatively simple approach to ethics. Just do a cost-benefit analysis on the effects of the act or practice being evaluated, and you have your answer about whether something is ethical. But utilitarianism raises complex issues of theory and practice before it can even be applied to a problem. For example, what are we to count as a good or bad consequence?

In economic analysis costs and benefits can often be measured in monetary profits and losses, but what is to count as a cost or benefit in ethics? Should pleasure and pain be the criteria, as classical utilitarians such as Jeremy Bentham and John Stuart Mill suggested? Are there other criteria, such as excellence in performance, achievement, or knowledge, that should also count? For example, is a well-played sports contest of greater intrinsic value than a poorly played one, and is this so even if the participants of both games experience the same levels of pleasure and pain? If we say that only pleasure and pain count, our theory may be too narrow. If we add other goods, such as excellence of performance, how are we to aggregate them with pleasure and pain to reach an overall total?

Moreover, even if we can agree on criteria of good and bad consequences, they may admit of different interpretations. For example, should we identify benefits with what actual participants seem to want or with what they would want if they were better informed and more rational? Suppose, for example, that Jones, who sees herself as a potential superstar, despises practices because of her coach's emphasis on teamwork but would value the practices if she were better informed about the benefits of teamwork and more honest about her own abilities.

Finally, what if the pursuit of the greatest good requires harming a minority? Suppose, for example, that a coach could motivate his team by bullying a weaker player, thereby getting the others to perform at a higher level through fear of being the next target. Is this fair to the victim or does it respect the rights of players, regardless of whether it is efficient in promoting better play?

None of this totally discredits utilitarianism. We all sometimes assess the consequences of behavior on our own lives and others. An ethical theory that ignored the consequences of actions or practices on human life would be hard to defend. Utilitarians, moreover, have developed versions of their theory that they claim protect the rights of minorities against the majority, although it remains controversial whether they are entirely successful.[30] But even though any satisfactory ethic must give some weight to the effects of acts or policies on human life, the choice of what framework we should adopt for evaluating the consequences will often be controversial.

In addition, if we are to evaluate the effects of competition in sports, another problem arises: Just what practices are we evaluating? Competition in sports can range from professional athletic contests to interscholastic competition to backyard contests among friends. Moreover, it is important to distinguish competition as it is practiced and as it ought to be practiced. Thus, even if competitive practices often have bad consequences, we should not necessarily conclude that competition in sports is morally indefensible. Perhaps competition in sports as carried out in one way has harmful consequences that could be avoided if that competition were instead carried out in another more ethical manner.

Accordingly, any utilitarian evaluation of competition in sports will rest on sometimes unstated and often controversial assumptions. An exhaustive analysis of the consequences of competition in sport is beyond the scope of this study, but it is important to remember the philosophical and methodological assumptions underlying such work. Given that the presuppositions of any utilitarian analysis are likely to be controversial, utilitarianism by itself probably cannot provide a decisive evaluation of competition in sport.

For example, we know that proponents of competitive sport claim that participation promotes loyalty, discipline, commitment, a concern for excellence, and a "never say die" attitude. That athletics offer unique opportunities for character development is a common general assertion. However, such claims are difficult to document. Thus, with regard to altruism, one early but influential study concluded, "Most athletes indicate low interest in receiving support and concern from others, low need to take care of others, and low need for affiliation. Such a personality seems necessary to achieve victory over others." More generally, the authors reported, "We found no empirical support for the tradition that sport builds character. . . . It seems that the personality of the ideal athlete is not the result of the molding process, but comes out of the ruthless selection process that occurs at all levels of sport. . . . Horatio Alger success—in sport or elsewhere—comes only to those who already are mentally fit, resilient, and strong."[31]

Although no study is by itself decisive and conclusions such as the one quoted above will be challenged later in this book, this study does have significant methodological implications. In particular, even if participants in competitive sport do manifest desirable character traits to an unusual degree, it does not follow that participation in sport caused these traits to develop; they may have been there all along. Correlation should not be confused with causation.[32]

However, the claim that preselection fully explains the virtues many athletes exhibit can cut in different directions. For one thing it can also be used to discount some of the consequentialist criticism of competitive sports. For example, competitive athletics may not promote selfishness or cheating, as critics of competitive sport may claim; rather, some successful athletes may already be selfish and predisposed to cheating before becoming successful in sport. There may be no causal effect, only correlation.

Thus, it is important not to confuse a factor associated or correlated with intense athletic competition with something that such competition causes.

Accordingly, if critics of competitive sport are right to explain away evidence that participation in sport develops virtues as simply the result of preselection, they cannot also consistently claim that participation in sport causes all the vices or harms involving athletes. If preselection is plausible at all, it applies to both the good qualities and the bad qualities associated with sport participation. It should not be used to dismiss the possibility of sport causing the good qualities while asserting that sport must cause the bad qualities.

But is the preselection theory plausible, even if applied consistently? In fact, even though there may be no direct and demonstrable connection between participation in competitive sports and desirable character development, there may be more subtle and indirect connections. Harry Edwards, while acknowledging that competitive sports do not build character from scratch, suggests that participation may reinforce and encourage the development of preexisting character traits.[33]

Similarly, it is not easy to show that a liberal arts education affects the values of students rather than preselecting students who already demonstrate desirable character traits. We do not conclude, however, that there are no effects. We surely need to be careful about a double standard in attributing the positive character traits of athletes to preselection while refusing to apply the same argument to our own favorite social and educational practices. Professors are rightly reluctant to assume they have no real influence on their students. But then why not be equally reluctant to assume that all the good qualities many athletes exhibit are entirely the result of preselection rather than at least partially the result of their participation in sports and the influences of their coaches?

Thus, the commonsense position Edwards suggests surely has force. Although it is true that both college coaches and admissions officers at selective schools recruit students who have already demonstrated a capacity for success, these individuals also may develop significantly because of the influence of coaches and professors. Surely the most intuitively plausible model is one of interaction. Experiences at college, whether in the classroom or on the playing field, often promote students' development, although the students selected to study and play sports at the institutions in question have already demonstrated some potential for success. The "add-ons" that college provides, whether in studies or in sport, in all likelihood make the educational experience valuable.

What should we conclude, then, about the consequentialist thesis that participation in athletics may promote moral and intellectual growth? For one thing we have learned that whether the thesis is true or false is not an issue easily settled and raises many complex questions. Much will depend on context. On one hand, if athletics are conducted in an unethical manner and if winning at all costs is the only goal emphasized, then participation may impede moral development rather than advancing it. On the other hand, if what is emphasized is the pursuit of excellence, if winning is considered an important goal but not the only goal, if respect for opponents and the best values of sport are emphasized, and if athletes are taught to think critically and reflectively about their performance, then participation might well have beneficial effects on participants and spectators alike.

Finally and of great importance, even if competitive sport have less impact on character development than many have claimed (for example, if the preselection theory is justifiable after all), it still may play a major role in expressing and illustrating our values and even help to justify them; we might call these the expressive and the justificatory functions of sport.[34] For example, athletic competition may illustrate the value of dedication and teamwork by publicly manifesting the excellence attained through the cultivation of those traits. Similarly, a highly talented team that never plays to its potential because its players are too selfish to work together or who cannot put aside their differences to cooperate in a common cause may show others all too clearly the costs of failure to cooperate in pursuit of a common cause.

In summary, we have seen that evaluating the social practice of competitive athletics by seeing whether its consequences are harmful or beneficial raises such complex issues that a decisive and uncontroversial consequential analysis is currently unavailable. However, we have also seen that those who are skeptical about the beneficial consequences of participation in competitive athletics have not necessarily won the day. On the contrary, there is much that believers in the benefits of sport participation can say in reply to the skeptics.

Most importantly, consequentialism itself may not be the most significant part of the ethical story. Competition, the critics contend, cannot satisfy legitimate ethical requirements that are nonconsequential in character. Are they right? Maybe if we look beyond consequences (especially if we construe "consequences" narrowly) to other sorts of principles, ones that regard factors other than consequences as morally significant, we can come to a defensible moral assessment of competitive sport.

Competition as a Mutual Quest for Excellence: An Interpretivist Approach

In the first part of this chapter we suggested that a broad internalist or interpretivist framework might help us better understand and assess moral issues in sport. In what follows, we suggest there is an account of competition in athletics that fits or explains key features of sport, such as Suits's suggestion that the constitutive rules create challenges often worth pursuing for their own sake and that presents competition in its best moral and aesthetic light.

Competition, Selfishness, and the Quest for Excellence

Perhaps the most important criticism of the moral worth of competition is that it is inherently selfish and egoistic. Because competitive activities are zero-sum games, one person's victory is another's defeat. The critics argue, then, that the goal of competition is to enhance the position of one competitor (or one small group of competitors, such as a team) at the expense of others. Thus, by its very nature, competition is selfish. Because selfish concern for oneself at the expense of others is immoral, it follows that competition is immoral as well. The point of this criticism is not that the consequences of competition are undesirable but that competition by its very nature is imbued with values we should reject.

These nonconsequentialist critics of competitive sports do not argue only against debased forms of competition, such as cheating. After all, virtually everyone acknowledges that competitive sports are morally objectionable when players are taught to cheat to win, to bribe officials, or to intentionally injure opponents to get them off the field of play. The critics, however, object to competitive sports at their best. Even supposing that the participants are playing fairly, is competition in sport still not selfish and egoistic?

The argument that competitive sports are selfish by their very nature is not without some intuitive force because in athletic competition if X wins, Y loses. Nevertheless, even if the argument that competition is essentially selfish is justifiable when applied to economic competition in the market, which is hardly self-evident, it faces special difficulties when applied to athletics.

For one thing the idea of competition in sport as an unrestricted war of all against all seems grossly inaccurate. Even though team sports involve competition between opponents, they also involve cooperation among team members. In many sports, even at the professional level, it is common for even opponents to encourage and even instruct each other in the off-season or between contests. Critics might reply that such examples show that even professional athletes find it morally impossible to live according to a strict competitive ethic. But, as we will see, such cooperative behavior can be regarded as part of a defensible competitive ethic that is based not on the idea of a war of all against all but on the value of meeting the challenges provided by competition in sport.

Moreover, as we have seen, competition in sport takes place within a context of binding constitutive rules. Constitutive rules are those that define what counts as a legitimate move within the game and what counts as winning and losing. Good competition requires competitors to forgo breaking the constitutive rules for momentary advantages (although, as we will see in the next chapter, strategic fouling may sometimes be permissible). Commitment to this ideal is perhaps best illustrated by the behavior of athletes in individual sports, from weekend tennis players to professional golfers, who call penalties on themselves in the heat of competition, sometimes at great financial cost. In many sports officials enforce rules. But although it is legitimate to question officials' calls, no one believes they ought not to apply the rules at all or that they should apply them arbitrarily or selectively.

In addition to obligations to obey the constitutive rules of the sport there are obligations of competitive fairness that also restrict selfishness in sports. Thus, competitive success seems insignificant or even unethical if it is obtained by stacking the deck against one side—say, by bribing an official or scheduling vastly inferior opponents for all or much of one's season.

Finally, selfishness in competitive sports is often criticized. The basketball player who is overly concerned with how many points she scores rather than with whether her team wins is criticized for being selfish; coaches often tell such players that they must become team players instead of trying to be the star. This response would make no sense if selfishness was the norm in competitive athletics.

At this point critics might concede that normative restrictions apply to selfish behavior in athletic competition, although they might still argue that, just as limited war is still war, so minimally constrained selfishness is still selfishness. Moreover, loyalty to one's team may be viewed as a kind of constrained selfishness similar to arbitrary discrimination against others: only my group or team counts fully; opponents are simply obstacles or things to be vanquished in the pursuit of victory. Even if this arguably narrow attitude is not selfishness, critics may maintain that it nevertheless is a morally indefensible attitude. Surely, one's opponents are persons with moral standing equal to that of one's own teammates.

To answer this point, we need a fuller account of competition in sport. Let us begin by considering a Yale-Princeton football game played in 1895. Princeton was winning 16–10, but Yale was right on the Princeton goal line with a chance to turn the tide on the very last play of the game:

> The clamor ceased once absolutely, and the silence was even more impressive than the tumult that had preceded it. . . . While they [the Yale players] were lining up for that last effort the cheering died away, yells both measured and inarticulate stopped and the place was so still . . . you could hear the telegraph instruments chirping like crickets from the side. Yale scored to win the game on a brilliant run. It is not possible to

describe that run. It would be as easy to explain how a snake disappears through the grass, or an eel slips from your fingers, or to say how a flash of linked lightning wriggles across the sky.[35]

Is the important point here simply that Yale won and that Princeton lost? Edwin Delattre, former president of St. John's College of Annapolis, Maryland, has drawn a different lesson from this episode and the many like it that take place in all seasons and at all levels of competition:

> Such moments are what make the game worth the candle. Whether amidst the soft lights and sparkling balls of a billiard table, or the rolling terrain of a lush fairway, or in the violent and crashing pits where linemen struggle, it is the moments where no letup is possible, when there is virtually no tolerance for error, which make up the game. The best and most satisfying contests maximize these moments and minimize respite from pressure.[36]

According to Delattre, these moments of testing rather than victory or defeat are the source of the value of competition in sports:

> The testing of one's mettle in competitive athletics is a form of self-discovery. . . . The claim of competitive athletics to importance rests squarely on their providing us opportunities for self-discovery which might otherwise have been missed. . . . They provide opportunities for self-discovery, for concentration and intensity of involvement, for being carried away by the demands of the contest . . . with a frequency seldom matched elsewhere. . . . This is why it is a far greater success in competitive athletics to have played well under pressure of a truly worthwhile opponent and lost than to have defeated a less worthy or unworthy one where no demands were made.[37]

Delattre's comments suggest that although it is essential to good competition that the competitors try as hard as they can to achieve victory, the principal value of athletic competition lies not in winning but in overcoming the challenge a worthy opponent presents. On this view, good competition presupposes a *cooperative* effort by competitors to generate the best possible challenge to each other. Each has the obligation to the other to try his or her best. Although one wins the contest and the other loses, each gains by trying to meet the challenge.

If this view has force, competition in sports should be regarded and engaged in not as a zero-sum game but as *a mutually acceptable quest for excellence through challenge.* Underlying the good sports contest, in effect, is an implicit social contract under which both competitors accept the obligation to provide a challenge for opponents according to the rules of the sport. Competition in sport is ethically defensible, on this view, when it is engaged in voluntarily as part of this mutual quest. This does not mean that all competition in sport is ethically defensible; actual practice may not satisfy the requirements of the mutual quest for excellence. It does say, however, that competition in sport is ethically defensible when it satisfies such requirements.

Competitive sport as a mutual quest for excellence not only emphasizes the cooperative side of athletic contests and the acceptance of the challenge from the point of view of all the competitors but also explains much of our society's fascination with competitive sports. A. Bartlett Giamatti, former president of Yale and former commissioner of major league baseball, emphasized the quest for excellence:

> When . . . a person on the field or fairway, rink, floor, or track performs an act that surpasses—despite his or her evident mortality, his or her humanness—whatever we have seen or heard of or could conceive of doing ourselves, then we have witnessed . . . an instant of complete coherence. In that instant, pulled to our feet, we are pulled out of ourselves. We feel what we saw, became what we perceived. The memory of that moment is deep enough to send us all out again and again, to reenact the ceremony, made of all the minor ceremonies to which spectator and player devote themselves, in the hopes that the moment will be summoned again and made again palpable.[38]

We propose, then, that competitive athletics is best conceived as a mutual quest for excellence, an activity that is significantly cooperative in that all the participants consent to be tested in the crucible of competition for both the intrinsic value of meeting interesting challenges and for what we can learn about ourselves and others through the attempt to meet the competitive test. This proposal, which we will call *mutualism,* arguably best fits and explains key features of competitive sport, such as why the constitutive rules create artificial challenges, and also presents athletic competition in its best moral and aesthetic light. Although mutualism can be viewed as an independent account of competitive sport, we also suggest it is justified on broad internalist grounds as the best interpretation of competitive sport.

A Criticism: Mutualism Is Not a Theory of Competition

At this point critics of competition in sport may become impatient. Sports events, conceived as part of a mutually acceptable quest for excellence, may indeed be ethically defensible, they might reply, but such a view does not justify competition in sport; rather, they might claim, it replaces competitive sport with something else. What has been done is a verbal trick. "Competition" has been so redefined that it no longer refers to true competition at all. By emphasizing the quest for excellence, we have changed the aim of the sports contest from that of defeating opponents to the quest for self-development and achievement. The aim is no longer to defeat opponents but rather to reach certain standards of performance or to gain self-knowledge and development through trying to satisfy those standards. Competition in sport has been replaced by so-called competition with oneself. Is this charge correct? Let us consider the issue further.

This rejoinder faces two serious criticisms. First, "competition with self" is not as independent from comparison with others as the criticisms suppose. Second and more importantly, the mutual quest for excellence emphasizes defeating an opponent and, thus, is concerned with competition after all.

"Competition with self" suggests that athletes play against ghostly images of their earlier selves. Because there are no ghostly images and no presently existing earlier selves with whom to compete, this expression is potentially misleading. It is perhaps less paradoxical to speak of individuals as striving for self-development or self-improvement than to speak of individuals competing against earlier versions of themselves.

Should participants in sports strive mainly for self-development or personal improvement? In aiming for improvement we do not necessarily aim to beat others. We can all improve together, so the element of the zero-sum game is missing. Because all can improve together, to aim at improvement does not appear selfish. Intending to beat others seems selfish, at least to the critics, because it seems to value success of the self or of one's team without regard to the interests of others.

There are two defenses against such an approach. The first, as we have seen, is that competition thought of as a mutual quest for excellence is not necessarily selfish or a total zero-sum game. Although only one party can win, each cooperates in providing a mutually acceptable challenge to the other. Although not all competitors can win, there is a sense, as we will see, in which all the competitors in a well-played contest can meet the challenge and achieve excellence.

Perhaps of most significance, we can question the degree to which the quest for self-improvement differs from competitive sports in an ethically important way. At the very least the two approaches share some central features. For one thing, an especially significant criterion of improvement is change in one's competitive standing when measured against others' performance. Perhaps the best way of judging one's progress is to see whether one is doing better against opponents now than in the past. Doing better against opponents is not merely a contingent sign of improvement; often, what counts as playing well is logically determined by what counts as an appropriate competitive response to opponents' moves. For example, it would be incorrect to say that Susan is playing good tennis if Susan is hitting crisp ground shots when intelligent play calls for charging the net. Similarly, it would be incorrect to say that she is improving if she continues to make such competitively inappropriate moves in match after match.

The conceptual point, then, is that achievement, improvement, or development cannot easily be divorced from comparison with others' performance. Robert Nozick provided a pertinent illustration: "A man living in an isolated mountain village can sink 15 jump shots with a basketball out of 150 tries. Everyone else in the village can sink only one jump shot out of 150 tries. He thinks (as do the others) that he's very good at it. One day along comes Jerry West."[39] (West was an All American for West Virginia University and one of the great professional players of all time in the NBA, where he played from 1960 to 1974.)

Nozick's example illustrates that what counts as a significant achievement requires reference to others' performance. It further suggests that judgments about what counts as a significant improvement also presuppose comparative evaluations about others' performance. Before the arrival of a great professional basketball player such as Jerry West, the village star may have thought that improving his average to 17 out of 150 shots would constitute significant improvement. After the visit, even if it is acknowledged that no villager can ever match West's skill, the very criterion of significant improvement would have radically changed.

Accordingly, those who value "competition with self" because it seems not to involve (possibly negative) comparisons with others' performance may need to rethink their position. The quest for improvement and the quest for victory both share an element of comparison with others' performance. That is why the rhetoric of competition with self can be misleading; the appropriate reference group is not only an earlier self but also a reference class of fellow competitors.[40]

Mutualism not only acknowledges that improvement often is measured by comparison to how well others perform; it also recognizes that winning often, perhaps generally, is the major criterion for meeting the test of the contest. Exhibiting better strategic skills than the opposition, as illustrated by the example of Susan's bad tactics cited above, is crucial to meeting the test the opposition presents. Although opponents can each meet the challenge of competition by playing their best against each other, normally the winner has done the better job of meeting the challenges of the sport.

Suppose dancers were given the following advice: "It's unimportant whether you are good or bad dancers—just try to get better and better every day." Surely it is important that dancers improve their performance, but isn't the level of achievement they have attained also important? In the dance we appreciate personal development, but we also value achievement and a skilled performance. If athletic performance is regarded as significant, skilled performance is important in sport as well. Competition is the mechanism by which achievement is measured and determined. Improvement is a desirable goal, but achievement is no less important or noble. Improvement, then, is a worthy goal toward which all competitors ought to strive. But it is not the only goal; high achievement in athletics can be equally worthy, sometimes inspiring, and, as Giametti has suggested, even ennobling as well.

Finally, the mutualist account of athletic competition avoids the charge of selfishness, as it conceives of athletic contests as mutually acceptable activities to which the participants freely consent. Although each participant aims at winning, mutualism implies that they see each other not as enemies or mere things or obstacles but rather as persons who facilitate the ability to test oneself through challenge. Noted golfer and 2001 British Open Champion David Duval expressed how a good competitor should view opponents when he discussed the possibility of contending against Tiger Woods in a major championship: "One of the great things about golf is that you don't have to have any ill-will in this game. If I come head-to-head against him at say, the U.S. Open, I want him to be playing as good as he can play because I want to beat him when he's playing his best. It would be a heck of a lot better, if you know he gave you all he's got, and you beat him."[41] Mutualism, then, condemns viewing opponents as enemies or reducing them to obstacles to success while at the same time supporting our best efforts to meet the challenges a worthy opponent presents.

Winning, Competitive Success, and the Mutual Quest for Excellence

In athletics we often speak of successful coaches, successful seasons, and success in particular contests. But how should we understand "success"?

On one view, success can be identified with winning. The successful coach is the winning coach, and the most successful season is an undefeated one or at least one in which many more games are won than lost.

But such a view surely goes too far. Is a game in which an athletically superior team plays sloppily and commits many careless errors but narrowly defeats an overmatched opponent truly successful? Is a team that wins only because of a series of bad calls by officials successful? Is a player unsuccessful if she loses because of an unlucky break in spite of playing just as well as her opponent? Nicholas Dixon surely is right to point out that "playing down" to inferior opponents, bad calls, and luck can deprive winning of much of its significance in many sporting contexts.[42] It is also arguable that a win achieved by aesthetically ugly play, such as frequent body checking in an ice hockey game by a team of inferior skaters for the sole purpose of preventing the team of better skaters from employing their skills, is less meaningful than one achieved through primary skills of hockey, such as excellent skating and puck handling.

On the mutualist account, winning normally is a major criterion of competitive success but hardly the only one. In a hard-fought contest between worthy opponents, both can meet the challenge of competition through exhibiting excellence even though only one can win. Of course, it is justifiable in such a case for the losers to be deeply disappointed, as they may rightly believe victory could have been achieved through the use of different tactics or better execution, but surely if they played a nearly flawless game, it is too harsh to regard their effort as a *failure*.

Although we believe this mutualist account of the significance of winning is largely correct, we also note that it has been the subject of some recent critical discussion. Does mutualism as we have presented it give adequate weight to winning?

The main theses of mutualism is that athletic competition is best conceived of (and often is) a significantly cooperative activity in which the parties freely engage in order to meet the challenge framed by the constitutive rules of the sport. On this view, although only one party can win, all can succeed or gain. Although winning normally is a major criterion of success, the losers also can be successful—for example, if they exhibited excellence in their play, lost only because of bad calls, or took an athletically superior opponent to the limit. Both parties can also learn about themselves and others often from their failures in meeting the test of competition.

But does this account give enough significance to winning? One line of criticism follows the suggestion of Scott Kretchmar and Tim Elcombe, according to whom winning requires the use of special strategic skills over and above the athletic skills the sport tests.[43] Competitors need to learn how to win, and this involves mastering such strategic skills as knowing how to make a run when behind, learning to keep one's cool when the opponent develops a hot hand, making good tactical choices, and playing one's best in high-pressure situations. These skills require a great degree of mental discipline and intelligence and can be distinguished from purely athletic or technical skills. For example, making good decisions under the pressure of a close game is not a physical skill. Does mutualism fail to emphasize the special skills involved in "knowing how to win"?

Kretchmar in a later paper raises two additional points. Although he acknowledges that both parties in an athletic competition can gain in the ways mutualists suggest, he adds that "sport is structured to produce a . . . ranking, a 'better than' and 'worse than' kind of conclusion" and adds that "the very poignancy of sport is predicated on the fact that this . . . matters." It matters, according to this argument, because if we do not immerse ourselves in the frame of the sporting contest, sport has no chance to move us and, thus, loses its dramatic and emotional impact. Not to give ourselves to the contest, Kretchmar points out, is like going to a dramatic play or movie or reading a gripping and emotionally wrenching novel and consistently reminding ourselves that it is all make believe and just a mere story. By immersing ourselves in the story as if it were real and by taking the sporting contest seriously, we add depth and intensity to our experience that is an important source of richness in our lives. As Kretchmar puts it: "the dramatic power of sport derives from is zero-sum frame."[44]

Moreover, Kretchmar argues, the possibility of a rematch to test and perhaps overturn the outcome of the earlier contest creates the possibility of redemption for the loser and through hope of victory the next time the competition takes place.[45] If we just emphasized the mutual benefits of the contest, this hope of redemption and the value of "playing again" would make no sense. For example, the nearly eternal hope of Chicago Cubs fans that their team will rise to the top of Major League Baseball would be virtually unintelligible if we focused only on the mutual benefits that arise from competition.

We accept Kretchmar's points about the significance of winning, which serve as a needed correction to dismissal of its importance. In fact, earlier editions of this book may have been guilty of underemphasizing its significance. Nevertheless, we suggest that his account is not incompatible with mutualism and does not call for a reassessment of its major tenets. Thus, winning is not everything for the reasons we already have provided. Athletic competition can and should provide benefits for winners and losers and, above all, is a significantly cooperative activity in which competitors voluntarily agree to test themselves against the challenges of their sport. Competitors contribute to the pursuit of excellence with each other and, thus, are facilitators rather than enemies or mere obstacles to victory. As Kretchmar argues, the possibility of winning and losing gives competitive sport much of its dramatic force and creates opportunities for demonstrating human excellence and redemption in playing again (rematches). Nevertheless, the pursuit of victory takes place (or should take place) within a mutually acceptable framework created by the challenges of each sport, within which competitors test themselves against one another. Thus, Kretchmar's emphasis on winning is not incompatible with mutualism but instead adds to the richness of the theory.

Concluding Comments

This chapter has examined different approaches to understanding sport and has argued for a broad internalist or interpretive approach as both an explanation of the broad appeal of sports and as basis for assessing their value and for approaching controversial normative issues that arise in athletic competition. In particular, we suggest the conception of athletic competition as a mutual quest for excellence is a strong candidate for the normatively most defensible account of competitive sport. Although one can accept mutualism as a stand-alone approach, we have argued that it also is justifiable on broad internalist or interpretivist grounds; that is, it both explains key features of sport, such as the importance of the challenges the constitutive rules provide, and provides an ethically and aesthetically justifiable account of athletic competition itself. Specifically, it answers the critics of competition by undermining the charge of selfishness, by explaining why opponents should be regarded as facilitators rather than enemies, and by emphasizing the importance of the process of meeting the challenges for their own sake as well as for any external rewards that may flow from competitive success.

Our discussion indicates that critics of competition in sport may have taken their points too far by ignoring the perhaps equally deleterious effects of underemphasis. Although we agree that sport need not always be played in an intensely competitive manner, competition in athletics is not necessarily immoral; indeed, if participants normally are told that "it doesn't matter how you do—just go out and have fun," the subtle message being conveyed may be that doing well is unimportant. If participation in competitive sport can be a form of human excellence, if it can contribute to self-development and self-expression and, perhaps, reinforce desirable character traits, performance may well matter after all. As William Bennett has observed, "Serious playing and watching . . . are rarely if ever doing nothing, for sports is a way to scorn indifference, and occasionally, indeed, one can even discern in competition those elements of grace, skill, beauty, and courage that mirror the greatest affirmations of human spirit and passion."[46]

This remark suggests that competitive sport, at its best, involves applying standards of excellence to challenges that people regard as worthwhile in themselves. This idea should be taken seriously. If competitive sport is understood on the model of a mutual quest for excellence through challenge, it not only can be an activity of beauty and skill but also can represent a striving for human excellence, and in so doing it can be a paradigmatic way of respecting each other as persons, of taking our status as persons seriously.

Of course, the mutualist approach to competitive sport sets an ethical standard that may be and indeed too often is violated in actual practice. In the real world winning may be overemphasized, rules may be broken, athletes may be exploited, and unfair conditions for competition may preclude genuine challenge. If so, the mutualist ideal provides grounds for the moral criticism of serious deviations from it. In the remainder of this book we will apply the ideal to the moral evaluation of actual practices in sport.

QUESTIONS FOR REVIEW

1. What is a theory of sport? Do you agree that such a theory might be useful in the ethical evaluation of issues arising within athletic competition? Why?
2. What are constitutive rules, and what role do they play in Bernard Suits's analysis of the nature of games? How might Suits distinguish games from other practices that might have constitutive rules, such as taking a standardized test for admission to college?
3. Distinguish formalism, conventionalism, and broad internalism from one another. What criteria might broad internalists appeal to in order to justify a theory of sport?
4. What is the relationship between broad internalism and mutualism in competitive athletics?
5. Explain William J. Morgan's defense of conventionalism. Explain a major criticism of his view.

Notes

1. Mike Ammann, goalkeeper of the Metro Stars of Major League Soccer, quoted by George Vecsey, "Backtalk: When Is It Gamesmanship and When Is It Cheating?" *New York Times*, August 8, 1999, sec. 8, p. 13.

2. The material on theories of sport that follows borrows from Robert L. Simon, "Theories of Sport," in Cesar R. Torres, ed., *The Bloomsbury Companion to the Philosophy of Sport* (London: Bloomsbury, 2014).

3. Ludwig Wittgenstein (1889–1951), although not well known to the general public, was extraordinarily influential in philosophy in part because in his later work he stressed understanding the use we make of philosophically puzzling concepts in our ordinary discourse and how removing confusions arising from misuse of language can dissolve many philosophical problems.

4. Ludwig Wittgenstein, *Philosophical Investigations* (New York: Macmillan, 1953), 33e (sec. 66).

5. Bernard Suits, *The Grasshopper: Games, Life, and Utopia* (Toronto: University of Toronto Press, 1978). This book was reissued with an introduction by Thomas Hurka in 2005 by Broadview Press, Buffalo, New York. A series of articles by Suits also has been particularly influential in developing the idea of constitutive rules as central to the idea of games (and most sports). See, especially, "What Is a Game?" *Philosophy of Science* 34, no. 2 (June 1967): 148–156; and "The Elements of Sport," in *Philosophic Inquiry in Sport*, ed. William J. Morgan and Klaus V. Meier (Champaign, IL: Human Kinetics Press, 1995), 8. For criticism, see Klaus Meier, "Triad Trickery: Playing with Sport and Games," *Journal of the Philosophy of Sport* 15, no. 2 (May 1988): 11–30. Volume 35 (2008) of that journal contains a symposium devoted to Suits's work.

6. William J. Morgan, *Leftist Theories of Sport: A Critique and Reconstruction* (Urbana: University of Illinois Press, 1994), esp. ch. 5.

7. Internalism as a theoretical approach to the analysis of sport is discussed more fully in Robert L. Simon, "Internalism," in *The Handbook of the Philosophy of Sport*, ed. William J. Morgan and Mike McNamee (New York: Routledge, 2013).

8. This kind of example, only with a squash player who forgets her racquet rather than a golfer whose clubs are lost, was employed by Robert Butcher and Angela Schneider in "Fair Play as Respect for the Game," *Journal of the Philosophy of Sport* 25, no. 1 (May 1998): 6, but for an even earlier use of it, see A. S. Lumpkin, S. Stoll, and J. Beller, *Sports Ethics: Applications for Fair Play* (St. Louis, MO: Mosby, 1994). Also, see, for example, Warren Fraleigh, "Why the Good Foul Is Not Good Enough," in *Philosophic Inquiry in Sport*, ed. William J. Morgan and Klaus V. Meier (Champaign, IL: Human Kinetics Press, 1995), 185–187.

9. For example, see the influential paper by Fred D'Agostino, "The Ethos of Games," in *Philosophic Inquiry in Sport*, ed. William J. Morgan and Klaus V. Meier (Champaign, IL: Human Kinetics Press, 1995) 36–49.

10. For Dworkin's criticism of Hart, see "The Model of Rules," in Dworkin's *Taking Rights Seriously* (Cambridge, MA: Harvard University Press, 1977). Hart's views are developed in his noted work *The Concept of Law* (Oxford: Clarendon Press, 1961).

11. Much of what follows in this section is taken from and more fully developed in Robert L. Simon's "Internalism and Internal Values in Sport," *Journal of the Philosophy of Sport* 27 (May 2000): 1–16.

12. Butcher and Schneider, "Fair Play as Respect for the Game," 9.

13. Ibid., 11.

14. Ibid., 18.

15. J. S. Russell, "Are Rules All an Umpire Has to Work With?" *Journal of the Philosophy of Sport* 26, no. 1 (May 1999): 27–49.

16. Ibid., 28.

17. Ibid., 14.

18. Ibid., 15.

19. Morgan's *Leftist Theories of Sport*, cited above, in part is an argument for this conclusion.

20. Cesar R. Torres has developed the role of aesthetic consideration within broad internalism in his paper, "Furthering Interpretivism's Integrity: Bringing Together Ethics and Aesthetics," *Journal of the Philosophy of Sport* 39, no. 2 (October 2012): 299–319.

21. For recent statements of this position, see W. J. Morgan, "Broad Internalism, Deep Conventions, Moral Entrepreneurs," *Journal of the Philosophy of Sport* 39, no. 1 (May 2012): 65–100; and "Interpretivism, Conventionalism and the Ethical Coach," in *The Ethics of*

Coaching Sports: Moral, Social, and Legal Issues, ed. Robert L. Simon (Boulder, CO: West-view Press, 2013), 61–77.

22. Morgan, "Broad Internalism, Deep Conventions, Moral Entrepeneurs," 70–79.

23. Morgan, "Interpretivism, Conventionalism and the Ethical Coach," 66–73.

24. Ibid., 70–71.

25. Robert Simon has developed this view in "From Ethnocentrism to Realism: Does Discourse Ethics Bridge the Gap?" *Journal of the Philosophy of Sport* 31 (2004): 122–141.

26. What Lombardi is claimed to have actually said is "Winning isn't everything, but wanting to win is." Scott Morris, ed., *The Book of Strange Facts and Useless Information* (New York: Dolphin, 1979). The statement by Rice is from *John Bartlett's Familiar Quotations* (Boston: Little, Brown, 1951), 901, and the remark from Evashevski is from *Sports Illustrated*, September 23, 1957, 119. For discussion, see James Keating, "Winning in Sport and Athletics," *Thought* 38, no. 2 (1963): 201–210.

27. Judy Cooperstein, as quoted by Gerald Eskanai, "Judy Cooperstein Still Has the Tempo," *New York Times*, July 2, 1981, B12.

28. Quoted by John Loy and Gerald S. Kenyon, *Sport, Culture, and Society* (New York: Macmillan, 1969), 9–10.

29. Utilitarianism is really the name of a family of related positions. For example, utilitarians disagree among themselves over whether we ought to evaluate the consequences of specific actions (act utilitarianism) or of general compliance with rules or social practices (rule utilitarianism). There are different versions of both act and rule utilitarianism. Some philosophers believe that each approach will evaluate the same act differently, as when a specific violation of a promise will have good consequences even when it breaks the rule that promises ought to be kept. Others suggest that a defensible set of rules will have so many exceptions that the very distinction between act and rule utilitarianism blurs or even collapses. For a helpful introductory discussion of utilitarianism, see James Rachels, *The Elements of Moral Philosophy* (New York: McGraw-Hill, 1993), 90–116.

30. For example, they might claim that in the long run, enforcement of rules protecting individual rights produces better consequences than violating the individual whenever it seems to be in the short-term interests of the majority to do so. For discussion see Rachels, *The Elements of Moral Philosophy*.

31. Bruce C. Ogilvie and Thomas Tutko, "Sports: If You Want to Build Character, Try Something Else," *Psychology Today*, October 1971, 61–62.

32. This point is argued forcefully by James L. Shulman and William C. Bowen in their influential study of the effects of participation in athletics at academically elite colleges and universities, *The Game of Life: College Sports and Educational Values* (Princeton, NJ: Princeton University Press, 2001), esp. ch. 4.

33. Harry Edwards, *Sociology of Sport* (Homeward, IL: Dorsey Press, 1973), 324.

34. The idea of an expressive function of punishment is suggested by Joel Feinberg in "The Expressive Function of Punishment," in his *Doing and Deserving* (Princeton, NJ: Princeton University Press, 1970), 95–118. The idea of an expressive function of sport is examined by David Fairchild in his article "Prolegomena to an Expressive Function of Sport," *Journal of the Philosophy of Sport* 14, no 1 (May 1987): 21–33.

35. Richard Harding Davis, "Thorne's Famous Run," in *The Omnibus of Sport*, ed. Grant-land Rice and Harford Powel (New York: Harper and Brothers, 1932), quoted by Edward J. Delattre, "Some Reflections on Success and Failure in Competitive Athletics," *Journal of the Philosophy of Sport* 2, no. 1 (May 1975): 134–135.

36. Delattre, Ibid., 134.

37. Ibid., 135. Similar themes are developed by Paul Weiss in his *Sport: A Philosophic Inquiry* (Carbondale: Southern Illinois University Press, 1969), one of the pioneering works in twentieth-century philosophic study of sport.

38. A. Bartlett Giamatti, *Take Time for Paradise: Americans and Their Games* (New York: Simon and Schuster, 1989), 35–36.

39. Robert Nozick, *Anarchy, State, and Utopia* (New York: Basic Books, 1974), 240.

40. Can't we just see whether our current performance improves relative to our past performance? Thus, if I shot a 90 in golf last month and an 89 today, haven't I shown improvement? Perhaps so, but whether that improvement is significant or worth noting depends on comparisons with an appropriate reference group. If players of similar athletic ability and training normally improve from 90 to 82 in one month, I may have no justification for regarding my improvement as worth noting or of significance at all.

41. Clifton Brown, "Golf: Golf's Titanium Twosome; Rivalry Between Duval and Woods Towers over PGA Tour," *New York Times*, February 3, 1999, D4, www.nytimes.com/1999/02/03/sports/golf-golf-s-titanium-twosome-rivalry-between-duval-woods-towers-over-pga-tour.html.

42. Nicholas Dixon, "On Winning and Athletic Superiority," *Journal of the Philosophy of Sport* 26, no. 1 (May 1999): 10–26.

43. See, for example, Scott Kretchmar, "In Defense of Winning," in *Sports Ethics*, ed. Jan Boxill (Malden, MA: Blackwell, 2002), 130–135.

44. Scott Kretchmar, "Competition, Redemption, and Hope," *Journal of the Philosophy of Sport* 39, no. 1 (April 2012): 104–106.

45. Ibid., 108–113.

46. William J. Bennett, "In Defense of Sports," *Commentary* 61, no. 2 (1977): 70.

=3=

Ethics in Competition

CHEATING, GOOD SPORTS, AND TAINTED VICTORIES

We began the last chapter by presenting some examples of controversial cases that arise in athletic competition, namely, Spygate, which involved the New England Patriots of the NFL using electronic devices to spy on opposing coaches to learn what plays would be used against them; Briana Scurry's illegal move in the goal to help the US Women's team win the World Cup in soccer; and Colorado's victory over Missouri when they were erroneously given one more down than the rules allowed, enabling them to score the winning touchdown. How should we assess these cases and other often related ethical issues that arise in athletic competition? Is the theoretical framework we developed in the last chapter helpful in such an endeavor?

Some may think all these cases involve cheating and, thus, are wrong. We can begin our examination, then, by examining the notion of cheating itself.

Cheating, Breaking the Rules, and Tainted Victories

What is cheating, and what makes it wrong in athletic competition? Can the ethic of the mutual quest for excellence ever allow cheating?

Although moral skeptics often appeal to disagreement on controversial moral issues, not all moral issues are controversial. Thus, most people agree that straightforward cheating in sports is to be condemned. And although cheating might be hard to define, sometimes we know it when we see it; for example, a golfer who deliberately fails to count all her strokes in an important tournament clearly is cheating, as is a basketball coach who, in the confusion of a last-second foul call, intentionally deceives referees and opponents by directing his best foul shooter to go to the line even though it was another player, a particularly poor foul shooter, who was fouled.

An Analysis of Cheating

What makes these examples paradigm cases of cheating? Because rules can be broken by accident or ignorance, cheating cannot mean simply breaking the rules; it must have other components. Sometimes, for example, cheating is identified with deception, as when an unfaithful spouse deceives his or her partner or when a basketball team sends its best foul shooter to the line even when she was not the player who was fouled. Or it could involve breaking an explicit or implicit promise, as when someone consciously violates an agreement made with others, as in sports when a tennis player dishonestly calls a shot by an opponent out of bound after having agreed before the match to make accurate calls.

However, as philosopher Bernard Gert has pointed out in a perspicuous analysis, cheating does not necessarily involve either deception or promise breaking.[1] For example, an athlete who has power over her competitors might cheat quite openly, or an athlete might deny that he ever promised to obey a particular rule. The latter would be like, say, a spy who cheated on a civil service examination to attain a powerful position but who then denied that he had ever promised, even implicitly, to obey the rules laid down by the government he despised. More generally, the idea of an implicit promise may be too vague to support charges of cheating.

Cheating, Gert suggested, is best identified with the intentional violation of a public system of rules to secure the goals of that system for oneself or for those for whom one is concerned.[2] Cheating is normally wrong, but not only because it usually deceives or violates a promise, although these may contribute to its wrongness. The distinctive element in the general presumption that cheating is wrong is that the cheater behaves in a way that no one could rationally or impartially recommend that everyone in the activity emulate; that is why the public system of rules prohibits it in the first place. Thus, cheaters make arbitrary exceptions of themselves in order to gain advantages over others, in effect treating those others as mere means to their own ends or their own well-being.

Cheaters, in other words, fail to respect their opponents as persons, as agents with purposes of their own, by violating the public system of rules that others may reasonably expect to govern the activity in question. A golf tournament would not truly be an athletic contest if everyone cheated nor would it determine who the best player was. The rules of golf are the public system under which it can reasonably be presumed the participants expect to compete. It may be difficult to say what is or is not cheating in borderline cases, but in paradigm cases cheaters arbitrarily subordinate the interests and purposes of others to their own and, thus, violate the fundamental moral norm of respect for persons. This illustrates the close connection between the general moral principle that requires respect for persons and the idea of athletic competitions as mutual quests for excellence; persons are respected because their choice to compete is not coerced and the rules and principles of a well-designed sport create a test or challenge all parties normally consider well worth pursuing.

Cheating, therefore, at least in paradigm cases, involves violating a public system of rules that every participant in an activity may reasonably assume will govern the activity in question, and a cheater does so in order to obtain benefits for oneself, one's teammates, opponents, fans, or others for whom one cares. The cheating is wrong because other participants in the activity could not reasonably accept it. Cheaters disregard the legitimate interest that other competitors have in a fair contest and may use other competitors as mere means to an end or tools for their own benefit.

Ethical Cheating?

Contrary to what was said above, some have suggested that cheating in athletic competitions is not always wrong. On this view, cheating may undermine fair play, but it still might make for good sports. As one commentator has maintained:

> Many competitions . . . would be more interesting if cheating takes place within it or if several players try to stretch the rules. Such deviant behavior adds a new dimension to the game which can also add to its interest. . . . Insofar as the contest is one of wits as well as one of skill and strategy, it can be exciting to compete with and against someone who uses his wits to try to cheat and it can be exciting for an audience to observe such intelligent behavior.[3]

For example, what about the use of the illegal spitball pitch in baseball? If, when it is used by a Major League pitcher such as Gaylord Perry, who was well known for throwing spitballs, it can make the game more fascinating and exciting, isn't its use justified?

This position is open to the objection that cheating undermines the idea of the sport contest as a test of skill as mutualism claims. Sports do, however, serve other purposes in our society, such as providing entertainment and giving professional players an opportunity to secure financial gains. But these other purposes are parasitic in that what ought to be entertaining about our sports and what makes them sometimes worth paying to see is the test of excellence they provide. Pitchers who throw the illegal spitball are taking an advantage for themselves that is unavailable to competitors who play by the rules, and they are, therefore, undermining the idea of competition as a fair quest for excellence.

Perhaps, however, what is being endorsed is not solitary acts of cheating that deceive opponents or in some other way violate the public system of rules that players are entitled to have apply to the game. Thus, "if . . . cheating is recognized as an option which both sides may morally take up, then in general the principles of equality and justice are not affected."[4] Perhaps the practice of strategic fouling in basketball fits such a description, in that players expect other players to foul strategically in appropriate situations.

If, however, all sides acknowledge, expect, and engage in the practice openly, it is far from clear that strategic fouling is cheating at all. If all players acknowledge that other competitors will engage in the action at issue, if all are willing to accept the penalty, and if the rules contain just compensation for violation, why is the act one of cheating? The difficulty for those who believe that cheating in sports is sometimes justified because it makes for better sports is to find behavior that clearly is cheating and that is also morally permissible. Strategic fouling may be morally permissible (we will discuss this more fully in what follows), but it is far from clear that it is a form of cheating.

Thus, proponents of the thesis that cheating in sports sometimes is permissible and even desirable face the following dilemma. On one hand, insofar as the actions in question are thought to be acceptable for all participants, are committed openly, are known and expected by participants and officials alike, and are compensated for by fair penalties prescribed by rules, such actions are not cheating. On the other hand, if the actions do not fall under such criteria, are not done openly with a willingness to accept the penalty, and, thus, cannot be part of the publicly acceptable framework (constitutive rules and principles) applying to the sport, they are not morally permissible. Rather, as in the case of throwing the spitball, it is not an acceptable violation of the public rules that all participants may reasonably expect to govern the game. Thus, we have not been shown that some acts in athletic competitions are both genuine cases of cheating and also morally acceptable. Hence, our conclusion that cheating is not a morally acceptable form of behavior in athletic competition still stands. Let us test this thesis by considering the Spygate scandal discussed in Chapter 2.

Spygate and the Nature of Cheating

The Spygate scandal, remember, involved the New England Patriots of the NFL using electronic devices to snoop on the conversations of opposing coaches during games in order to steal their strategies. If successful, this would enable the Patriots to anticipate the plays their opponents would run and, hence, counteract the strategies of the competition. Is this cheating? If so, is it wrong, or does it simply make the game more interesting as suggested in the discussion above?

Clearly, because it violated a rule of the NFL and was done intentionally to gain a competitive advantage, the Patriots' hacking certainly seems to be cheating. But we need to pursue the question further to illuminate what was seriously wrong with the behavior. In particular, we need to consider whether the rule should be changed to allow such behavior. Would anything be wrong with the Patriots' spying if every team was permitted to do the same, if secretly taping of the kind carried out was made part of the public system of rules governing the sport? Thus, in baseball or softball, if an opposing pitcher's behavior gives away what pitch will be thrown and teams pick up on the "tell" and anticipate what will be thrown, their behavior seems perfectly acceptable. Why does the ethics of the situation change when the case is hacking into coaches' instructions to their team? Is there a relevant difference?

We maintain there is a difference. If a pitcher tips off the opposition to what kind of pitch will be thrown, that is a fault in the player's technique. The pitcher is inadvertently revealing his or her intention by the way the ball is gripped or by telltale mannerisms that sharp-eyed players on the opposing team can pick up. In other words, such a pitcher is deficient in what we earlier called strategic skills; this player lacks knowledge and technique relevant to knowing how to win. Good coaches can train pitchers to conceal their grip or avoid exhibiting physical "tells." Pitchers who tip off the opposition are deficient in skills relevant to playing the game well.

However, intercepting electronic communication among coaches about strategy and play calling during games is not a skill of football. It is not regulated by constitutive rules, there are none of Suits's "unnecessary obstacles" to its use specified in the rule book, and, therefore, it is totally extraneous to the game.

Even more importantly, any plausible interpretive (broad internalist) account of football would include the choice of strategies and the calling of clever plays to be a central part of the game. If each team knew what plays the other would call in advance, the strategic element would be removed. Hence, secretly taping of the kind the Patriots carried out could not be permitted as part of any public set of rules applying to football without destroying a key element of the sport—the matching of wits and ingenuity through the choice of strategies and counter-strategies.[5] Finally, strategic skills are not only key factors that make sports such as football interesting and challenging; they also add an aesthetic dimension to athletic contests. Strategies can be "elegant," "well designed," and beautiful to watch in action, or they can be ugly, as when they slow down a game by leading to the excessive calling of penalties.

Accordingly, if our account of cheating and its application to Spygate is sound, the NFL was correct to condemn and punish the action. Although secretly taping of the kind at issue may make the game more interesting to some fans, it cannot be made into a universal practice because it undermines fundamental values of athletic competition by removing the elements of strategy and play calling from the competition.

Strategic Fouling and the Ethics of Athletic Competition

What does our discussion suggest about the ethics of strategic fouling? Strategic fouling is an example of the intentional violation of the rules of a sport for a competitive advantage. Specific instances of strategic fouling already mentioned include Scurry's save at the World Cup, a losing team intentionally fouling to stop the clock in the last minutes of a basketball game, and a football team deliberately incurring a delay of game penalty to get a better position for an attempt at a field goal. Is strategic fouling a case of cheating, though? If it is not, is it unethical in some other fashion?

The debate about the ethics of strategic fouling is not just a narrow controversy that is of interest to only a few "purists" who fail to understand the practice of competitive athletics; rather, the critics of strategic fouling are implying that we have become so consumed by the pursuit of victory in sports that we embrace even highly questionable tactics in trying to win. The prevalence of strategic fouling, on this view, is evidence not of smart play but of the corruption of athletic competition by the cult of achieving victory by whatever means necessary.

Although many, perhaps most, athletes see nothing wrong with strategic fouling and view it as part of the game, some philosophers would unequivocally assert that strategic fouling is unethical and perhaps a form of cheating. For example, in an early discussion of the issue Warren Fraleigh analyzed the basketball example by maintaining that "intentional holding, tripping, and so on are not part of the game or within the rules of basketball. . . . [Therefore] the 'good' foul is a violation of the agreement which all participants know that all participants make when they agree to play basketball, namely, that all will pursue the . . . goal of basketball by the necessary and allowable skills and tactics and will avoid use of proscribed skills and tactics."[6] In a similar vein Kathleen Pearson wrote that strategic fouling "destroys the vital framework of agreement which makes sport possible."[7] These comments reflect the formalists' central emphasis on the rules. Indeed, formalists might go further and argue that cheaters aren't even really playing the game, as the rules constitute the game. Be that as it may, Fraleigh's and Pearson's remarks suggest that strategic fouling is a form of cheating because it intentionally violates the framework of rules that make the game possible and that the participants have agreed (either implicitly or explicitly) to obey.

However, if the analysis of cheating presented earlier is on the right track, this formalist approach to strategic fouling may be seriously questioned. One criticism is that the formalist approach does not give sufficient weight to the conventions associated with specific sports: the "ethos" of the game. Thus, in basketball, players understand that losing teams will foul at the end of the game to stop the clock. Virtually all players expect the losing team to foul to stop the clock when such behavior is strategically appropriate; the players expect it of themselves and of their opponents. Similarly, in soccer the goalies generally try to move into position a bit more quickly than the rules allow in order to reduce the shooter's angle for a favorable shot. Thus, one could argue that Scurry's action in the World Cup conformed to a convention widely accepted among participants.

But just because such behavior is conventional does not make it morally right or in the best interests of the game. Nevertheless, if cheating means violating a public set of norms to gain an advantage for oneself or one's team, and these norms include conventions as well as rules, then strategic fouling is not always a form of cheating. This is partly because conventions exist that sometimes make such behavior normal and expected. But, more importantly, it is also because the strategic fouler acknowledges such behavior is appropriate for all participants, including opponents. This is quite a different situation from that of the cheater who, say, wants to get an advantage by falsifying the scorebook, behavior that could not possibly be made universal without destroying the game itself. In addition, strategic fouling, especially but not only in basketball, is done openly. The strategic fouler in basketball in fact wants the referee to call the infraction, stop the clock, and award compensatory foul shots to the other team.

Theorists such as Fraleigh and Pearson could object that conventions, unlike rules, are too vague to form a basis of the common understanding presupposed by players who commit themselves to respecting the game. For example, is there really a convention or common understanding in international soccer that goalkeepers can bend the rules as Scurry did in the World Cup? How are we to tell?

Sigmund Loland and Mike McNamee provided an example of just such a difference in understanding. In a major soccer competition in England between Arsenal FC and Sheffield United, when an Arsenal player became injured, a Sheffield United player, following the prevailing convention, deliberately kicked the ball out of bounds so that during the ensuing pause in play the injured player could receive medical treatment. According to the convention, once the ball is back in play, the receiving team, in this game Arsenal, would turn the ball over to the opposition so Sheffield would suffer no competitive disadvantage. But this time, according to Loland and McNamee, an Arsenal player, a recent recruit from another continent (and presumably a different cultural setting) "intercepted the ball, crossed it to one of his teammates, who instinctively (so it is said) . . . scored."[8] Apparently the understanding of the convention was not common to all players. Similarly, in the women's World Cup situation, for example, perhaps the Americans, the Chinese, and the World Cup officials did not all understand Scurry's strategy in the same way. If that is the case, then her decision to use the strategy would seem ethically questionable, whereas it would seem more appropriate if all these participants shared the same view of it as an example of a convention that was commonly accepted.

Thus, Fraleigh and Pearson's claim that conventions are too vague to form the basis of a common understanding surely has force. Nevertheless, the idea that strategic fouls are different from paradigm examples of cheating still seems plausible. Strategic foulers are conforming to a general practice they are willing to condone even when it works against them, whereas cheaters are violating rules in ways they do not want others to emulate. Moreover, cheaters could not reasonably want such violations to be part of the public system of rules and principles governing the sport. How could anyone reasonably advocate a rule allowing falsification of the scorebook, for example, as this would destroy the ability for anyone to tell who really won the contest?

But even if strategic fouling is not a form of cheating, it may be morally unacceptable on other grounds. After all, just because behavior is conventional does not mean it is ethical. Strategic fouling may be unethical because it is unsportsmanlike or because it shows disrespect for principles that should govern conduct in competition. Let us explore these possibilities more fully.

Penalties as Sanctions and as Prices

Perhaps a strong moral defense of strategic fouling is that such behavior really does not violate the rules to begin with. For example, in basketball, one could argue, the strategic foul is part of the game because an explicit penalty—foul shots—is provided for in the rules. Pearson has considered this rejoinder and pointed out that "the obvious rebuttal to this position is that penalties for breaking the law are contained within the law books, but no sensible person concludes, therefore, that all acts are within the law."[9] For example, we surely would not say that the law allows murder simply because it prescribes penalties for murder.

But is this reply decisive? The parallel drawn between sanctions in law, such as punishment for criminals, and penalties for strategic fouls is questionable. In particular, some penalties in sport do not play a role analogous to criminal sanctions in law. A jail sentence for a crime should not be thought of as the price the law charges for a particular act, such as a felony. That would make the felony a permissible option for those criminals who were willing to bear the cost of a jail sentence if caught. Rather, a felony is a prohibited act, and a jail sentence is not the price for allowable commission of the act but rather a punishment for committing it.

However, in addition to penalties for crimes, the law also sometimes requires payment or fees for actions that are permissible, such as obtaining a hunting license. Thus, it would be absurd to regard the fee the state charges for issuing a driver's license as a penalty or punishment for driving; rather, it is more like the price of having one's driving legally sanctioned. Similarly, not all penalties in sport are punishments or sanctions for prohibited acts; instead, some may be the price to be paid for exercising a strategic option. Thus, the stroke penalty in golf for extracting one's ball from an unplayable situation, such as when it is wedged tightly between two rocks, clearly is not a penalty, as the rule is explicitly designed to allow play to continue but compensates your competitors for your opportunity to move the ball without making a golf stroke.[10]

But are the penalties for strategic fouls punishments or prices? If the penalties for the fouls in at least some contexts can be regarded as prices for exercising a strategy rather than sanctions for violating a rule, then strategic fouling, in those cases, rather than being unethical, would be a permissible strategy of play.

Although it is sometimes difficult to tell whether a penalty should be regarded as a sanction or a price, the notion of a *fair price* might help us distinguish the two. The intuitive idea here is that if a pricing penalty is fair in sports, then it should provide equitable compensation to the opposing player or team. The penalty for intentional fouling in basketball is probably best regarded as a price rather than a sanction if the foul shots awarded are fair compensation for the violation. Sports authorities can more clearly distinguish sanctions from prices by making the penalty for prohibited acts more severe than mere fair compensation would require.

This analysis of strategic fouling in basketball in effect rests on a broad internalist theory of the game that views foul shots as fair compensation for the team that was fouled for strategic reasons. A good team should be able to convert the foul shots and be no worse off than before the infraction was committed. Inability to convert the foul shots indicates a weakness that rightly puts that team's lead in jeopardy.

The strategic violation Briana Scurry allegedly committed might be analyzed in a similar fashion, but it is arguably more complex. The penalty for illegal movement by the goalkeeper allows the shooter to make another attempt to score if the original shot was missed (otherwise the goal stands), so the rules call for restoring the situation to what it was before the infraction was committed. This suggests that the prescribed penalty is a price rather than a sanction, although this may not demonstrate that beyond a reasonable doubt.

Another relevant factor is that officials seldom call the kind of infraction Scurry committed. In the World Cup finals the officials should have suspected that the goalkeepers would seek every edge in the shootout; however, either they did not notice the infraction or deliberately ignored it. Do referees tend not to make this call because they believe the shootout is too heavily weighted in favor of the offense and that goalkeepers have no real chance to stop a shot without moving illegally? If so, the referees, by refraining from calling all but blatant goalkeeper violations, may be trying to restore competitive balance to what they regard as an unfair restriction imposed by the rules.

Conversely, one might wonder whether strategic fouling is less acceptable in a low-scoring game such as soccer than in a high-scoring one such as basketball, where one play has much less effect on the outcome. Clearly, there is much room for further discussion on the ethics of strategic fouling in different sports.

A Counter-Argument Against Strategic Fouling

Before leaving the topic of strategic fouling, however, we will consider a more recent argument by Warren Fraleigh for the view that the practice is unethical.[11] This new argument relies on a distinction made in an article by Cesar R. Torres between a sport's basic, or constitutive, skills and its restorative skills.[12] Constitutive skills are the skills that the game is designed to test. In basketball these would include dribbling, passing, rebounding, and shooting. Restorative skills are those that are used to restore the status quo after a rules infraction has been committed. These would include foul shooting in basketball and taking a penalty shot in soccer.

In his paper Torres argued that constitutive skills normally require a more complex set of abilities to execute and are more interesting than restorative skills. Thus, running a fast break in basketball is more complex, difficult, and interesting than shooting a foul shot; similarly, running the bases intelligently in baseball is more complex, difficult, and interesting than being awarded a base as compensation for a fielder's interference with a runner.

Although Fraleigh's argument is complex, his basic point is that strategic fouling ruins the game by making the less complex and less difficult compensatory skills more central and the basic, constitutive skills less central to the outcome. It is perhaps for this reason that fans at a basketball game will feel the game has been made boring or has been ruined by referees who call fouls excessively. Such fans often will yell "Let them play," indicating that they do not regard foul shooting as being as interesting or as central to the game as the more complex basic skills exercised in the normal course of play. In addition, Fraleigh argued that strategic fouling often will deprive a player of an advantage earned through excellent use of basic skills, as when a hockey player, who has been fooled by the brilliant skating move of an opponent, trips the opponent from behind to prevent a breakaway shot on the goal.

This new argument of Fraleigh's is broad internalist in spirit. It advances an interpretation, based on Torres's distinction, about which skills are the most important skills in a sport and indicates why it is important to keep those skills at the center of play. On this view, strategic fouling, while certainly not cheating, shows a fundamental disrespect for what is really valuable about athletic competition—the quest for excellence—and gives undue priority to winning even at the cost of harming the game.

Nevertheless, although Fraleigh's argument is an important one, it may not carry the day, or at least it may not apply to all cases of strategic fouling. For one thing, not all exercises of restorative skills are routine or require less skill than constitutive skills require. Running a good power play in ice hockey clearly requires the use of both physical and mental abilities of a high order, but arguably it is restorative because it compensates an offended team for a rule violation by the opposition. Even shooting a foul shot in basketball, under pressure at the end of a close game, can test the composure and shooting ability of the player on the line.

More importantly, the assumption that team strategy should never make restorative skills central to determining the outcome of contests is itself questionable. Let's say, for example, that Team A and Team B are meeting for the third time in the basketball season. Team A won the first game by three points, and Team B won the second by four points. So far, in the third and deciding contest, the teams are evenly matched. Suppose that it is evident from all three games that the two teams are evenly matched in constitutive skills. However, Team B is awful at foul shooting, a restorative skill. Team B has possession of the ball and is ahead by two points, with ten seconds to go. Team A's coach realizes that his squad has little chance of stealing the ball and scoring in only ten seconds. He orders his team to strategically foul in order to stop the clock, reasoning that if the poor foul shooters on Team B miss, his team will have a chance to at least tie the game.

Regarding this strategy as unethical or ruining the game is unwarranted. After all, if we are trying to find out which team is better, and they are roughly equal in constitutive skills, why shouldn't a difference in restorative skills then be relevant? If the teams are equally skilled at the constitutive level but one team is clearly better at the restorative level, isn't that the better team? Moreover, it is hard to see how fouling at such a point in a close game ruins the game or makes it less interesting than simply letting the team with the ball hold it and run out the clock. It fact, it may make the game more exciting for fans and players alike.

Of course, this example is an extreme case, but it does suggest the following thesis. According to the Strategic Fouling Thesis, strategic fouling is permissible in a competitive athletic contest when the following four conditions are satisfied. First, the teams playing have demonstrated, perhaps by the closeness of the contest, that they are roughly equal or well matched in constitutive skills. Second, the team that strategically fouls has no other strategy based on the use of constitutive skills that gives it a reasonable chance to win. Third, it must be reasonable to regard the penalty for the strategic foul as a price rather than a punishment. Last, the foul must not take away a major advantage earned by the use of constitutive skills, such as would be the case if a hockey player on a breakaway was tripped from behind.

This suggests that in close contests, particularly in high-scoring sports such as basketball, the judicious use of strategic fouls not only may be morally allowed but also may enhance the challenge of the athletic contest. Although the extent to which this argument applies to other sports needs to be debated case by case, we suggest that the distinction between judicious and indiscriminate use of strategic fouls is important. Thus, the Strategic Fouling Thesis might not justify a hockey team that was vastly inferior to its opponent in skating and shooting skills if it were constantly taking penalties designed to deprive the opponent of advantages earned through superior skills or turning the game, in effect, into a wrestling match to prevent the opponent from demonstrating its constitutive superiority.

What, then, does our extended discussion suggest about the morality of strategic fouling? One conclusion is that strategic fouling cannot be equated with cheating. One reason is that it rests on implicit practices all the players have reasonably accepted, whereas in cheating, the cheater tries to gain an advantage through actions that could not reasonably be accepted by all players as a universal practice. Moreover, in many contexts in sport strategic fouling may constitute a strategic option for which the rules exact a price rather than impose a sanction. It might even be argued that strategic fouling sometimes improves the game by creating interesting tactical choices or, as in the example of the movement at issue in the World Cup, even improves the competitiveness of the game. Finally, although strategic fouling in some circumstances can undermine the sports contest by making the exercise of constitutive skills secondary and restorative skills primary, this does not have to be the case. Although strategic fouling may sometimes be unethical, judicious use of strategic fouls not only may be morally acceptable but also may reinforce the idea of the sport contest as a worthy challenge or test of excellence.

Sportsmanship and Responsibility in Athletic Competition

So far in this chapter we have been examining what is prohibited (cheating) and what arguably is permitted (strategic fouling) in athletic competition. Some behavior, however, may not be prohibited or wrong to do but may be encouraged or sometimes even morally required. Let us consider one kind of behavior that falls under the heading of sportsmanship. Although the term *sportsmanship* itself may carry connotations of gender or class bias and could be replaced by sportspersonship instead, we will use the original term to refer both to men's and women's sports because of its frequent use in the rhetoric of sport educators and participants in athletics alike and its long history in the evolving ethics of athletic competition.

What values ought to govern competitors' behavior in athletic competition? Sportsmanship is one value people often appeal to in such contexts. Moral thinkers have given sportsmanship relatively little attention, and, as just noted, it probably suffers today because of associations with the morality of an elite upper crust and perhaps from concerns that a male bias is built into the meaning of the term.[13] Nevertheless, sportsmanship is a value coaches, players, and sports commentators frequently cite. It should not be simply dismissed as out of date or only for the socially or economically elite without first trying to understand what it might involve. So what is sportsmanship? Does it apply equally to intense athletic competition and informal games among friends?

James W. Keating has provided a particularly interesting analysis of sportsmanship. Keating properly warned, first of all, that we must not make our account of sportsmanship so broad as to make it virtually identical with virtue. Not every virtue is an instance of sportsmanship, and not every vice is unsportsmanlike. Keating observed that a formal code of sportsmanship promulgated earlier in this century included such diverse injunctions as "Keep yourself fit," "Keep your temper," and "Keep a sound soul and a clean mind in a healthy body." The trouble with such broad accounts of sportsmanship, as Keating points out, is that they do no specific work because they cover virtually all positive values and, thus, amount to no more than the injunction to be ethical. We cannot say conduct is ethical because it is sportsmanlike, for *sportsmanlike* has just become another way of saying *ethical*. The idea of sportsmanship has been characterized so broadly that there is no particular aspect of morality that is its specific concern.[14]

Keating argued that a more useful account of sportsmanship would develop the rather vague suggestion of the dictionary about behavior expected of a sportsman or sportswoman. To develop this idea, he introduced a crucial distinction between sport and athletics: "In essence, sport is a kind of diversion which has for its direct and immediate end fun, pleasure, and delight and which is dominated by a spirit of moderation and generosity. Athletics, on the other hand, is essentially a competitive activity, which has for its end victory in the contest and which is characterized by a spirit of dedication, sacrifice, and intensity."[15]

Sportsmanship, then, is the kind of attitude toward opponents that best promotes the goal of sports as defined by Keating—namely, friendly, mutually satisfactory relationships among the players. "Its purpose is to protect and cultivate the festive mood proper to an activity whose primary purpose is pleasant diversion, amusement, joy."[16] In Keating's view the supreme principle of sportsmanship was an injunction to "always conduct yourself in such a manner that you will increase rather than detract from the pleasure found in the activity, both your own and that of your fellow participant."[17]

Sportsmanship, Keating said, was a virtue that applied to the recreational activity of sport, as he understood it, but not to the more serious and competitive activity of athletics. To Keating, sportsmanship and athletics did not fit together easily: "The strange paradox of sportsmanship as applied to athletics is that it asks the athlete, locked in a deadly serious and emotionally charged situation, to act outwardly as if he was engaged in some pleasant diversion."[18]

On Keating's theory sportsmanship only applies to athletics in an attenuated way involving adherence to the value of fair play, which to Keating implies adherence to the letter and spirit of equality before the rules. Because the athletic contest is designed to determine which competitor meets the challenge best, fair play requires that competitors not intentionally disregard or circumvent the rules. Broadly understood, perhaps more broadly than Keating would recommend, fair play requires that victory be honorable. So fair play should be expected of the serious athlete in intense competition. However, to require that the serious athlete also attempt to increase the pleasure of the opponent in the contest is to ask too much.

But what is honorable behavior in competitive sport? Is it ethically required? Do we act wrongly, in a way that is morally prohibited, if we behave dishonorably, or do we just fail to live up to an ideal that is above and beyond the call of duty? And what is fair play? Does it mean simply following the rules, or does it require more than that? Did Scurry act unfairly in the decisive play in the World Cup championship game? What precisely is the relationship between unfair and unsportsmanlike conduct? Did the University of Colorado act dishonorably in accepting its disputed victory over Missouri that we referred to in Chapter 2? Finally, is the line between sports and athletics as sharp and as ethically significant as Keating's account suggests?[19]

The Sports-Athletics Distinction: A Critique

Is Keating's distinction between sports and athletics sound? More importantly, even if there is something to the distinction, does it follow that the ethical norms applicable to each differ as radically as Keating suggests?

Clearly, sports can be played with more or less competitive intensity. The NCAA championship softball game undoubtedly differs in many respects, perhaps including the ones Keating suggested, from a recreational softball game at a company picnic. Nevertheless, the distinction may not be a sharp one, and some principles of sportsmanship may apply virtually across the board. If so, we have a spectrum of activities ranging from elite competition at the highest levels down to recreational contests played with little competitive intensity, but nevertheless, positive ethical obligations to opponents may apply in different ways at all or at least most levels of competitive intensity.

Thus, referring back to our earlier example, Annika should lend the spare set of clubs to clubless Josie whether the contest is a club championship, the US Amateur, or even a major professional event for precisely the reasons articulated in Chapter 2. This suggests that even in what Keating calls athletics, participants may have positive duties or, if not duties, good moral reasons to not merely refrain from prohibited behavior such as cheating but rather to take positive steps to respect and support the underlying values of the game.

Consider an actual and not merely a hypothetical example involving the competition at the 2008 high school state track championship in Washington state. A senior, Nicole Cochran, thought she had won the girl's 3,200-meter title but was disqualified by a highly questionable call by an official, who ruled she had stepped outside her lane once during the race. According to reports of the incident, even her competitors thought the judge had made an egregious error, and a video of the race later confirmed the error.

As a result of the disqualification the winner was sophomore Amanda Nelson of Spokane, who had finished second but was moved up to first as a result of the disqualification. Nelson, however, thought this decision was unacceptable. As Nelson said, "It wasn't fair. She deserved it. She totally crushed everybody."[20] So when Nelson received the medal she left the podium and placed the first-place medal around the neck of the person she regarded as the rightful winner, Cochran. Moreover, the other girls who placed all did the same thing, removing their medals and placing them around neck of the runner who would have placed ahead of them if Cochran had not been disqualified.

Although it may go too far to say that Nelson had a moral duty to give up the first-place medal or that she would have wronged Cochran if she had kept it, her action surely was praiseworthy and exhibits the kind of behavior that should be encouraged in many sporting contexts. That is especially the case if we regard athletic competitions as mutual quests for excellence through challenge, as Cochran met the challenge of the contest better than her opponents. Moreover, on a plausible interpretation of athletic competition, principles underlying mutualism call on us to protect the integrity of the contest: merely appearing to win when one hasn't would not be assigned the same value as demonstrated in a hard-fought victory legitimately earned.[21]

Our discussion suggests then that even in those kinds of sporting contests that fall under or resemble what Keating calls athletics, athletes should be encouraged to take steps to support the deeper values underlying sporting competition. Although failure to do so may not necessarily be punishable by penalties, positive steps that respect the game sometimes are morally called for. However, determining when such positive acts are called for may be controversial, and some will exceed even broadly construed theories of what sportsmanship requires. For example, a batter who strikes out during a softball game surely should not be given another chance (an extra pitch) just because she was unlucky enough to get dust in her eye just as the pitch was released. We can further explore the issues involved and develop an account of sportsmanship itself by considering yet another example, the Colorado-Missouri intercollegiate football game discussed briefly in Chapter 2.

The Fifth Down: A Tainted Victory?

The example we will now consider involved a top-ranked university football team winning a game on a fifth-down play that was run because officials lost count and didn't notice that the allotted number of downs had already been used up. (Football teams are allowed only four plays, or downs, to advance the ball at least ten yards.) Should the winning team, the University of Colorado, have accepted the victory, or, as many critics of the university suggested, should it have refused to accept a tainted win?

Proponents of one view might begin by appealing to Keating's distinction between sport and athletics. They might argue first that because a major intercollegiate football game is clearly an example of athletics, neither team is under an obligation to make the experience pleasurable or enjoyable for the other. Generosity should not be expected either; after all, if a referee had made an incorrect pass interference call in their favor, Missouri would not have been urged to refuse to accept the penalty. Second, Colorado did not cheat, as least as we have defined cheating. There was no intent to violate a public system of rules to gain an advantage. The Colorado team seemed unaware of the true situation. Tapes of the game reveal that on the fourth-down play the Colorado quarterback looked to the sideline, noticed the play was officially marked as a third down on the official scoreboard, and intentionally grounded a pass to stop the clock. Had the quarterback believed the play was his team's last down, he surely would have gambled by attempting a touchdown pass, perhaps successfully.

However, we have provided reasons for questioning Keating's distinction between sport and athletics. Contests need not be classified exclusively as athletics or exclusively as sports but may share elements of each. Thus, to refer back to another previous example, Josie's opponent ought to lend her the clubs whether it's for a friendly match or a round of a major tournament.

Moreover, our discussion indicates that sportsmanship, although certainly not an all-encompassing value, covers more than generosity toward opponents. In particular, if athletic contests ought to be regarded as mutual quests for excellence, along the lines argued in Chapter 2, implications follow for sportsmanship. Thus, opponents ought to be regarded as engaged in a cooperative enterprise designed to test their abilities and skills, and, regardless of whether they are owed generous treatment, they should be treated as partners in the creation and execution of a fair test. To treat them differently is to reject the presuppositions of the very model of athletic competition that ought to be observed.

Arguably, the Missouri team was not treated in such a fashion. The rules of the game did not allow the play that won the game. Even though the officials were mistaken about how the rule applied, that does not alter the fact that Colorado did not win the test as defined by the rules. Moreover, there is no common convention acceptable to all participants that covers the situation. According to its critics, Colorado, by accepting the victory, did not treat its opponents as partners or facilitators in a common enterprise (as runner Amanda Nelson seems to have done in the example discussed above) but instead treated them as a means for attaining the kind of external rewards that go with victory in big-time college games.

In a famous game played forty years before the contest between Colorado and Missouri a similar incident led to a dissimilar resolution. In the late fall of 1940 an undefeated Cornell team, also in contention for the national championship and a Rose Bowl bid, played a Dartmouth team that was hoping for a major upset. Although trailing late in the fourth quarter, Cornell apparently pulled out a victory with a scoring pass on the game's last play. But did Cornell really win? Film of the game indicated without a doubt that the referee, who admitted the error, had allowed Cornell a fifth down! The game should have ended a play earlier, and Dartmouth should have pulled off a major upset.

Although no rule required that Cornell forfeit the victory, soon after the game film's release "Cornell officials (including the Director of Athletics) telegraphed Hanover formally conceding the game to Dartmouth 'without reservation . . . with hearty congratulations . . . to the gallant Dartmouth team.' Another loss the following Saturday to Pennsylvania helped the Cornell team drop from second to 15th in the Associated Press polls, its season ruined but its pride intact."[22] Should Colorado take pride in its victory? Should Cornell be proud of its loss?

We also need to consider the role of officials and referees in sport. Should we conclude that because opponents in many forms of organized competition delegate responsibility for enforcement of the rules to officials in full knowledge that officials sometimes make mistakes, officials' decisions should be accepted as ethically final? Alternately, do participants have obligations not to accept unearned benefits arising from particularly egregious official errors, especially those that involve misapplication of the rules rather than "judgment calls" about whether a rule was violated?[23]

Although these questions do not admit of easy answers, an argument can be made that Colorado's victory was tainted. Although there was no intention to violate rules and, therefore, no cheating in a general sense, and although the referees bear heavy responsibility for what happened, Colorado still had to decide after the game was over whether to accept the victory. Although it may not have been morally required for Colorado to forfeit the game as Cornell did in a perhaps more innocent era of intercollegiate sports, it seems just as clear that Colorado's victory was significantly less meaningful than it otherwise would have been. It would seem, then, that Colorado's reasons for wanting the full benefits of victory had more to do with securing the external benefits of a win, including national rankings and a bid to a bowl game, than to intrinsic pride in a well-earned victory. It is at least questionable, then, whether Colorado met the challenge its opponent set or whether Missouri failed to meet it simply because the final score was in Colorado's favor.

Sportsmanship and an Internal Morality of Sports

Cases such as those discussed above are likely to be controversial, and discussion of them may generate disagreement, but it is important to remember that such disagreement occurs against a general background of deeper agreement on sport ethics. None of the parties to the discussion endorses cheating, blatant examples of unfair play, or unsportsmanlike behavior; rather, the disagreement concerns "hard cases" that help us define the boundaries of the values we are exploring.

Although we have not offered a general theory of sportsmanship, our discussion certainly supports the view that sportsmanship involves more than either generosity toward opponents or fidelity to the rules and, thus, calls into question any sharp distinction between sport and athletics. In particular, it also involves not only respect for but also some forms of positive action to protect and even enhance the principles that ethically defensible athletic competition presupposes (which, from our broad internalist perspective, includes the mutual quest for excellence).

In fact, our discussion in Chapters 2 and 3 supports the internalist view that competition in sport properly conceived of and carried out commits us to both moral and aesthetic norms that are presupposed by a justifiable interpretation of the nature of sports and their lusory purposes. Although these norms, such as fairness or respect for opponents as persons, surely are not unique to sport, they are central to conducting sport well. That is, some values are such that all competitive athletes have strong reason to commend and act upon them. What can be called the inner moral-aesthetic compound of competitive athletics comprises the normative features that are indispensable to athletic competition that is morally defensible and committed to the pursuit of excellence through challenge. This inner morality of sport supports a form of life, competition in sport, that not only is a worthwhile enterprise in its own right but also, as we will see, has truly significant educational benefits as well.

Although the mutualist conception of sport we have developed represents an ideal often not implemented in practice, it, like other ideals, can serve as a basis of criticism of actual behavior in sport that does not conform to its precepts. In other words, it provides grounds for criticizing actual practice when that deviates significantly from what mutualism requires. In what follows in succeeding chapters we will apply the theoretical framework we have developed in Chapters 2 and 3 to controversial issues that arise in sporting practice.

We hope, however, that our discussion in this chapter illustrates that although it sometimes is difficult to always draw the line between what sportsmanship and fair play permit and what they forbid, those values are not vacuous and do apply broadly to competitors' behavior in sport. A defensible sport ethic, one that respects participants as persons, should avoid the twin errors of, on one hand, leaving no room for such tactics as the judicious strategic foul or, on the other hand, assuming that any behavior that contributes to victory is morally acceptable.

QUESTIONS FOR REVIEW

1. Explain the authors' analysis of cheating.
2. Do you agree with the argument that sometimes cheating in sport may be morally acceptable? How do the authors evaluate that claim?
3. What is James Keating's analysis of sportsmanship? Explain one criticism of it.
4. Do you think strategic fouling sometimes is morally acceptable? Defend your view by considering one criticism of it.
5. Do you think beneficiaries of egregiously bad calls in close contests should accept a resulting victory? How would you apply your analysis to the case of the fifth down and the different reactions to it by the University of Colorado and Cornell, as described in the text?

Notes

1. Bernard Gert, *Morality: Its Nature and Justification* (New York: Oxford University Press, 1998), 191–195.

2. Ibid., 196.

3. Oliver Leaman, "Cheating and Fair Play in Sports," in *Philosophic Inquiry in Sport*, ed. William J. Morgan and Klaus V. Meier (Champaign, IL: Human Kinetics Press, 1995), 195.

4. Ibid., 196.

5. In this regard, remember the principle suggested by John Russell discussed in Chapter 2 that states "rules should be interpreted in such a manner that the excellences embodied in achieving the lusory goal of the game are not undermined but are maintained and fostered."

6. Warren Fraleigh, "Why the Good Foul Is Not Good Enough," in *Philosophic Inquiry in Sport*, ed. William J. Morgan and Klaus V. Meier (Champaign, IL: Human Kinetics Press, 1995), 185–187.

7. Kathleen Pearson, "Deception, Sportsmanship, and Ethics," in *Philosophic Inquiry in Sport*, ed. William J. Morgan and Klaus V. Meier (Champaign, IL: Human Kinetics Press, 1995), 184.

8. Sigmund Loland and Mike McNamee, "Fair Play and the Ethos of Sports: An Eclectic Philosophical Framework," *Journal of the Philosophy of Sport* 27, no. 1 (May 2000): 63–80. The material in the parentheses is my own paraphrase of the original quotation.

9. Pearson, "Deception, Sportsmanship, and Ethics," 184.

10. Of course, as Warren Fraleigh has pointed out in conversation, this situation is not strictly parallel to strategic fouling because one is not breaking a rule by moving the unplayable ball but rather exercising an option the rules allow. However, as our discussion will suggest, the same may be true of some cases of strategic fouling as well.

11. Warren Fraleigh, "Intentional Rules Violations—One More Time," *Journal of the Philosophy of Sport* 30, no. 2 (2003): 166–176. The following discussion draws on Robert Simon's paper "The Ethics of Strategic Fouling: A Reply to Fraleigh," *Journal of the Philosophy of Sport* 32, no. 1 (2005): 87–95.

12. Cesar R. Torres, "What Counts as Part of the Game? A Look at Skill," *Journal of the Philosophy of Sport* 27, no. 1 (May 2000): 81–92.

13. As used here, "sportsmanship" will designate a virtue that can be exemplified equally by all athletes, in particular by males and females of all races, ethnic groups, and socioeconomic backgrounds.

14. James W. Keating, "Sportsmanship as a Moral Category," in *Philosophic Inquiry in Sport*, ed. William J. Morgan and Klaus V. Meier (Champaign, IL: Human Kinetics Press, 1995), 144–151.

15. Ibid., 146.

16. Ibid., 147.

17. Ibid., 147.

18. Ibid., 149.

19. This distinction will be criticized later in the chapter. For additional criticism of Keating's position, see Randolph M. Feezell, "Sportsmanship," in *Philosophic Inquiry in Sport*, ed. William J. Morgan and Klaus V. Meier (Champaign, IL: Human Kinetics Press, 1995), 152–160.

20. This incident was widely reported. For an online account, see Dan Daly, "Sportsmanship Exists When Money Doesn't," *Washington Times*, June 3, 2008, www.washingtontimes .com/news/2008/jun/03/dany-daly-sportsmanship-exists-when-money-doesn't.

21. John Russell has argued recently for the thesis that coaches in particular have a duty to try to correct officials' egregiously wrong calls in their favor. For his provocative argument, see his essay, "Coaching and Undeserved Competitive Success," in Robert L. Simon, *The Ethics of Coaching Sports: Moral, Social, and Legal Issues* (Boulder, CO: Westview Press, 2013), 103–119.

22. This incident also was widely reported. For an account, see Ken Johnson, "The Forfeit," *Dartmouth Alumni Review* (October 1990): 8–16.

23. For discussion, see Russell, "Coaching and Undeserved Competitive Success."

=4=

Drugs, Genes, and
Enhancing Performance in Sport

In the summer of 1998 Major League Baseball (MLB) was abuzz with talk of the home run race between Chicago Cubs star Sammy Sosa and Mark Mc-Gwire of the St. Louis Cardinals. McGwire would end up with 70 home runs and Sosa with 66, both eclipsing the single-season record for home runs set in 1961 by Roger Maris, who had scored 61. Maris had broken Babe Ruth's previous record of 60 homers in a single season, a record that itself had stood for forty years. Maris's record had stood for thirty-seven years. Yet McGwire's record was eclipsed just a few years later by Barry Bonds, who hit 73 home runs in 2001. Bonds went on to later eclipse Henry Aaron's record of 755 career home runs, finishing his career with 762.

The race between Sosa and McGwire attracted tremendous attention from baseball fans, but by the time Bonds set his career record all of these figures in the game had become controversial and the significance of their records were called into question. Increasingly, evidence suggested that their achievements were not due entirely to skill but also to the players' use of performance-enhancing substances.[1]

Concern about the use of performance-enhancing drugs in sport is hardly new, but it perhaps first came into the public eye through allegations, since confirmed, of drug use by Olympic athletes, primarily the East German women's swimming team and other East German athletes in the 1960s, 1970s, and 1980s. But the use of performance-enhancing drugs was hardly restricted to

East German swimmers, at least by the end of that period. A highly publicized incident took place in the 1988 Summer Olympics in Seoul, South Korea, in a long-awaited track race between Canadian star Ben Johnson and American star Carl Lewis. In a hard-fought hundred-meter race, Johnson defeated Lewis and apparently won the gold medal.

Urinalysis tests subsequently revealed that Johnson had been taking the steroid stanozolol to enhance his performance. To the shock of Canadians, to whom Johnson had become a national hero, and the rest of the sports world, Johnson was disqualified and had to forfeit his medals from the 1988 Olympics, including the medal he had been awarded for his race against Lewis.

Of course, it is now well known that a perhaps significant proportion of Olympic athletes as well as professional athletes in many sports have used performance-enhancing drugs. Most major sports associations have instituted testing programs to keep sports "clean," or drug-free. However, some MLB stars' use of steroids and other performance enhancers, such as the more difficult-to-detect human growth hormone, captured the general public's attention in the United States in a way few other cases have and generated lively discourse regarding the moral status of performance-enhancing substances and techniques in elite sport.

Initially many people ridiculed star player Jose Canseco's assertions about the relatively widespread use of steroids in baseball, made in his 2005 book, *Juiced: Wild Times, Rampant 'Roids, Smash Hits, and How Baseball Got Big.* However, subsequent revelations supported many of Canseco's claims. Soon, players' admissions emerged in the face of various investigations, including inquiries from Congress. McGwire himself was observed with androstenedione ("Andro"), a hormone that boosts testosterone production, in his locker during his sensational 1998 season. He was reticent and evasive, according to virtually all observers, during his testimony on the issue before Congress in 2005. However, in January 2010 McGwire acknowledged using steroids in 1998, when he set the then single-season record for home runs, although he denied the drugs were responsible for his achievements as a slugger.

Examples of admitted users include Canseco, 1996 National League MVP Ken Caminiti (who died prematurely in 2004, perhaps as a result of his use of performance enhancers), Jason Giambi of the Yankees, and McGwire. All acknowledged the use of performance enhancers at some point in their careers. Alex Rodriguez admitted being a user from 2001 to 2003 before he became a Yankee and was suspended for the entire 2014 season and postseason for his association with Biogenesis of America, an anti-aging clinic that MLB accused of supplying illegal performance-enhancing substances to its players, and for his alleged attempt to obstruct the League's investigation of that clinic. Barry

Bonds and seven-time Cy Young Award–winning pitcher Roger Clemens remain under heavy clouds of suspicion as well.

According to an influential report for MLB authored by former senator and diplomat George Mitchell, anonymous tests conducted in 2003 found that 5 to 7 percent of MLB players were using anabolic steroids.[2] The actual figure of those using performance-enhancing drugs was probably much higher, however, as the tests employed were incapable of detecting human growth hormone. Bonds in particular has been widely thought to have benefited from the use of steroids and other drugs, partly because of his involvement in the Bay Area Laboratory Cooperative (BALCO) scandal, described below, and partly because of the remarkable improvement in his home run statistics at an age when most athletes in his sport are in decline.

According to many observers Bonds may have started using performance-enhancing drugs before the 1999 season, perhaps, as some speculate, as a reaction to McGwire's and Sosa's record-setting seasons the year before.[3] He was thirty-four years old at the time, an age when most baseball players' performance starts to deteriorate. Yet four of his five best seasons came after he was thirty-five. During the 2001 season he batted .318 and hit his record-setting seventy-three home runs. No other player in the history of baseball had done so well at that age or later; according to one analysis, "by what should have been the end of his baseball career, Bonds became a significantly better hitter than at any time in his life."[4]

In 2003 a team of federal and state law-enforcement agencies raided BALCO, which had been the subject of an investigation since 2002. BALCO was suspected of supplying several MLB players with performance-enhancing substances, and the raid turned up records showing that Bonds and other Major Leaguers had been supplied with substances designed to frustrate discovery through tests. Testimony from Bonds's trainer, Greg Anderson, to a grand jury is alleged to have also confirmed the hypothesis that Bonds used performance enhancers.[5] Bonds himself denied knowingly having used steroids, however, and Anderson has recanted some of his testimony before the California grand jury investigating BALCO, but it is also worth noting that in 2007 Bonds was indicted for committing perjury in his testimony and was convicted of obstruction of justice in 2011.

Regardless of whether Bonds used performance-enhancing substances, subsequent revelations and player admissions clearly indicated that the use of performance-enhancing drugs was a big problem for MLB. As a result of widespread concerns about the legitimacy of competition and of the records set during the so-called steroid era, in 2004 Major League Baseball instituted random drug testing of players. It was one of the last major American professional sports organizations to adopt such a policy, and the organization as well as the players' union, which for a long time opposed testing, has been widely criticized for not reacting more quickly.[6] However, MLB strengthened the penalties for violating the rules concerning banned substances in subsequent years and also instituted a policy of random in-season testing of players for the use of performance-enhancing substances.

Our major concern, however, is not primarily how many elite athletes use performance enhancers or the extent of such use in MLB but rather the ethics of such use. Many sports fans, commentators, and ethical theorists regard the use of performance enhancers as unethical or a form of cheating. Others, however, including some philosophers of sport, argue that prohibitions on the use of performance enhancers in sport are arbitrary and unjustified. Why shouldn't athletes be free to explore how far they can go in setting records and improving achievement in sport? Why is the use of performance enhancers unethical but the use of new technology, such as graphite-shafted titanium golf clubs, fiberglass poles for vaulting, and high-tech running shoes, acceptable?

Is the use of performance-enhancing drugs in sport a form of cheating or unethical in some way? Or are restrictions on the use of performance-enhancing drugs illegitimate restrictions on athletes' freedom to pursue excellence in their own way? Are records set by users of performance-enhancing drugs legitimate, or should they be discounted? In the next section we will pursue in some depth the ethical issues performance-enhancing drugs raise. We will conclude the chapter by examining the issues another form of enhancement brings up: genetic enhancement of athletic abilities.

The Ethics of Using Performance-Enhancing Drugs and the Quest for Excellence

A principal conclusion of Chapters 2 and 3 was that competition in sports is ethically defensible when it involves participants in a mutual quest for excellence through challenge. In effect, competitors should view themselves as under moral obligations to their opponents. Competitors are obligated to try their best so opponents can develop their own skills through facing a significant test. In this view, sports are of interest and significance in large part because they fully involve our minds and bodies in meeting a challenge, one regarded as worth meeting for its own sake. Whether one is a recreational softball player imagining himself or herself as a Major Leaguer or a hacker on the golf course who for once hits a perfect shot, participants in sports all take part in the quest for excellence, although with various degrees of intensity. In great part what distinguishes the fun we have through sport from mere exercise is the presence of standards of excellence and the challenge presented by the play of others.

Many athletes at the most skilled levels of professional and amateur competition love the challenge sport provides and seek constantly to improve their performance. Often they seem to compete as much for the love of competition as for financial reward. Some professional athletes—Michael Jordan during the peak of his career and Tiger Woods, at least until highly publicized personal problems involving infidelity surfaced in late 2009, being especially prominent examples—seem to play as much for the love of the challenge and the desire to compete as for external rewards such as fame and fortune. Indeed, could anyone rise to the top in a highly competitive sport unless love of the game and dedication to excellence provided the motivation for the hours of practice, drills, and preparation required?

The danger, of course, is that the drive to win will lead some dedicated athletes to use dangerous and arguably unethical means to achieve success. Losing becomes identified with failure, and anything that promotes winning is also seen as promoting success. But is winning achieved by any means success or simply the illusion of it?

We need to ask how excellence might be achieved. In particular, is the use of drugs, such as anabolic steroids, an ethically permissible method for achieving excellence in sports, or, as most sports authorities argue, should the use of such drugs be prohibited in organized athletic competition?

What Is a Performance-Enhancing Drug?

Before we can turn to a discussion of the ethics of the use of performance-enhancing drugs in sports, we need to be clearer about what counts as a performance enhancer. Are vitamins performance-enhancing drugs? What about a cup of coffee that stimulates a sleepy athlete before a match? What about medication that alleviates allergy symptoms, thereby allowing an athlete to compete more effectively? If we want to forbid the use of performance enhancers, what defines these substances?

Unfortunately there does not seem to be a clear and simple definition that distinguishes the kind of performance-enhancing drugs that officials of major sports organizations want to prohibit from the legitimate use of other substances such as vitamins or allergy medicine. The situation is complicated further by the fact that a substance that might enhance performance in one context or sport and may fail to do so or even harm performance in another. Thus, while the enhancing effects of stimulants are more evident in sports that require quick bursts of speed and power, like sprinting and weightlifting, such effects are murkier in sports like gymnastics and figure skating, in which athletes must hit exact marks in moving with precision as well as speed and power. And although moderate use of a depressant like alcohol would normally affect performance adversely, it can be enhancing in sports such as archery and shooting, in which a slower heartbeat may translate to a steadier hand on the shooting range.

Moreover, it is of little help to say that athletes should be permitted to take only what is "natural"; steroids are derivatives of the hormone testosterone, which does occur naturally in the human body, whereas many legitimate medications that athletes ought to be allowed to take are synthetic and not present in a normal or natural diet. The term *natural* is too vague and open textured to be of much help in this area. In addition, what of practices such as blood doping, where athletes inject stored samples of their own blood in an attempt to boost their oxygen-carrying capacity? It is doubtful whether one's own blood can be classified as *unnatural*, yet major sports organizations regard blood doping as an unethical form of performance enhancement.

We might also try to distinguish the use of substances that merely assist in restoring normal function, such as aspirin, from those like steroids that enhance performance. Although this suggestion has promise, the line between restoratives and enhancers is not a sharp one or, at the very least, is unlikely to be uncontroversial. What if a proponent of performance enhancement through steroid use argued that steroids simply restore the body's abilities to work out more intensely and recover sooner from workouts that imperfections in the human body subvert in a manner similar to the way a headache might subvert the ability to concentrate intensely to study for an academic test?

Rather than search for a precise definition to distinguish the substances we intuitively believe are illegitimate performance enhancers from those that are not, it seems more useful to examine anabolic steroids, prohibited by major sport organizations. We can then ask what factors, if any, morally justify this prohibition. If the prohibition is justified and if we can isolate the moral reasons for it, then any other substances to which the same reasons apply should also be prohibited. Thus, rather than search for an abstract definition, we should first decide what ought or ought not to be allowed to affect athletic performance.

Understanding the Problem of Steroid Use

Anabolic steroids are a family of drugs that are synthetic derivatives of the hormone testosterone that stimulate muscle growth and repair injured tissue. They are among the most widely discussed performance-enhancing drugs. Although not everyone would agree that the controlled and medically supervised use of steroids to enhance performance is dangerous, the American College of Sports Medicine as well as other major medical organizations warn against serious side effects. Some of these are, at least in high doses, liver damage, arteriosclerosis, serious hypertension, a lowered sperm count in males, and development of masculine physical characteristics in women. The regular and prolonged use of steroids is also asserted to produce such personality changes as increased aggressiveness and hostility.

What is particularly frightening is that world-class athletes are reported to be taking steroids at dosages so high that it would be illegal to administer them to human subjects in legitimate medical experiments. Some athletes are said to "stack" various forms of steroids along with other kinds of performance enhancers, such as human growth hormones, in attempts to find the most effective combinations. Moreover, many, perhaps most, athletes who use steroids do so without medical supervision. Such athletes are likely to ignore claims that steroids have little effect on performance when such claims are based on studies that administer only low doses of the relevant drugs.

Evaluating the Use of Steroids

Various reasons are cited as justifications of the claim that competitive athletes ought not use performance-enhancing steroids. Among the most frequently cited are the following: (1) use of steroids to enhance performance is harmful to athletes, who need to be protected; (2) use of steroids to enhance performance by some athletes coerces others into using steroids; (3) use of steroids to enhance performance is unfair or a form of cheating; (4) use of steroids to enhance performance violates justifiable norms or ideals that ought to govern athletic competition; and (5) use of steroids demeans or cheapens achievement in sport, for example, by making home runs too common and too easy to hit in baseball. Let us examine each kind of justification in turn.

Paternalism, Informed Consent, and the Use of Steroids

Why shouldn't athletes be allowed to use performance-enhancing steroids? According to one argument, steroids, particularly at the high dosages believed necessary to enhance performance, can seriously harm those who use them. For example, according to the Mitchell Report, "Steroid users place themselves at risk for psychiatric problems, cardiovascular and liver damage, drastic changes to their reproductive systems, musculoskeletal injuries, and other problems." The report adds that "users of human growth hormone risk cancer, harm to their reproductive health, cardiac and thyroid problems, and overgrowth of bone and connective tissue."[7] Let us accept the factual claim that steroids as performance enhancers can be seriously harmful and consider whether potential harm to the user justifies prohibiting their use.

The principal criticism of prohibiting steroid use to protect athletes from themselves is that it is unjustifiably paternalistic. Paternalistic interference prevents athletes from making decisions for themselves. After all, would any of us want to have our liberty interfered with whenever some outside agency felt that our personal decisions about how to live our lives were too risky? If widespread paternalism was practiced, third parties could prohibit us from eating foods that might be harmful, playing in sports that carried even slight risk of injury, or indulging in unhealthy lifestyles. Our lives would be monitored—for our own good, of course. The difficulty is that we might not conceive of our own good in the same way as the paternalist.

The trouble with paternalism, then, is that it restricts human liberty. We may believe, with John Stuart Mill, the great nineteenth-century defender of human freedom, "that the only purpose for which power can be rightfully exercised over any member of a civilized community, against his will, is to prevent harm to others. His own good, either physical or moral, is not a sufficient warrant."[8]

If each of us ought to be free to assume risks we think are worth taking, shouldn't athletes have the same freedom? In particular, if athletes prefer the gains in performance the use of steroids allegedly provides, along with the increased risk of harm, to the alternative of less risk and worse performance, what gives anyone else the right to interfere with their choice? After all, if we should not forbid smokers from risking their health by smoking, why should we prohibit track stars, baseball players, or weight lifters from taking risks with their health in pursuit of their goals?

Although these antipaternalistic considerations have great force, we cannot yet dismiss paternalism as a justification for prohibiting steroids as performance enhancers. First we must consider some difficulties with this view. Even Mill acknowledged that the kind of antipaternalism articulated in his Harm Principle (the principle stating that the only justification for limiting liberty is to prevent harm to others) had limits. Mill excluded children and young people below the age of maturity as well as those, such as the mentally ill, who may require care from others. Moreover, Mill would surely exempt those who are misinformed or coerced from the immediate protection of the principle. To use one of his own examples, if you attempt to cross a bridge in the dark, not knowing that the bridge has been washed away by a flood, I do not violate the Harm Principle by preventing you from attempting the crossing until I have explained the situation to you.[9]

In particular, before accepting the antipaternalistic argument, we need to decide whether athletes who use steroids to enhance performance really are making a free and informed choice. If behavior is not the result of free and informed choice, it is not really the action of a rational autonomous agent. If it is not informed, the person does not truly know what she is doing, but if the behavior is coerced, it is not what the agent wants to do in the first place.

Is there reason to believe athletes who use steroids are either uninformed about the effects of the drug or are coerced or otherwise incompetent to make rational decisions?

First, those below the age of consent can legitimately be prevented on paternalistic grounds from using performance-enhancing steroids. In the same way that parents can prevent children from engaging in potentially harmful behavior, even if the children want to take their chances on getting hurt, so sports authorities can prohibit the use of harmful performance enhancers by those who are less capable of accurately weighing risks and potential harms against possible benefits due to their youth.

Moreover, elite athletes often are role models for younger athletes, who may strive to imitate their idols or hope to eventually achieve similar levels of success. When elite athletes use performance-enhancing drugs to better their own performance, their use may encourage minors, whose reasoning capabilities have not yet fully developed, to use them as well. As the Mitchell Report points out, even if steroid use by high school athletes is declining, as has been reported, and only 3 to 6 percent of such young people are using steroids, it still would be the case that hundreds of thousands of young people are using such drugs.[10] Therefore, instead of trying to justify restrictions on the use of performance-enhancing drugs by appealing to paternalism toward competent adult athletes, we can justify the restrictions with the claim that we must fulfill our duty to protect younger athletes, who often cannot completely comprehend the short-term and long-term risks involved in steroid use, from themselves. One point that could be raised here is that, although young athletes may be negatively influenced by the examples of athletes who use steroids and other illegal performance enhancers, they may also be dissuaded from using such substances by high-profile cases of those athletes caught and sanctioned for using them. The fall from grace of American cycling icon Lance Armstrong, for example, provides a cautionary tale of how using illegal enhancers can destroy an athlete's career and legacy. It could be argued that such examples serve to persuade young athletes that illegal performance enhancers should not be used in their pursuit of excellence and advancement in sport.

A second possible problem with the role model argument is that it is not completely consistent with our practices in other areas. We don't prevent adults from consuming alcohol, for example, even though adult drinkers may serve as models for alcohol abuse by underage drinkers. Adults normally are not prohibited by law from being bad role models for young people. Why should we apply a double standard to athletes? The above points suggest that although we cannot ignore the effects of star adult athletes' steroid use on young people, the claim that prohibitions on competent athletes' use of performance enhancers can be justified solely on the basis of the need to protect younger, less competent individuals is dubious. Such a consideration may factor into the ultimate case against allowing steroid use, but it cannot bear the whole weight of the argument.

What about the requirement of informed consent? Are athletes who use steroids adequately informed about the serious potential side effects of these drugs? Some athletes, particularly teenagers, may be uninformed or skeptical about the information available, but it is hard to believe that most adult users of steroids could be ignorant of the risks involved. Even if H. L. Mencken may not have been totally off the mark when he suggested it was impossible to go broke by underestimating the intelligence of the American people, it is difficult to believe, in view of the amount of publicity devoted to the use of performance enhancers, that the majority of mature athletes could be unaware that steroid use can be dangerous. However, even if ignorance about the effects of steroids were widespread, antipaternalists still might argue that fostering informed choice through improved drug education is a better remedy than simple prohibition.

Accordingly, paternalism alone probably does not provide a strong enough justification for prohibiting competent athletes' use of harmful performance-enhancing drugs, although it does justify prohibiting those below the age of consent from using them. However, we should leave open the possibility that paternalism, when conjoined with other premises, may provide partial support for prohibition. For example, if steroid use by some people reasonably may be thought to threaten harm to others as well as to the users, and if it is less clear than suggested above that adult users give free consent to assuming the risk of use, then a limited kind of paternalism may play a supporting role in the prohibitionist argument. The argument for prohibiting steroids might then be similar to the argument for requiring automobile drivers to wear seatbelts: we may justifiably require automobile drivers to wear seatbelts because it is for their own protection, because the decision not to buckle up may not result from thoughtful consideration of the dangers involved, and because of the high costs associated with collisions, which place a burden on the health care system as well as the taxpayers who support it.

Coercion and Freedom in Sports

What about the requirement of free choice? Are athletes really free to not use steroids? At least some analysts would argue that athletes are coerced into using steroids. Consider professional sports. The professional athlete's livelihood may depend on performing at the highest level. Athletes who are not among the best in the world may not be professionals for very long. Thus, as one writer concluded, "the onus is on the athlete to continue playing and to consent to things he or she would not otherwise consent to. . . . Coercion, however subtle, makes the athlete vulnerable. It also takes away the athlete's ability to act and choose freely with regard to informed consent."[11]

Although this point may not be without force in specific contexts, the use it makes of the term "coercion" seems questionable. After all, no one literally is forced to become (or remain) a professional athlete or to participate at elite levels in amateur athletics. If we want to use "coercion" so broadly, are we also committed, absurdly it seems, to saying that coaches coerce players into practicing or training hard? Do professors similarly coerce students into studying hard? Isn't it more plausible to say that although there are pressures on athletes to achieve peak physical condition, these no more amount to coercion than do the pressures on law or medical students to study hard? Rather, the athletes (or the students) have *reasons* to try hard to achieve success; the pressures are self-imposed.

At best it is unclear whether top athletes are coerced into using steroids or can freely decide that the gains of steroid use outweigh the risks. Surely we are not entitled to assume that professional athletes as a class are unable to give informed consent to steroid use unless we are willing to count similar pressures in other professions as forms of coercion as well. And if we use "coercion" that broadly, it becomes unclear who, if anybody, is left free.

Sometimes, however, in particular contexts athletes may be victims of coercion. For example, some of Lance Armstrong's teammates alleged that he pressured them to use illegal performance enhancers. With the power he accrued over time as seven-time Tour de France winner, such pressure could be perceived as coercion, as it seems that refusal to dope could have resulted in a cyclist's dismissal from the team; specific overt or even implied threats do imply coercion. Apart from such specific situations, however, it appears doubtful that the athlete's general desire to be successful at his or her profession can by itself undermine the capacity for free choice.

But is this conclusion too hasty? A critic might point out that even if the athlete's own internal desires for success do not rule out free choice, coercion from other competitors could be present. That is, even if we agree that internal pressures generated by the athletes are not coercive, we might suspect that their competitors create external pressures that are. It is sometimes argued that even if some sophisticated athletes do give informed consent, their drug use may force others into taking steroids as well. Athletes who would prefer not to become users may believe that unless they take the drugs, they will not be able to compete with those who do. Athletes may believe they are trapped because they are faced with a choice in which neither option is attractive: don't take steroids and lose, or take them and remain competitive.

Note that the argument here is no longer that we should interfere with athletes on paternalistic grounds—to prevent them from harming themselves—but that we should interfere with them to prevent them from coercing others. Such an argument is in accord with Mill's Harm Principle: liberty is restricted, but only to prevent harm to others.

Do pressures generated by athletes who use drugs coerce other athletes into using performance enhancers too? One reason for doubting they do is that it once again appears as if "coercion" is being used too broadly. One might just as well say that students who study harder than others "coerce" their classmates into studying harder in order to keep up or that athletes who practice longer hours than others "coerce" their competitors into practicing longer hours as well. The problem with such claims is that all competitive pressure becomes "coercive." As a result, the term "coercion" is deprived of any moral force. Indeed, if all the competitive behaviors that were "coercive" in this way were put into a list, virtually no competitive behaviors would be left over that were not coercive.

Critics might reply that there is a difference between weight training and extra studying, on one hand, and steroid use, on the other. As one writer has pointed out, "Steroids place regard for enhancement of athletic performance above regard for the health of the athletes themselves."[12] Weight training should make athletes stronger and more resistant to injury; studying normally enhances the intellectual ability of students. But steroid use, even if it enhances athletic performance, also presents serious risk of harm to the user.

These differences are important and suggest that the use of steroids does present athletes with a difficult choice. But is this enough to show that a user *coerces* other athletes into also becoming users? Much depends upon how we understand the term "coercion."[13] If we understand coercion to mean imposing difficult choices on others when we have no right to do so and if we assume the user has no right to impose the choice of using or not using on other athletes, then perhaps a strong form of the coercion argument can be defended.

But before any such argument can be made good, we need to consider whether steroid users do have a right to impose the choice of becoming a user on others. And even if they have such a right, would it be wrong for them to exercise it? Rather than engaging in a conceptual analysis of the notion of "coercion," perhaps it will be more profitable to consider directly whether it is morally wrong for athletes who use steroids to place other athletes in a situation in which they must choose between becoming users themselves or becoming competitively disadvantaged.

Unethically Constrained Choice

The appeal to coercion as a justification for prohibiting the use of steroids is open to the charge that it uses the notion of coercion far too broadly. Perhaps the argument can be reconstructed or modified without unacceptably stretching the term "coercion."

Whatever the proper definition of coercion, what seems to make coercion presumptively wrong is that it unduly, illegitimately, or in some other way improperly interferes with the freedom of another. Thus, if we are reluctant to say that the student who studies harder than his peers or the athlete who trains harder than her competitors is coercing them, perhaps it is because we do not think the student or the athlete is acting improperly to begin with. Both have a right to work harder, so their working harder does not coerce others to do the same or, if it does, does not do so improperly or wrongly. Accordingly, we have no reason to prohibit the behavior of the student or the athlete (and even have reason to encourage it because it leads to superior achievement). In fact, their hard work may be inspiring to others and thus make a positive social contribution.

But consider another situation in which competitive pressures are imposed improperly. Suppose you work in a firm where young employees compete for promotions to higher levels. Up to a point, if some work harder than others, no ethical issue is involved, because it is not wrong and usually highly desirable for some workers to try to perform better than others. But now suppose that some workers work all the time, including weekends. Everyone feels the pressure to keep up, and soon all the workers give up their holidays and evenings for fear they will lose their jobs if they do not. In this situation it is more plausible to conclude that the workers are coerced or, if not "coerced," then at least unjustifiably pressured into putting in many hours of overtime.

Let us go further. Suppose some of the workers start taking stimulants—drugs having harmful side effects—so they can work even harder. Other workers feel that to keep up they too must take the stimulants. They ask the employer to set limits on the amount of time they are expected to work because they are being coerced into taking the stimulant to keep their jobs.

In this example it is unclear whether the workers who take the stimulants are behaving properly. Arguably, they are putting undue pressure on other workers to risk harming themselves so they can keep their jobs. If so, the workers taking the stimulants are violating the freedom of their fellow workers, and their behavior may be regulated in the interests of protecting the freedom of all.

Is the practice of steroid use in competitive sports like that of our last example? Do users of dangerous performance-enhancing drugs behave improperly when they put pressure on others to keep up competitively? Some would say "No!" As one writer has argued, "the ingestion of steroids for competitive reasons cannot be distinguished from the other tortures, deprivations, and risks to which athletes subject themselves to achieve success. No one is coerced into world class competition. . . . If they find the costs excessive, they may withdraw."[14]

Although such a rejoinder has force, it may not be decisive. Although steroid use is not strictly "coercive" because athletes can always withdraw from the competition, the choice of either using a potentially harmful drug or being noncompetitive may be unethical if it is imposed on others. Perhaps a prohibition on steroids can be justified as a means of protecting athletes from being placed in a position in which they have to make such a choice. To the extent that we think it is wrong or illegitimate to present athletes with such a dilemma, then to that extent we will find the argument from coercion to have a point. Regardless of whether we want to apply the term "coercion" in such a context, we need to consider whether it is morally wrong to insist that athletes risk harming themselves to compete. If so, a prohibition on steroid use may be justified as a means of protecting athletes against having such a choice imposed upon them and protecting them from competitive pressures that, if unregulated, are far too likely to get out of hand.

Such considerations may not satisfy those who think steroid use is permissible. They would reply that athletes are not considered unethical if they engage in demanding training and thereby impose hard choices on other competitors. How can we justifiably condemn the users of performance-enhancing drugs for confronting competitors with difficult choices when we do not make the same judgment in similar situations?

This rejoinder does need to be explored further, but it is far from decisive. Perhaps we can distinguish the risks inherent in stressful training programs from those inherent in the use of steroids. As M. Andrew Holowchak remarked in a passage quoted earlier, we might distinguish between steroid use, which can be harmful, and training, which, if done properly, promotes conditioning and reduces the chances of injury.

Although we have not arrived at an uncontroversial justification for prohibiting the use of steroids in organized athletic competition, we have discovered an argument that is well worth further examination. According to this argument, athletes who use steroids have no right to put other athletes in the position of either damaging their health or competing under a significant disadvantage. Whether it will survive the test of further critical discussion remains to be seen, but perhaps it is strong enough to create at least a presumption in favor of prohibiting steroids in athletic competition, especially when we also consider the effects of elite athletes using steroids on impressionable young athletes as an added reinforcing factor (the "role model" argument is discussed more fully in Chapter 8). Perhaps this presumption can be strengthened when conjoined with another argument of a different but not totally unrelated kind.

Fairness, Cheating, and the Use of Performance Enhancers

Many of those who object to the use of performance-enhancing drugs in sport do so not (or not only) because they believe users coerce others into using these drugs but (also) because they believe that such use is cheating. What reasons, if any, can be given for regarding the use of drugs such as steroids as an unfair competitive practice?

Those who assert that users of performance-enhancing drugs are cheating their opponents are doing more than claiming that users are breaking existing rules. For instance, many fans of Major League Baseball claim that players who used steroids and other performance enhancers before the explicit prohibition of their use prior to the 2004 season were cheating.[15]

Of course, if the existing rules prohibit the use of such drugs, then their use is cheating. Those who secretly violate the rules take unfair advantage of those who don't. The interesting philosophical issue is whether sports organizations should adopt the rules prohibiting the use of performance-enhancing drugs in the first place, or if such rules already exist, they should be changed to allow the use of performance-enhancing drugs. Would allowing the use of performance-enhancing drugs be unfair even if such drugs were available to all participants in a sport?

Many of us share the feeling that use of performance enhancers provides an unfair advantage, but we need to ask whether there are good arguments to support this intuitive conclusion. We also need to consider just where the unfairness lies. Roger Gardner made a perceptive distinction when he asked whether steroid use was unfair to *competitors* because of the advantage it provides or was unfair to *the game* because it made success too easy. It will be useful to keep this distinction in mind as we explore the topic further in what follows.[16]

One line of argument suggests an analogy with differences in the equipment available to competitors. For example, if one player in a golf tournament used golf balls that went significantly farther than balls opponents used, even when struck with the same force, and the same ball was available for others to use, the tournament arguably would be unfair. One player would be able to avoid one of the major challenges of golf not through skill but by using a superior product. Perhaps the use of steroids provides a similar unfair advantage.

The problem with this argument is that it is, at best, unclear that such a golf tournament was unfair. If the ball was acceptable under the rules and available to other competitors, the user indeed would have an advantage over players who were using ordinary equipment, but what would make the advantage unfair? Other players could use the same brand of golf ball if they wished to do so. There are all sorts of differences in equipment, past experiences, training facilities, coaching, and diet that can affect athletic performance but are not regarded as unfair. Until we can say why the advantages steroids provide are illegitimate and the advantages other conditions provide are legitimate, the charge of unfairness must be dismissed for lack of support.[17]

A similar difficulty affects the view that performance enhancers make sports too easy. Thus, we might say that the trouble with the "hot" golf ball is not that it gives some competitors unfair advantages over others but that it makes golf significantly less challenging than it would be otherwise. Similarly, perhaps the trouble with steroids, we might claim, is that they reduce the challenge of sports by making achievement to too great a degree the result of taking a pill rather than the result of skill. But, as Roger Gardner pointed out, the same claim can be made about equipment, such as perimeter-weighted golf clubs that expand their "sweet spot," thereby reducing the skill needed for a desirable shot, as well as about diets promoting carbohydrate loading, high-tech running shoes, streamlined designer swimsuits, and top-of-the-line practice facilities, all of which are regarded as acceptable parts of athletic competition.[18] The difficulty, then, is that of finding a principled way of drawing the line between the illegitimate use of steroids and other performance enhancers, on one hand, and factors that provide legitimate competitive advantages, on the other.

In fact, some advances in equipment can make the game too easy and should be prohibited in the interest of preserving the game's inherent challenge, but other innovations should be allowed. Major League Baseball does not allow the use of aluminum bats, and golf regulates how "hot" golf balls may be made as well as the degree to which clubfaces can flex, adding unearned distance to the shot. Perhaps steroid use is on one (prohibited) side of the line and effective dieting is on the other (permissible) side. The problem is to draw the line properly in the first place. Just when does an innovation make the game too easy?

Although a simple answer to such a question is unlikely to exist, the charge of unfairness should not be dismissed too quickly. Perhaps by expanding the considerations mentioned in our discussion of the potential coercive effects of steroid use we can develop a different analysis of the unfairness involved. This analysis may be able to help us develop a reasonable—although perhaps not conclusive—case that steroid use should be prohibited in competitive sports.

That some athletes' steroid use creates a situation of unpalatable choices for others was suggested earlier: either use steroids and risk harm, or cease to be competitive (or at least assume a significant competitive disadvantage). In a sense the steroid user, though perhaps not like the robber who demands your money or your life, at least creates a dilemma like that facing the workers who must use harmful stimulants to keep pace with their drug-induced, energetic colleagues. We may conclude that neither athletes nor workers should face such choices and that we should enact legislation to protect them from such a cruel dilemma.

Does a similar line of argument also suggest that the use of performance-enhancing steroids is *unfair*? Suppose we ask whether it would be rational for all athletes to support either the rule "Use of steroids should be prohibited in athletic competition" or the rule "Use of steroids should be permitted in athletic competition." Let us stipulate one artificial but plausible and morally justifiable limitation on their choice: namely, the athletes vote as if in ignorance of how the use or nonuse of steroids would affect them personally, but with knowledge of the general properties of steroids. The use of this limited "veil of ignorance," suggested by John Rawls's theory of justice, forces the athletes to be impartial and unbiased rather than to vote according to personal self-interest.[19] How would rational and impartial athletes vote?

Can it be established that a vote for the rule permitting steroid use would be irrational under such circumstances? One might argue for such a view by pointing out that all athletes would know of the general harmful effects of steroids, but because of the requirement of limited ignorance, none would have any reason to believe steroids would be especially beneficial to them personally. Widespread use would, at best, yield only minimal gains for any one competitor, as the advantages gained by some would be largely canceled out by roughly similar advantages gained by others. However, the risk of serious effects on health would be significant for all.

Under such circumstances a rule allowing the general use of steroids seems collectively irrational. Why would rational individuals choose to run great risks for minimal gains, gains that, from behind the veil of ignorance, they have no reason to believe will benefit them rather than their competitors? It seems that significant competitive advantage can be secured only if some athletes use steroids covertly. Allowing steroid use would not be supported by the informed, impartial choice of all athletes and would provide only minimal gains relative to the risk of serious harm. The use of steroids as performance enhancers is unethical precisely because rational and impartial athletes would not agree to it as a universal practice.

Thus, steroid use may seem rational if users think only about themselves and hope to secure advantages over nonusers. But if they must think impartially about what is an acceptable universal practice, steroid use no longer seems rational. This is why the use of steroids seems to many to be a form of cheating. The user operates from principles that could not be consented to as principles applying to all.

In effect this argument appeals to a hypothetical contract among rational and impartial athletes. It is hypothetical because it attempts to specify what would be agreed to under specified but not necessarily real or actual conditions of choice. Although it is hypothetical rather than actual, writers such as Rawls have suggested that such a contract nevertheless is binding on us in that the hypothetical conditions reflect considerations we think ought to apply to moral reasoning. The veil of ignorance, for example, reflects our belief that moral reasoning should be impartial rather than biased in our own favor and should not be unduly influenced by our social class, race, gender, religion, or genetic endowment.

Unfortunately for those who oppose the use of performance-enhancing steroids, this sort of argument is hardly free from criticism. In particular, it assumes, perhaps incorrectly, that the only outcomes athletes would consider behind the veil of ignorance would be risks to health versus competitive gains over other athletes. Some athletes might consider other issues. For example, some might believe that a universally higher level of competition generated by using steroids more than compensates for health risks. Others may value their greater strength as a result of steroid use, regardless of competitive gain over others.[20] Thus, it is not as uncontroversial as it first appeared to suppose that impartial and reasonable athletes would unanimously agree to prohibit steroid use; their deliberations behind the veil might even be indeterminate because of conflicting views.

This critique indicates that the contractual version of the argument from fairness is open to reasonable objection. However, further development of the argument may undermine some of the objections to it. For example, we might consider whether the official rule-making bodies of sports, such as the National Collegiate Athletic Association (NCAA) or the International Olympic Committee (IOC), are obligated to ignore the idiosyncratic values of individual athletes and simply consider steroid use from the standpoint of promoting good competition. If we can justifiably rule out the preferences of athletes who value increases in strength or in overall athletic achievement over risks to health and only consider the issue from the standpoint of weighing competitive advantages and disadvantages (which arguably is the point of view that rule-making bodies should take), then our original conclusion seems to follow. From the standpoint of collective impartial choice about the conditions of competition, users of steroids are exempting themselves from rules to which they would not consent under conditions of free, impartial choice. Because they are making exceptions of themselves arbitrarily, their behavior may be regarded as unfair. Users who engage in a behavior they could not rationally endorse as a policy for others to follow treat their fellow athletes merely as a means to their own success.[21]

Sports organizations such as MLB or the IOC are justified in considering things from this perspective—and discounting the possible desires of those athletes who would like to see the overall level of play improve as a result of drug use—because their job as organizations is not to make play better and better but rather to regulate competition fairly. This conclusion, as we have seen, may not follow if, behind the veil of ignorance, we take into account the fact that athletes may take a point of view based on some value not directly connected to competitive success, such as raising the limits of human performance. However, because sports organizations regulate fairness in competition, it seems reasonable for them to ignore such idiosyncratic values when making regulations about steroid use.

Performance-Enhancing Drugs, Respect for Persons, and the Ethic of Competition

Even if the contractual version of the argument from fairness has force, it may seem to miss part of the issue the use of performance enhancers raises. For one thing, it depends heavily on the harmful effects of prolonged steroid use to the user. But we may believe the use of performance enhancers would be wrong even if the drugs were not harmful. If there were a "magic pill" that, if taken properly, would improve athletic ability without significant risks to health, would using such a pill be ethical? Doesn't the use of steroids run counter to the ethic of good competition outlined in earlier chapters, even if the potential dangers to the user are discounted?

To many people steroid use seems a way of avoiding the challenges sport presents rather than overcoming them. This belief does not seem to rest upon claims that the use of steroids is coercive or that such use is unfair but instead seems to arise independently from concerns about the basic ethic of athletic competition. Can such intuitions about the wrongness of performance-enhancing drugs be justified?

If competition in sports is supposed to be a test of the athletic ability of persons, isn't the very heart of competition corrupted if performance-enhancing drugs affect results? Presumably, we would not accept a new high-jump record if the winner wore special mechanical aids that added spring to her shoes.

Similarly, consider home runs produced through the use of a high-tech baseball bat programmed to make square contact with the ball (perhaps through an implanted sensor and computerized control chip) so it will fly out of the park regardless of the batter's skill. In both of these examples we are inclined to say that success would not reflect the skill of the athlete but rather the operation of the special equipment.

Isn't it the same with the use of performance-enhancing drugs? Where such drugs lead to improved play, it is not the person who is responsible for the gains; rather, it is the drug that makes the difference. Isn't this similar to the examples of the mechanical track shoes and the high-tech baseball bat? Isn't the ethic of competition violated because the skills of the athlete are replaced with technological aids that turn the contest from one of competing persons into one of machines? The logical extension of such a route would be to gradually replace flesh-and-blood athletes with part-human and part-machine cyborgs or even robots designed to maximize performance in every category. What we would have, if such a situation ever became reality, might be enhanced performance, but would it be sport?

Those who believe the use of performance-enhancing drugs should be permitted may not be convinced by such an argument. They might raise four important objections. First, we do allow new equipment in sport, even if such equipment does enhance performance. Fiberglass poles for vaulting, tennis racquets composed of composites, and the replacement of wooden golf shafts with steel ones are examples of technological innovations that enhance performance.[22] How does the introduction of performance-enhancing drugs differ? Second, changes in diet are widely believed to enhance performance. If runners can "load up" on carbohydrates before a race to improve their times, why can't they take steroids as well? Third, steroids and other performance enhancers are not magic bullets that immediately produce results. They yield improvement only in conjunction with hard training and a demanding work ethic. In fact, they allow muscles to recover faster and, therefore, permit users to engage in more intense and more frequent workouts than nonusers are able to manage. Finally, why isn't the decision to use steroids just as much a person's decision to make as the decision to use weight training? What reason do we have to say that weight training reflects our status as persons who can make free choices and the use of steroids does not?

Let us consider the point about technological innovations in equipment first. Although it is doubtful whether any one principle explains when an innovation in equipment is acceptable and when it is not, some distinctions can be made. For example, some technological improvements in equipment remedy previous defects. Old wooden shafts in golf clubs twisted to varying degrees under the pressure of the golf swing, producing arbitrary results. The same player could make two equally good swings but get different results because of too much torque in the wooden shaft. Steel golf shafts remedied this defect, providing more consistent results because they do not twist under the pressure of the stroke. Similarly, improved athletic shoes remove the defects of unnecessary weight and faulty structure. Although both innovations made it easier to perform better, neither changed the basic character of the game and both can be regarded as removing handicaps faulty equipment created that were extraneous to the challenges set by the sports in question.

Other changes in equipment that have been regarded as permissible cannot so easily be seen as simply removing defects in materials used earlier. The use of hypoxic oxygen chambers that simulate the effects of high-altitude training is controversial. Their use is allowed by the World Anti-Doping Agency (WADA) but prohibited within the confines of the Olympic Village since the Sydney Olympics of 2000.[23]

In golf the sand wedge, a club with a specially designed flange, invented by professional Gene Sarazen, made escaping from sand bunkers far easier than before. Many skilled professionals would rather have a missed shot land in the sand than in a difficult lie on grass because the sand wedge has made highly accurate recoveries likely for the advanced player. Similarly, fiberglass poles have made it possible for pole-vaulters to achieve heights previously considered unreachable. In 2008, both at the Olympics and the European Short Course Championships as well as in 2009 at the World Championships, special streamlined full-body swimsuits, which improved buoyancy, were widely believed to contribute to the plethora of records set during these competitions. Graphite and other composite materials have contributed to advances in play in golf, tennis, and other sports. In other words, it does not appear true that all technological advances in sports equipment are simply remedies for defects in earlier materials. Why should such advances be allowed and steroids prohibited?

In reply, as noted above, sometimes sports authorities prohibit advancements in equipment. It simply is not true that all technological advances in equipment are allowable regardless of their effects on the game. Some technological advances are prohibited because they make the game too easy or reduce its challenges in some significant way. Other advancements can make the game more competitive or make its challenges more reasonable. Thus, the use of the sand wedge in golf can be defended on the grounds that without it, bunker shots were simply too difficult. The game was made better by allowing the equipment. Nevertheless, in 2009 the United States Golf Association prohibited the use of wedges and other irons with specially designed grooves in professional and certain other elite competitions (although their use is allowed until 2024 for less elite play). This is because the special grooves allowed top players to get backspin on the ball even after hitting from the rough (an unmowed or less closely mowed area of the course). This allowed elite golfers to control the ball better and, hence, reduced the penalty for inaccurate drives that missed the fairway. In effect, the special grooves significantly reduced the penalty for lack of skill in a key area of the game and reduced the challenge of the contest to an arguably unacceptable degree. Similarly, since 2010 the Fédération Internationale de Natation, the international governing body of aquatic sports, has banned the use of full-body swimsuits.

Performance-enhancing drugs, it might be argued, also change the nature of those who use the equipment and, thus, undermine the challenge sport presents. Instead of meeting the challenge of the test, we change the nature of the test takers to minimize the challenge they face. For example, if steroids were permitted in sports in which strength and speed play a significant role (sprint races in track and swimming, field events such as shot put and hammer throw, and power lifting, for example), the way the drug affected athletes would significantly influence outcomes in these sports. But this seems irrelevant when determining which contestant is the better player. Jones should not defeat Smith because Jones's body processes steroids more efficiently than Smith's. We want the winner to be the best athlete, not the individual whose body is best attuned to a performance-enhancing drug! Thus, it could be argued that performance enhancers turn sports like those above from contests among persons into contests among "designer" bodies that are manufactured through a technological fix[24] and that winners in these sports tend to be the individuals whose bodies react best to the available drugs. This hardly seems to be what is meant by sport as a mutual quest of persons for excellence through challenge.

However, a proponent of the use of performance enhancers might ask whether the same thing isn't true of, for example, special diets. Thus, "carbohydrate loading," or consuming unusually large amounts of carbohydrates before competition, seems to be a common and accepted practice among long-distance runners, but clearly some competitors may gain more from the practice than others. Is this an example of athletically irrelevant qualities unfairly affecting outcomes? Or if it is permissible to adhere to a performance-enhancing diet, why isn't it also acceptable to use performance-enhancing drugs?

Even if this point is ignored, proponents of steroid use might charge that the argument against steroids is inconsistent in another way. Competition in sports has been defended here because it is expressive of our moral status as persons. But by prohibiting athletes from using performance-enhancing drugs, it can be argued that we show disrespect to them as persons. That is, we deny them the control over their own lives that ought to belong to any autonomous, intelligent, and competent individual. In other words, aren't athletes persons? If so, shouldn't their choices, including the choice to use drugs to enhance performance, be respected?[25]

The debate so far raises several key issues. Just when are changes in equipment allowable and when should they be prohibited? Is there a bright, clear line that tells us when changes in equipment or in the persons using it reduce the challenge of the game to an unacceptable extent? Why does steroid use "change the nature of persons" but training, diet, and vitamins do not? And why should our current conception of persons (assuming it is clear enough to be useful) be sacrosanct? It appears that both the proponents and the critics of the use of performance-enhancing drugs in sport have advanced points well worth considering but that the arguments presented by both sides are still inconclusive. However, as will be argued later, that does not mean they are equal in rational force—only that no one argument taken by itself is decisive.

Performance-Enhancing Drugs and the Legitimacy of Records

One of the complaints many sports fans, particularly baseball fans, bring against the use of performance-enhancing drugs is that they undermine our ability to make comparisons between achievements of the past and those of "the steroid era." Many fans question whether the home run records Barry Bonds set—assuming Bonds was using performance enhancers when the records were set—are truly legitimate. Is it fair to Roger Maris, the holder of the single-season record for home runs for many years, or to career home run leaders such as Babe Ruth and Hank Aaron, that Bonds be regarded as the home run king of all time?

A somewhat different but related situation arises in what Sigmund Loland has called "record sports," sports such as swimming or track and field, in which the goal of many athletes is to set new records, but the difference between the old performance and the new, record-setting performance is almost infinitesimal, perhaps made possible only by new technology capable of detecting minute differences in performances. In such sports athletes may be tempted to use performance enhancers simply to set new records and raise the bar higher. Loland surely is correct when he asks whether such tiny differences in performance are really all that significant.[26]

However, baseball has a long history and a tradition in which fans debate the merits of different players from different eras of the sport. How do the center fielders of today, for example, compare with stars of the 1950s and 1960s, such as contemporaries Duke Snider of the Brooklyn Dodgers, Willie Mays of the New York Giants, and Mickey Mantle of the New York Yankees, three of the great center fielders of all time who graced New York with their play? In baseball, at least before the steroid era, records often lasted for decades. Many knowledgeable observers doubt that Joe DiMaggio's fifty-six-game hitting streak, set in 1941, will ever be surpassed. Should we regard records like those of Aaron, Maris, and Ruth as having been surpassed when it is reasonable to suspect they were broken only with the aid of performance enhancers?

We doubt whether a decisive answer can be provided to this question, but it will be useful to consider some of the arguments on both sides. Those who argue that indeed the records of the past were genuinely broken by today's sluggers, regardless of whether they used performance enhancers, might make three different points.

First, they might argue that other past changes in baseball also affected performance but that no one ever argued that records set under these changed conditions were illegitimate. Thus, in 1968 MLB lowered the height of the pitching mound in order to rejuvenate the offensive side of the game. Bringing the pitcher down to the level of the batter reduced the advantage of the hurler over the hitter. Also, when Ruth set his records baseball was a racially segregated sport in which white batters never had to compete against all the top pitchers of the time, some of whom were excluded from the Major Leagues because of their race. Were Ruth's records somehow illegitimate because he did not always play against all the best players of his time as a result of excluding minorities from the field of play? In other words, different eras of baseball differ from others in a variety of ways that can affect performance.[27] The steroid era, on this view, is only one more change, and it is not totally dissimilar to those of the past; it does no more to delegitimize present achievement than any other significant change did throughout the history of the sport.

Second, batters have not been the only users of performance-enhancing drugs; pitchers have been among the alleged users as well. So even if some of the batters improved their performance by using steroids or other performance enhancers, so did some of the pitchers they batted against. This makes their slugging achievements even more impressive, not less so, than if only batters were using steroids, the person arguing for acceptance of records made under the influence of steroids might say.

Third and finally, performance-enhancing drugs are not magic pills. Bonds, McGwire, and other sluggers, regardless of whether drug use enhanced their performance, demonstrated enormous talent in performing one of the most difficult feats in all of sport—namely, making powerful contact with the kinds of pitches thrown by elite pitchers who also were at the top of their game.

All of these considerations support the view that records set even by users of performance-enhancing drugs are entirely legitimate, even in Major League

Baseball. But are these arguments persuasive? Let's consider the other side of the case before deciding. What might the person say who is against including records made under the influence of performance-enhancing substances?

First of all, the barrage of home run records that have been set during the steroid era was unprecedented. For the first 122 years of Major League Baseball only Ruth, with sixty, and Maris, with sixty-one, hit more than fifty-nine home runs in a season. But from 1995 to 2001 this was done six times by three different players. It is unlikely that all these achievements have been due to a sudden improvement in the athletic abilities of the players without the assistance of performance-enhancing drugs. More importantly, it is unlikely that these records were set on a level playing field. When the mound was lowered in 1968, reducing the advantage of the pitcher over the hitter, all hitters and all pitchers performed under the same set of conditions. However, many—perhaps a great majority—of Major League players have not used performance-enhancing drugs.

In addition, if the contractual argument presented earlier is plausible, those who did use performance-enhancing drugs were acting in a way they could not reasonably universalize. As we have seen, impartial athletes (deliberating behind the veil of ignorance) would not adopt a rule allowing everyone to use performance-enhancing drugs of the kind at stake. As such, they achieved their records by using an arguably unethical method and operated egoistically rather than ethically.

Moreover, although baseball did not have an explicit antidrug policy at the time when many of the records were set, there were rules in place that implicitly—and after 1991 explicitly—prohibited the use of performance-enhancing drugs. Thus, as the Mitchell Report points out, "Beginning in 1971 and continuing today, Major League Baseball's drug policy has prohibited the use of any prescription medicine without a valid prescription. By implication, this prohibition applied to steroids even before 1991 when Commissioner Fay Vincent first expressly included steroids in baseball's drug policy."[28]

This point can be pressed even further. If records were allowed to stand after being set with the help of methods that, for one thing, were against the rules and, for another thing, were arguably unethical, then less disincentive would be provided to deter future players from trying to achieve success outside the rules and moral framework of the sports involved. Moreover, the records of the players who did conform to proper standards of conduct should stand until they are broken by legitimate (non-drug-enhanced) performances. Why should their achievements be supplanted by performances achieved through illicit methods? Reducing the significance of some of the records, which it is reasonable to believe were achieved with the use of performance enhancers, would provide a guarantee that those who abide by an appropriate sporting code of conduct will not be disadvantaged by doing so and would help to restore the situation to what it would have been if performance enhancers had not been used. Thus, considerations of deterrence and considerations of fairness both support the claim that certain records achieved in the steroid era of Major League Baseball should not be viewed as legitimate.

How are we to weigh all of these conflicting considerations? As we suggested above, perhaps there is no clearly decisive answer to that question. Perhaps these records should simply be marked with an asterisk, indicating they may have been achieved with the use of performance-enhancing drugs. In addition, out of respect for the previous record holders, whose achievements were presumably not aided by the same types of performance enhancers, the surpassed records could also be displayed as a reference point and standard to which "clean" competitors could aspire. In this way the records would not be erased or eliminated; they would be allowed to stand, but with reservations attached to them. Under this reasonable compromise the record books would indicate to the game's observers that the way in which the achievements were made is open to serious moral question.

A Presumptive Case Against Performance Enhancers

We have provided some reason to believe that the use of performance-enhancing drugs in order to improve performance in sports is unethical. But have we proven our case? Are our reasons good enough to become the basis for action on the part of the sports organizations setting the rules for professional and amateur competitive sports? Why shouldn't the rules be changed to allow the use of such substances, perhaps under strict medical supervision?

We suggest that, although critics and proponents have advanced important arguments, neither side has won conclusively. However, although it is important to engage in further discussion to advance the argument, it doesn't follow that the debate should leave us paralyzed by analysis and unable to act. Although theorists have the luxury to continue debating arguments for and against prohibition of performance-enhancing substances, sports authorities cannot necessarily wait for them to come up with a definitive answer. They must promulgate rules about whether to permit the use of performance-enhancing drugs on the best information they have at present.

Policymakers often have to decide difficult issues over which reasonable persons of good will disagree. If we had to wait for the emergence of decisive arguments on controversial moral issues, we often would be intellectually paralyzed in circumstances demanding some action. In fact, we often have to draw lines between what is permissible and impermissible in areas where reasons for making the distinction do not apply in as sharp a fashion as we would like. For example, the democratic state must distinguish between those who are mature enough to vote and those who are not. Because it would be impractical to evaluate the maturity of all persons based on their merits and character, we attempt to draw a line reasonably. So long as the process by which the line is drawn is itself consistent with democratic values and the boundary is reasonable, there are good grounds for regarding it as justified. We need to avoid the fallacy of insisting that if we cannot find the perfect place to draw a line, we should draw no line at all. As the French philosopher Voltaire reminded us: "The perfect is the enemy of the good," and so to produce the most defensible policy we sometimes have to arrive at a reasonable decision, even when the grounds for doing so are not airtight.

Thus, we may want to give sports authorities the discretion to prohibit performance enhancers if their best judgment supports such a policy. If sports authorities, such as the NCAA or the IOC, have *reasonable* grounds for making distinctions between impermissible performance-enhancing drugs and permissible diets, equipment changes, and the like, and if they are not acting in an autocratic or dogmatic fashion, then even if no conclusive argument can be given for drawing the line in one place, their decision still has normative force.

Several points emerge from our discussion to support such a conclusion:

1. Athletes who choose to use harmful performance enhancers create a situation in which nonusers must either subject themselves to serious health risks or cease to be competitive. It is far from clear that users have the right to impose this choice on others.
2. It is doubtful whether rational and impartial athletes concerned with regulating competition would support a universal rule allowing the use of potentially harmful performance enhancers.
3. More controversially, the use of harmful performance enhancers moves sport closer to transforming persons into tools for athletic success than do special diets, weight training, or vitamin supplements.
4. Elite athletes' use of harmful performance enhancers is likely to encourage, by example, aspiring young athletes who are beneath the age of consent to use such harmful substances and so may be prohibited in order to prevent or minimize such dangerous consequences.
5. Finally, and perhaps more controversially, in some (perhaps many) sports, such as Major League Baseball, the use of performance-enhancing drugs can cheapen the achievements of the sport (for example, by making home runs too easy to hit), making it difficult or impossible to make a fair comparison of the performance of users and nonusers over time.

Thus, our discussion does suggest that, although no conclusive argument or knock-down proof is available, good reasons can be given for prohibiting steroids as performance enhancers and that official governing bodies in sports can, therefore, prohibit their use. Unless it can be shown that such decisions are arbitrary, dogmatic, or authoritarian, they are given moral weight because legitimate governing bodies promulgate them.[29] Rather than assigning the burden of proof to those who find the use of performance enhancers to be immoral, why not maintain instead that where the sports community is in deep disagreement, governing bodies' decisions are morally binding as long as they are not unreasonable, undemocratic, or arbitrary?

Moreover, the lines of argument we have considered for prohibiting the use of performance-enhancing drugs, although not determinative, might well be strengthened by extended discussion and debate. Although none of these arguments avoids serious objection, it is far from clear that the objections are decisive enough to justify total rejection of the arguments. Perhaps these arguments are cogent enough to show that the policies of those governing bodies of organized sports that prohibit the use of performance enhancers in their competitions are sufficiently reasonable, at least until the ethical issues involved are more satisfactorily resolved.

Enforcement

If the rules prohibiting the use of performance-enhancing drugs are to be effective, they must be enforced. Enforcement, however, raises a host of ethical issues. For example, drug use often can be detected through urinalysis and other scientific tests, although elite athletes have made attempts at chemically disguising evidence of drug use. But assuming that tests are often effective, should athletes be required to take them? Does this amount to forcing users to incriminate themselves, violating constitutional guarantees against self-incrimination? Do drug tests violate a right to privacy? Do rights to privacy of high school, intercollegiate, and professional athletes differ in this regard? What about the constitutional prohibition on unreasonable searches? Which methods of enforcement are ethical and which are not?

What are the principal ethical objections to requiring athletes to be tested for performance-enhancing substances? Clearly they have to do with liberty and privacy. One of the most cherished principles of Anglo-American law and of the liberal political theories from which it derives is that the presumption is on the authorities to prove the guilt of an individual.

To see why this principle is so important, consider the alternative. Under a presumption of guilt, individuals could be detained, their homes searched, and their lives disrupted simply because prosecutors decided they might find evidence of an infraction if they looked hard enough. Our liberty and our privacy would be minimal at best under such an arrangement. We would have them only to the extent that the authorities permitted us to keep them, which is to say we would not have them in any meaningful sense at all.

Requiring the individual to submit to drug tests seems to those concerned with our liberties to be similar to requiring individuals to open their homes to searches or to detaining individuals against their will, without evidence that, if it existed, might justify such intrusions. Accordingly, it seems that those of us who are committed to respect for the freedom of the individual must reject the required random testing of athletes for drug use.

But although this argument does have considerable force, it does admit of exceptions. For example, shouldn't those persons directly responsible for the safety of others be required to show that they are not under the influence of alcohol or other mind-altering drugs? Airline pilots, railroad engineers, surgeons, police officers, and firefighters are among those with special obligations to care for the safety of others. Requiring them to take drug tests seems to be an exception permitted even by Mill's Harm Principle because its purpose is to prevent direct injury to others.

This argument can be gradually extended until it becomes dangerously broad. Thus, although loss of worker efficiency due to drug use is a major national problem, could we justify required testing of all workers in an effort to prevent harm to fellow workers and to consumers? What happens to our civil liberties then?

Although we cannot pursue this important question in depth here, we ought not to be driven down the slippery slope too quickly. Although some workers' drug use on the job may indirectly injure consumers, lines can be drawn. The greater the threat of harm, the more serious the kind of harm at stake, and the more directly it is attendant upon drug use, then the greater the argument for required testing. Usually, either the threat of harm will be sufficiently indirect or weak, or other methods of protection and/or detection will be available. It is therefore doubtful that making exceptions to the general principle of noninterference in instances of direct and serious harm to individuals will undermine civil liberties generally.

Is there another kind of exception that might apply to organized athletics? After all, unlike airline pilots who use drugs, athletes who take steroids do not directly endanger the general public. Perhaps the idea of a collection of individuals voluntarily taking part in a joint activity requiring the mutual observance of common rules applies here. Thus, in professional baseball an umpire has the right to require a pitcher to empty his pockets so the umpire can check that the player is not carrying special prohibited substances that, when applied to the baseball, can alter its flight, making it more difficult to hit. Off the field the umpire would have no right to search the player, but he does have such a right in the special context of the game. This is because the game is fair only if all players observe the same rules. The umpire, with the consent of the competing teams, is charged with enforcing the rules, thereby ensuring a fair contest. As a result, umpires acquire rights in virtue of their role that they do not have as ordinary citizens. The civil rights of the players have in effect been limited in the context of the game because the players accept its rules and enforcement procedures.

A similar argument can be applied to testing for the use of performance-enhancing drugs in organized athletics. Participants consent to playing by publicly acknowledged rules. No one is forced to participate, but once consent is given to participation, players are owed protection from those who would intentionally violate the rules. Without enforcement, no protection would be provided. In particular, if effective means of detection were not used, then athletes would suspect each other of breaking the existing rules. Pressures would exist to use performance-enhancing drugs illegally in attempts to remain competitive.

Because participants voluntarily agree to participate and because they agree to play under the assumption that the rules will be applied fairly to all, they are owed protection against violators. Drug testing of athletes, in this view, seems not to be a violation of their civil rights but instead a reasonable protection against being unfairly disadvantaged. To the extent that requiring athletes to submit to drug tests can be defended, it is because each participant is entitled to play under the public conditions specifying the rules of the contest. If umpires in baseball can enforce such an entitlement by requiring pitchers to reveal whether they are carrying illegal substances that can alter the flight of the ball, why wouldn't sports authorities have a similar justification for drug testing to ensure that advantages prohibited by the rules are not obtained through ingestion of illegal substances of a different kind?

That said, room for debate remains about the circumstances or specifics of drug-testing programs. Although professional and elite amateur athletic associations may need to rely on random testing to promote compliance and reassure the public about the fairness of competition, things get trickier when we turn to the level of intercollegiate and scholastic sports. For example, should authorities have to have probable cause to suspect drug use before testing a high school athlete, or should they be allowed to conduct random testing of all athletes at a school, even if most are not under any suspicion whatsoever? To what extent must privacy be ensured, both during the testing itself and with the dissemination of the results? For example, should parents of a high school athlete be notified if the student is found to be using steroids? What if the student is using drugs but not those that would enhance athletic performance? Accordingly, even if there is a reasonable case for testing as a mechanism to ensure the fairness of competition, and even if athletes are informed about the possibility of being tested in advance, so they consent to be tested prior to play, there is plenty of room for debate about how tests may be conducted, to whom they may be administered, and what protections (say, for appeal) should be provided to those who are subjected to them.[30]

Our discussion in this section has explored important lines of argument for and against the view that the use of performance-enhancing drugs in sports is immoral. Although arguments for different positions on these issues need to be defended further, our examination provides provisional but not conclusive support for a prohibition on the use of such drugs and supports drug testing as a principal means of detection and enforcement in certain situations. Critics of the use of steroids and other performance enhancers will no doubt wish for an even stronger verdict on their behalf. Perhaps further critical reflection on the issues we have discussed will justify such a verdict. As we have seen, however, there are important criticisms of the arguments for prohibiting steroid use, not all of which have yet been answered satisfactorily. In the meantime, while debate continues, rules prohibiting the use of steroids in organized sports can be defended as permissible because they have not been shown to be arbitrary, unreasonable, or illegitimately imposed. To violate those rules covertly solely to gain a competitive advantage seems unjustifiable, regardless of whether the rules themselves ultimately should be revised.

Creating "Posthumans"?: The Ethics of Genetic Enhancement

Although athletes' use of steroids and other performance-enhancing substances has attracted widespread attention and generated much controversy, scientific advances in biology and genetics have raised even more profound issues in the ethics of sport. Potential advances in our ability to genetically enhance individuals may in time affect some of the very qualities we associate with being human. These advances promise many benefits outside the world of sport, especially in the area of medicine, and open up the possibility of curing diseases with genetic origins or prescribing treatments that are precisely designed to fit the specific genetic profile of the patient. However, these advances also open up what many fear is a Pandora's Box of dangers, ranging from the cloning of human beings to the production of genetically engineered superathletes capable of shattering all existing records in sport.

The specter of the eugenics movement, endorsed by many leading figures in the United States in the early part of the twentieth century and later adapted by the Nazis for their own purposes, often haunts discussions of genetic enhancement. The goal of the eugenics movement was to weed out "defectives," those regarded as possessing unhealthy or even undesirable traits that could be passed on to offspring, from the population by preventing them from reproducing in order to elevate the genetic fitness of the overall population.

Most reasonable people would agree that the therapeutic use of genetic techniques to cure disease and reduce human suffering is admirable and worthy of our support. But what about using these same techniques to enhance our memories, our attractiveness, our height, and other physical characteristics and abilities in a wide variety of areas perhaps leading to the creation of drastically altered posthumans? As philosopher Michael Sandel has pointed out, "the moral quandary arises when people use such [genetic] therapy not to cure a disease but to reach beyond health, to enhance their physical or cognitive capacities, to lift themselves above the norm."[31] For example, to cite an example discussed by Sandel, what if athletes utilized a genetic therapy used medically to help patients with muscular dystrophy and to reverse muscle loss associated with aging instead to enhance muscle mass and increase strength well above normal limits? Would such use of a legitimate medical therapy to enhance athletic performance be morally permissible?

Before turning to that issue we need to distinguish between genetic techniques that affect nonreproductive (somatic) cells, and, thus, are not passed on to offspring, and actual changes in reproductive or germline cells that are passed on through reproduction. The former (techniques affecting nonreproductive cells) would allow two types of cases: first, a competent adult who had a genetic abnormality would be able to choose to have the abnormality corrected, usually to avoid an illness or disorder associated with the abnormality, and second, a competent adult would be permitted to voluntarily agree to genetic enhancement. The latter (techniques affecting reproductive cells) would allow us to design our children to exhibit special abilities or characteristics that would give them advantages in life, say, in athletic competition, musical performance, or other activities in which enhanced cognitive and physical skills would enable those who possessed them to excel.

In what follows, the discussion will be largely restricted to enhancement of athletic abilities. However, it is clear that concerns about enhancement apply to many areas of human life. The possibility of making such changes raises the question of what it means to be human and whether we should exercise the power to perhaps bring a new kind of being, the enhanced posthuman, into existence. Of course, all of this is beyond our capabilities at present, and many forms of enhancement may not ever be safe enough for humans. Nevertheless, it is still important to engage in debate about genetic enhancement.

There are at least two reasons for this in our discussion of ethics in sport: first, it is always helpful to reflect on issues before they arrive right on our doorstep so we can be prepared for dilemmas we may face in the not-too-distant future; and second, the discussion will help sharpen our examination of performance enhancement in sports by enabling us to revisit some issues from a fresh perspective. In particular, in this discussion we will assume that techniques of genetic enhancement will be reasonably safe (thus eliminating those concerns about performance-enhancing drugs that arise from their safety) and medically feasible to perform.

Three Arguments Against Enhancement

Many people regard genetic enhancement as abhorrent on religious grounds. It seems to be "playing God" or tampering with God's design for humanity. However, many other religious people have no such theological objection to enhancement and may regard improving the human species as carrying out God's will. Moreover, theological concerns are not persuasive to atheists or agnostics.

Perhaps more importantly, in a religiously pluralistic society such as ours, we need to supplement religious concerns with arguments that appeal to reason if we are to influence policy in a fully legitimate way. Without rational arguments we run the danger of some religions imposing their theology on those who in good conscience do not share it and who may have opposing religious beliefs, and this would show a lack of respect for the religious concerns of those who dissent.

Another reason for the religious to look for reasoned arguments in this area is the idea that God would prohibit a practice on moral grounds only if it were actually unethical. Thus, we need to have reasons to think a practice is unethical before we can reasonably conclude that God prohibits it. Of course, some theists would want to rely on revelation rather than reason, but, as just noted, in a pluralistic society religions themselves disagree on many fundamental points, so appeals to revelation in areas of moral controversy are not likely to move others from different religious perspectives.

Similarly, arguments that genetic enhancement is unnatural are not helpful either. Should genetic therapies that fight disease and might save countless lives be prohibited because they are unnatural? Or, if it is claimed that therapies are natural but enhancement is unnatural, the whole natural-unnatural distinction seems arbitrary. What about medical interventions with antibiotics that cure infections that otherwise would be fatal? Are such interventions unnatural because they prevent nature from taking its course? Many people would argue that if we forsake the artificial for the natural, we would have to abandon many, if not all, of the medical and other technological breakthroughs that have saved countless lives since their development. Alternately, one could argue that genetic enhancement is natural because we achieve it through the use of human reason, part of our natural abilities.

The problem is that the idea of the natural is just too indeterminate to lead to solutions to moral dilemmas. Are airplanes unnatural because they wouldn't exist in a pretechnological stage of human development, or are they natural because they are possible through applying human reason to scientific laws of nature?

A second problem with arguments based on whether something is natural concerns their normative force. Even if something was unnatural, does that automatically make it wrong? If unnatural is taken to mean something like "not statistically normal in a pretechnological state," why does statistical abnormality create wrongness? Using electric shocks from a defibrillator to restart the hearts of people suffering cardiac arrest and save them from death may be unnatural in that sense, but it isn't morally wrong.

Accordingly, arguments based on theology or appeals to nature are unlikely to be philosophically or ethically pertinent. What we want to see, where appeal to religion is concerned, are the reasons why a religious perspective might condemn genetic enhancement.

Perhaps a second sort of argument supplies such a reason. We have already seen that liberal political thought attaches great weight to autonomy and freedom of choice by competent adults. Perhaps the problem with manipulation of germline cells in order to design our children—to assign them desirable traits such as height, strength, and speed so they might excel as athletes—is that it violates their future autonomy and freedom of choice. Indeed, many believe children have the right to an open future.[32] By designing children to fulfill certain functions or to excel at certain activities, we ensure that their future is no longer open but is instead fixed by the parents or designers. Isn't this wrong because, in effect, it makes the children mere means to ends desired by others, without giving them freedom of choice to decide their own futures?

This argument undoubtedly has some force. Many parents of budding young athletes already may push their children too far, sometimes unintentionally causing burnout and discouraging them from participating in sports at all. Wouldn't it be worse if the parents were allowed to design their children to excel in given activities? "Sure you want to play in a band," we can almost hear such a parent exclaiming, "but we created you to play ball. If we wanted a musician, we would have built in those talents, but we didn't!" Indeed, if we pursue this line of reasoning to an extreme, we might imagine parents building into their children the desire to enjoy excelling in areas where they were given genetic abilities, almost like the Gammas, Deltas, and Epsilons in Aldous Huxley's *Brave New World*, who were genetically designed to enjoy repetitive, boring tasks that others were unwilling to perform.

Although we should acknowledge that this argument from autonomy has force, it is not decisive. That is because parents can already put pressure on children to excel in areas the parents value more than the child does. Moreover, parents already can engage in forms of genetic selection, ranging from simply picking a mate who seems to have the desired inheritable traits to purchasing eggs or sperm on the market from donors who are likely to have those characteristics.[33] Finally, children who have characteristics likely to make them successful in a given area can still simply stand up to their parents and assert that they want to determine their future for themselves. (Robert L. Simon remembers one of his children, who had been a successful high school basketball player, telling his parents when they urged him to try out as a walk-on for his college team: "Mom and Dad, if I play, it will be because I want to, not because you want me to!" Why couldn't designer children do the same?)

Although these criticisms may diminish the force of the argument from autonomy so it is not decisive, they do not diminish its force to the vanishing point. That is because it is plausible to think that the pressure to conform to parents' desires may be greater for genetically engineered children than for others. That is because such children may feel more indebted to their parents, as they would not even have existed if not for their designers' plans. So although the autonomy argument is far from decisive, it may have some weight in a comprehensive evaluation of the practice of altering germline cells to produce a designer child. Just as the athlete who uses steroids, though not literally coercing opponents, may still pressure others to also use them, parents of designer children may not coerce their offspring or totally eliminate their autonomy but may more often than not make autonomy more difficult to exercise, which in itself is ethically questionable.

Consider a third argument against genetic enhancement. It is based on equality. If techniques for either making changes in the nonreproductive (somatic) cells of existing athletes (which the subjects themselves may freely choose) or in actual germlines turn out to be sufficiently expensive, the more affluent will have much more access to them than others. Is this inequality fair or just?

Perhaps it isn't, but proponents of genetic enhancement would have a point if they were to argue that many other inequalities in sport already result from differences in the resources supporting athletes. These include differences in coaching, training facilities, access to funds supporting travel, and the ability to purchase and maintain high-tech equipment. For example, not all runners can afford either to train at high altitude or to work in specially designed oxygen chambers that simulate high-altitude training, both of which raise the carrying capacity of the blood, thereby promoting endurance. Although such inequalities may not be totally fair, they are considered acceptable in sport. Why isn't the same true for genetic enhancement? Alternately, we might stipulate that genetic enhancement of athletes is acceptable only when access to it is equitable and fair.

Because none of the arguments we have considered against genetic enhancement of athletes seem decisive, should we conclude that the practice, were it to become both feasible and safe, is acceptable and, perhaps, even desirable? As one of our students wrote, "the promotion of intelligence, long life, attractiveness and athleticism coupled with the reduction of congenital disease or defect, strikes me as indubitably good. To escape the cruelties of nature and recast man as being beholden only to himself could prove to be the most profound (and exhilarating) moment of human existence."[34]

Theorists who welcome the prospects of genetic enhancement in a wide variety of areas but are also committed to the values of liberty, autonomy, and respect for persons have developed a position some call liberal eugenics. On this view, the benefits of genetic enhancement, not only or even primarily in athletics but also in a wide variety of areas, justify the practice, assuming the safety of the subjects is protected. The theory is liberal, however, because it contains certain safeguards associated with liberal political perspectives. For example, only general traits, such as enhanced cognitive or physical skills, may be promoted so that the autonomy of subjects is protected. We would be prohibited, for example, from producing slaves like those in *Brave New World*, who were genetically designed to love their position in life. In this way genetic enhancement would expand choice, not limit it, by opening new possibilities of achievement without closing doors to realizing a wide variety of plans of life. Second, access to genetic technology would have to be equitable so that wealthy elites could not attain a genetically dominant position over everyone else. Third, the government should be neutral with respect to what enhancements should be encouraged. The choice should be up to parents and families and not be backed by an ideal of human good or perfections promoted by the state.

Is liberal eugenics acceptable? Although such a broad question takes us well beyond the realm of sport, we can consider a more limited version restricted to sport and athletics. On this view, genetic enhancement of athletes, including engineering germline cells, is morally permissible if either the athletes themselves freely choose it (somatic enhancement) or it does not limit the autonomy of genetically enhanced children, promote unacceptable inequalities, or reflect a conception of the human good supported by the state.

Before offering a tentative assessment of such a view, let us consider a recent argument directed against genetic enhancement developed by Michael Sandel in his book *The Case Against Perfection*.

Sandel's Case Against Perfection

Sandel's full argument is too complex to do it full justice here, but we will consider one of his most important suggestions: debates in ethics need not always revolve around such values as liberty, justice, rights, equality, fairness, or autonomy. Thus, in addition to those sorts of considerations, which focus on ways we may wrong others, such as by treating them unfairly or violating their rights, we might also ask what human goods would be lost if we pursued human perfection through genetic enhancement. For example, if all people did was sit around all day watching the lowest level of mind-numbing TV shows, no one's rights might be violated, but such goods as achievement and the pursuit of excellence would be relegated to the scrap heap. Similarly, Sandel has argued that an extensive practice of genetic enhancement would compromise important human values, even if the principles of liberal eugenics were not violated.

What values does Sandel think would be threatened? Although Sandel's argument is quite complex, perhaps his main supporting point is that the *giftedness* of our genetic heritage, by which he means at least that it arises from the natural genetic lottery, would be undermined. Our nature would be something to be mastered and controlled, not a given that we receive but do not design. But why is that important? After all, we have already seen that the link between the natural and the moral is at best tenuous.

However, Sandel is not relying uncritically on the alleged moral value of the natural; rather, he thinks that if we ceased to admire our natural talents and abilities and viewed them instead as simply products of human design, we would lose humility and solidarity with our fellows. Moreover, the scope of our responsibilities would increase to a dangerous extent. We ourselves (or our parents or designers) would be responsible for our genetic design or innate nature itself. As more and more about our genetic makeup came under our control, the areas in which we could be praised or blamed would expand dramatically. "Today, when a basketball player misses a rebound, his coach can blame him for being out of position," wrote Sandel. "Tomorrow the coach may blame him for being too short."[35]

Because we do not genetically design our children, we, as parents, retain what Sandel called an "openness to the unbidden," or an appreciation of the fact that there are significant contingencies in life beyond our control. If we designed our children, we would come more and more to see ourselves as masters of our world, which we might come to view as "a gated community writ large."[36]

As more and more of our characteristics become our own achievement (or our own fault) or that of our designers, solidarity with our fellows is threatened. It would less and less frequently make sense to say of someone less fortunate than ourselves that "but for the luck of the draw, that could be me!" According to Sandel, "perfect genetic control would erode the actual solidarity that arises when men and women reflect on the contingency of their talents and fortunes," resulting in a hardened meritocracy in which those who did worse than their fellows in any competitive arena, business as well as sport, would have largely themselves (or their designers) to blame.[37]

Criticism of Sandel's Argument

Although a full evaluation of Sandel's overall case against genetic enhancement would take us too far afield, some major difficulties with it can be noted before we turn to its specific application to sport.

First, Sandel seems to assume a fairly sharp line dividing genetic therapies, which restore health but do not enhance abilities, from enhancement. Sandel approves of the former but not the latter. But surely that line is not always a sharp one. For example, would a genetic change in reproductive cells that leads to having offspring with less need for sleep than normal be a therapy for chronic insomnia or an enhancement that allows bearers to have more waking hours in which to be productive?

More importantly, the effects of genetic enhancement may not be as dire as Sandel suggested. For one thing, people might not lose their sense of humility in the face of chance because there would still be all sorts of contingencies that would significantly affect human life. These might range from accidents, disasters, and illnesses to various forms of good fortune, such as experiencing chance encounters with strangers who unexpectedly affect our lives, winning the lottery, or getting a lucky bounce on the golf course.

Finally, and perhaps most importantly, it is far from clear that solidarity with others would suffer simply because we ceased to regard other people as, in part, products of the natural genetic lottery. Philosophers influenced by the Kantian idea that we should never be treated as mere means would argue that people are owed respect precisely because they are persons, rational creatures capable of choosing a plan of life and of responding to moral imperatives.[38] The duties we have to others, then, may arise more from their status as autonomous persons who can experience happiness and suffering than with whether they themselves are the result of the genetic lottery or parental design. Accordingly, it is at best unclear whether Sandel's overall case against genetic enhancement is successful. But what about its application to the realm of sport?

To Sandel, one of the great attractions of sport is the value of the talents exhibited in the pursuit of excellence. Although we also appreciate the athlete with less innate talent who plays to his or her capacity because of hard work, the athletes who exhibit excellence to the highest degree are the ones who are regarded almost with awe. A Tiger Woods, LeBron James, Michael Jordan, Serena Williams, or Annika Sorenstam are in a class by themselves because of the excellence of their performance. And although none of these athletes could have succeeded without also working at least as hard as their opponents, natural ability also contributed to their success, or at least that is what Sandel would argue.

But if the physical basis of such excellence can be designed or engineered—if it can, in effect, be purchased on the market—its value is cheapened. Similarly, if everyone could be genetically designed to have an outstanding singing voice, such voices would be common, their value cheapened, and our appreciation for their excellence diminished. Thus, Sandel wrote that "a game in which genetically altered sluggers routinely hit home runs might be amusing for a time, but it would lack the human drama and complexity of baseball, in which the greatest hitters fail more often than they succeed."[39]

However, as readers by now might anticipate, Sandel's argument is open to objection. For one thing, as John Rawls famously argued, the natural genetic differences arising from the natural lottery seem arbitrary from the moral point of view.[40] Is it fair if one person is born with extraordinary hand-eye coordination that others, no matter how hard they work, can never come close to matching? Genetic enhancement would enable us to counteract the arbitrary differences arising from the natural lottery and make the playing field more level, at least in terms of innate ability. Competitive athletics would still be meritocratic, however, because differences in work ethic and in such mental characteristics as ability to stay cool under pressure and to develop superior strategic plans for competition would become crucial.[41]

This objection, however, does not seem as strong as it might at first appear. To begin with, some mental characteristics, such as the capacity to remain calm and control one's nerves under the pressure of competition, may also be subject to some degree of genetic enhancement. More importantly, we suggest that Sandel is right to think that athletics would lose much of their richness and complexity if we took enhancement to the extreme and reduced athletic competition to a kind of mental chess game between physically similar competitors. Indeed, one of the reasons sport is so fascinating is because it presents us with the opportunity to see athletes with very different sets of abilities try to maximize their assets, often in very different ways.

We will say more about this point below, but first we will look at a second objection presented by sport philosopher William J. Morgan that cuts to the heart of Sandel's position. Morgan acknowledged that many of us today think of sport the way we suggested above, as exhibiting a mixture of striving to excel and maximizing whatever package of natural assets nature has bestowed upon us. But even if this is the dominant conception, why is it sacrosanct? Morgan is ambivalent about whether the present conception also gives weight to the value of compensating for advantages bestowed arbitrarily by nature. But regardless of whether it does or doesn't, why shouldn't the dominant conception of sport as being dependent in part on natural assets be subject to change? Morgan wrote, "What would be morally amiss in re-envisaging sport, in true meritocratic fashion, as primarily a matter of striving for excellence in which, therefore, simply accepting one's talents as they come because they emanate from the genetic lottery is rejected in favor of genetic engineering?"[42]

After all, as Morgan pointed out, the ethos of sport has changed before, often for the better. To cite his own example, in the Academy Award–winning and cinematically spectacular film *Chariots of Fire* (1981), based on the actual careers of two English Olympic runners in the 1920s, one of the characters, Harold Abraham, is ostracized for using a coach. This was viewed as violating the gentlemanly account of sportsmanship and amateurism prevalent at the time. Are competitive athletics today morally worse because that code, perhaps itself founded on a kind of snobbery of social class, has been modified?

Morgan was suggesting that even if the moral ideal of sport Sandel proposed is dominant, there may be no reason to regard that ideal as morally superior to an alternative ideal that would allow for enhancement as an acceptable means of striving for excellence. How do we choose between ideals, assuming each is compatible with autonomy and the pertinent rights of all competitors?

There is no widely agreed upon answer to this question, which is why some philosophers endorse the idea that the state should not pick sides but remain neutral in such disputes. However, we suggest that sometimes there can be good reasons for preferring one ideal over another. Although we do not know of a knock-down rebuttal to Morgan's line of argument and believe it may ultimately turn out to be justified, we believe there are reasons for exercising caution before adopting it too quickly.

In particular, there seems to be a major difference between revising a paradigm of good sportsmanship to allow for coaching and revising a paradigm of relying on natural assets to allow for the genetic engineering of athletes. The former revision seems true to the educational function of sport, which surely is valuable, through which we learn to honestly face our weaknesses and strive to overcome them. It also coheres with training in other areas of life. Singers, for example, receive assistance from singing instructors to learn how to use their voices correctly; indeed, almost every other type of excellence relies on mentoring or instruction to harness natural talents and abilities.

Thus, critics of genetic enhancement can reply to Morgan that coaching helps us develop and use our abilities to meet the challenge of a sport, but genetic enhancement in effect builds us into creatures for whom the challenge of the sport is weakened or, in extreme cases, almost erased. Perhaps this is the point of Sandel's example, cited above, of the sluggers in baseball who cheapen the value of the home run. In effect they were designed to make home runs relatively easy to hit so home runs, when hit by the enhanced batters, are not the achievement they were when hit by the likes of Ruth, Maris, and Aaron. Indeed, if the enhancements became great enough, whole sports could become obsolete because they would have become too easy for enhanced athletes to find interesting and too boring for spectators to pay to watch. Or perhaps the sports would be made more difficult so spectators would still attend. Thus, ballparks would be made larger to make home runs harder to hit. As Sandel warned, sports might simply become mere spectacles, perhaps like slam-dunk contests in professional basketball.

Whether these worries are sufficient to undercut Morgan's important line of argument remains to be seen. After all, some of us already are better equipped by the natural genetic lottery than others to succeed in sport. Is genetic enhancement just continuing a benign process we already find in nature (or, as noted above, does it allow us to correct arbitrary genetic inequalities in athletic ability)? Or would genetic enhancement be, in effect, a game changer, substituting one practice with another? In the new practice the goal would not be to meet the challenge of the sport by using our abilities to the fullest but rather to reduce the challenge itself by building in abilities that render it moot.

Further discussion is needed to settle these issues and, indeed, many more that can be raised about genetic enhancement. However, we have identified several areas of concern that should lead us to proceed with caution in this area. First, the goal of producing "designer children" who result from engineered changes in germline cells may raise questions of autonomy that differ in degree, if not in kind, from those already raised by overdirective parents. Second, although such a result is not inevitable, widespread use of genetic enhancement may, just as Sandel suggested, weaken the ties that bind us by radically expanding the range of things in which bad outcomes are considered our fault. As noted earlier, Sandel warned that the future coach might blame the player for being too short, too slow, or too nervous to function well under the pressure of competition. (True, being too short or too slow already are weaknesses in many sports. But to the extent that they are not under the athlete's control, they are not the athlete's *fault* either.) Finally, genetic enhancement, if taken to the extreme, might cheapen the idea of a quest for excellence through challenge by undermining the strength of the challenge itself.

Concluding Comments

The ethical issues surrounding the use of performance-enhancing drugs and techniques are some of the most complex within the ethics of sport. Acknowledging this fact, we regard the use of performance-enhancing drugs in sport as problematic and agree with the conclusion that major sport organizations, such as the International Olympic Committee and Major League Baseball, have strong reasons to prohibit such use. However, we further believe that such a conclusion is more open to debate than it might first appear. We hope the preceding discussion has brought out the complexities of performance-enhancement issues in sport while demonstrating that if we work through them, we can still come to reasonable conclusions regarding these issues.

The future use of genetic techniques for purposes of enhancement in sport raises ethical issues perhaps even more complex than those relating to performance enhancement in sport today. There are many sport libertarians and others who will welcome the arguably revolutionary changes in sport brought about by technology and see no threat to athletics in this kind of enhancement. They believe it might simply lead to improved sports in which genetically enhanced athletes achieve new levels of excellence. Why not explore how far human or even posthuman athletes can go in setting new records and achieving what was at one time thought to be virtually impossible? Why not go where no one has gone before?

Our inclination is to be more cautious. We take seriously Sandel's warning about cheapening the idea of achievement in sport and have tried to extend it by considering the effect enhancement might have on the idea of challenge. Today athletes work hard to overcome what they consider to be worthy obstacles. But would enhancement produce athletes who found the challenges of sport easy and perhaps boring? Or is this worry groundless, as new challenges would always arise, perhaps even the challenge of playing against opponents who also were enhanced?

Of course, there are other possible problems with genetic enhancement in sport, including possible effects on the autonomy and freedom of athletes or of the children who have been at least partially genetically designed by others. The conclusions our very preliminary discussion of genetic enhancement suggest surely are tentative and open to criticism and revision. There are important arguments in favor of permitting genetic enhancement of athletes, so long as they are not forced on anyone and the techniques themselves are safe. And yet our discussion in this chapter suggests that the burden of proof still rests on proponents.

Perhaps a brave new world of enhanced athletes competing at ever higher levels will be exciting and ethically permissible (even desirable). But serious questions still remain, and it is unclear whether the arguments of proponents will be able to survive criticism in the extended debate that is sure to continue.

QUESTIONS FOR REVIEW

1. According to the authors, do organizations governing sports have the right to ban performance-enhancing drugs based on the risks they pose to either the users or to others in sport and society? Explain and assess what you think is an important criticism of this position.
2. What is the ethical difference, if any, between the advantages athletes gain over other athletes as a result of weight training and the advantage they gain from performance enhancers like steroids, which make the former fair and the latter unfair? Explain how you think the authors would respond to this question and assess what you think is an important criticism of their response.
3. Do the authors believe rational and impartial athletes would permit steroid use in competitive sport rather than prohibit it? Explain how they would attempt to justify their answer to this question and assess their justification, including their method of argumentation, by evaluating what you think might be an important criticism of it.
4. State the authors' presumptive case against performance enhancers and offer criticisms of that argument.
5. Based on the points discussed in the chapter, do you believe genetic enhancements should be preliminarily accepted or banned in competitive sports? Provide reasons to support your view.

Notes

1. See Tom Verducci, "Totally Juiced," *Sports Illustrated* 96, no. 23 (June 3, 2002): 34–48, http://sportsillustrated.cnn.com/vault/article/magazine/MAG1025902/; and Mark Fainaru-Wada and Lance Williams, *Game of Shadows: Barry Bonds, BALCO, and the Steroids Scandal That Rocked Professional Sports* (New York: Gotham, 2006). The latter is a report on the BALCO investigation, discussed later in the text, by two reporters for the *San Francisco Chronicle*. A major source of information about steroid use in MLB is the so-called Mitchell Report, more formally *The Report to the Commissioner of Baseball of an Independent Investigation into the Illegal Use of Steroids and Other Performance Enhancing Substances by Players in Major League Baseball*, by former Senator George Mitchell (December 13, 2003). This report will be referred to as the Mitchell Report hereafter.

2. Mitchell Report, SR-2.

3. See Fainaru-Wada and Williams, *Game of Shadows*, esp. the prologue.

4. Ibid., 296.

5. Testimony before a grand jury is supposed to be confidential, but reporters Fainaru-Wada and Williams leaked reports of Anderson's testimony as well as other details, as discussed in *Game of Shadows*.

6. For a history of Major League Baseball's reaction to claims of players' drug use, see the Mitchell Report.

7. Mitchell Report, SR-8.

8. John Stuart Mill, *On Liberty* (1849), quoted from the Dolphin edition (Garden City, NY: Doubleday, 1961), 484. Mill's Harm Principle, articulated in the quoted passage, also rules out interference with liberty to prevent acts that merely are offensive to others or to interfere with acts on grounds of their alleged immorality, independent of any harm to others they may produce.

9. Ibid., 576.

10. Mitchell Report, SR-8–9.

11. Carolyn E. Thomas, *Sport in a Philosophic Context* (Philadelphia: Lea and Febiger, 1983), 198.

12. M. Andrew Holowchak, "'Aretism' and Pharmacological Ergogenic Aids in Sport: Taking a Shot at the Use of Steroids," *Journal of the Philosophy of Sport* 27 (2000): 40.

13. For an excellent discussion of different senses of "coercion" and an argument that we should think of coercion normatively as the *illegitimate* interference with the freedom of others, see Alan Wertheimer, *Coercion* (Princeton, NJ: Princeton University Press, 1989).

14. Norman Fost, "Let Them Take Steroids," *New York Times*, September 9, 1983, A19. But see also Wertheimer, *Coercion*, ch. 1.

15. Mitchell Report, SR-24–26. It should be noted that this report states that earlier regulations implied the prohibition of performance enhancers.

16. Roger Gardner, "On Performance-Enhancing Substances and the Unfair Advantage Argument," in *Philosophic Inquiry in Sport*, ed. William J. Morgan and Klaus V. Meier (Champaign, IL: Human Kinetics Press, 1995), 225.

17. See Gardner, "On Performance-Enhancing Substances and the Unfair Advantage Argument," for versions of this sort of argument.

18. Ibid., 229.

19. The idea of a veil of ignorance is presented by John Rawls as part of a complex argument for a conception of social justice in his monumental work *A Theory of Justice* (Cambridge, MA: Harvard University Press, 1971). Part of his argument is that the principles of justice are those we would accept, if we were being rational, from a position of choice in which we were ignorant of our personal characteristics or position in society. This would guarantee that choice was impartial and uninfluenced by such accidents of fate as the wealth of our parents or our genetic endowment.

20. Strictly speaking, athletes behind the veil would be ignorant even of their own values but would have to take into account the possibility that in the real world they might have such values and vote accordingly.

21. Richard Werner suggested that a rule-consequentialist argument would lead to the same conclusion through a simpler argument; that is, a rule prohibiting the use of performance enhancers that are harmful to users would have better overall consequences than rules permitting use. However, such an approach would be open to objections of paternalism and, more important, would not explain the intuition of many of us that the use of performance enhancers is unfair. Moreover, the argument presented in the text can be

presented without reliance on the "veil of ignorance," which, as Rawls sometimes seems to suggest, can be best viewed as a heuristic aid to impartial thinking. The main point of the argument is simply that if athletes disregard the personal benefits or harms that might accrue to them through steroid use, then the use of steroids to enhance performance makes no rational sense as a general practice. Steroids provide the risk of significant harm to everyone who uses them but, at best, minimal relative gains in performance.

22. This sort of point has been made by Gardner, "On Performance-Enhancing Substances," 229.

23. For recent discussions, see Sigmund Loland and Arthur Caplan "Ethics of Technologically Constructed Hypoxic Environments in Sport," *Scandinavian Journal of Medicine and Science in Sports* 18, no. 1 (2008) Supplement 1: 70–75; and G. Lippi, M. Franchini, and G. C. Guidi, "Prohibition of Artificial Hypoxic Environments in Sports: Health Risks Rather Than Ethics," *Journal of Applied Physical Nutrition and Metabolism* 32 (December 2007): 1206–1207.

24. Does this argument imply that we also should prohibit athletes from using glasses or contact lenses or from having LASIK surgery? Just when does a technological aid provide an unearned benefit, and when should unearned benefits be prohibited? These are difficult questions. One kind of reply, worth exploring further, is that glasses do not modify the challenge of the sport or provide users with competitive advantages over others; they only allow athletes with poor vision to catch up with others. (Does this mean that steroids should be allowed but only by weaker athletes to make them competitive with naturally stronger ones?)

25. This sort of antipaternalistic argument has been made in a series of articles by Miller Brown. See, especially, W. M. Brown, "Paternalism, Drugs, and the Nature of Sport," *Journal of the Philosophy of Sport* 11, no. 1 (May 1984): 14–22.

26. Sigmund Loland, "Record Sports: An Ecological Critique and a Reconstruction," *Journal of the Philosophy of Sport* 28, no. 2 (October 2001): 127–129.

27. We would like to thank Ronald Weinfeld for making me appreciate the force of this point.

28. Mitchell Report, SR-10 and 11.

29. This point has been developed by Michael Lavin in his paper "Drugs and Sports: Are the Cultural Bans Justified?" *Journal of the Philosophy of Sport* 14 (1987): 34–43. See also David Fairchild's paper "Sport Abjection: Steroids and the Uglification of the Athlete" (*Journal of the Philosophy of Sport* 16 [1989]: 74–88) for further reasons in favor of prohibition as well as for some skeptical doubts about whether governing bodies in sport tend to be reasonable or nonarbitrary.

30. For an excellent discussion and summary of issues in this and related areas where legal issues bear on intercollegiate and interscholastic sports, see Matthew J. Mitten, "Rules Limiting Athletic Performance or Prohibiting Athletic Participation: Legal and Ethical Considerations," *Journal of Intercollegiate Sport* 2, no. 1 (2009): 99–113.

An especially controversial testing procedure is the "Whereabouts Program" implemented by the World Anti-Doping Agency. This out-of-competition program requires some elite athletes to select an hour per day (from 6 a.m. to 11 p.m.) every day of the week to be available for no-notice drug tests. These athletes should also provide the full address of where they will be available for such testing. For a critique of the program, see, for example, James Holt, "Where Is the Privacy in WADA's 'Whereabouts' Rule?" *Marquette Sports Law Review* 20, no. 1 (2009): 267–289.

31. Michael Sandel, *The Case Against Perfection: Ethics in the Age of Genetic Engineering* (Cambridge, MA: Harvard University Press, 2007), 8.

32. See Nicholas J. Dixon, "Sport, Parental Autonomy, and Children's Right to an Open Future," *Journal of the Philosophy of Sport* 34, no. 2 (2007): 147–159.

33. Sandel cited the example of an advertisement in the *Harvard Crimson* seeking an egg donor who was athletic, was at least five foot ten inches in height, and had combined SAT scores of 1400 as well as other traits regarded as highly desirable by the potential buyer. The ad offered a payment of $50,000. Sandel, *The Case Against Perfection*, 2–3.

34. Nelson Scott, in a review essay on *The Case Against Perfection*, Hamilton College, 2009.

35. Sandel, *The Case Against Perfection*, 87.

36. Ibid., 86.

37. Ibid., 92.

38. Such a conception of respect for persons plays a key role, for example, in the liberal political theory of justice developed by John Rawls in *A Theory of Justice* and his later writings, particularly *Political Liberalism* (New York: Columbia University Press, 1993).

39. Sandel, *The Case Against Perfection*, 36.

40. See Rawls, *A Theory of Justice*, especially p. 104, where he writes that "it seems to be one of the fixed points of our considered judgments that no one deserves his place in the distribution of native endowments any more than one deserves one's initial starting place in society."

41. A similar point can be made about performance-enhancing drugs. In a review of Sandel's book, William J. Morgan recalled a student coming up to him after class and "exclaiming he didn't see anything wrong in taking such substances to redress the natural inequalities of the genetic lottery." William J. Morgan, review of *The Case Against Perfection*, *Journal of Intercollegiate Sport* 1, no. 2 (2008): 288.

42. Ibid.

Gender Equity in Sport

WHAT DOES JUSTICE REQUIRE?

In all cases, excepting those of the bear and the leopard, the female is less spirited than the male . . . more shrinking, more difficult to rouse to action, and requires a smaller quantity of nutriment. . . . The fact is, the nature of man is the most rounded off and complete.
—ARISTOTLE, *HISTORY OF ANIMALS*, BOOK IX

Games and recreation for all types of girls, by all means, which develop charm and social health, but athletic competition in basketball, track and field sports, and baseball? No!
—FREDERICK R. RODGERS, *SCHOOL AND SOCIETY*, 1929

The passages quoted above express attitudes that have probably been dominant in most periods of Western civilization. For example, the belief that women are naturally sedentary was reinforced by the customs of Aristotle's culture, which kept women largely confined to the home. But the view that women are neither fit for nor interested in sport or that participation in serious athletic competition is somehow not appropriate for women was a dominant one even in our own society well into the late twentieth century, and it still influences policy in many parts of the world.

These attitudes have sometimes been challenged, although the challengers frequently have shared more with proponents of the dominant outlook than they might have acknowledged. For example, a Women's Division of the National Amateur Athletic Federation was formed in 1923 to stress "sports opportunities for all girls, protection from exploitation, enjoyment of sports, female leadership [and] medical examinations."[1] The purpose of this "creed," as it was sometimes called, was to promote greater participation in sport for all women rather than to promote intense competition for highly skilled female athletes. "Soon female competitive athletics began to decrease. . . . In place of competition, play days and sports days were organized. This philosophy of athletics for women and girls continued into the early 1960s."[2]

As a result, women and girls who really did want to participate in competition were usually made to feel strange or unfeminine. Former tennis star Althea Gibson described what it was like to be a female athlete in high school in the South in the 1940s: "The problem I had in Wilmington was the girls in school. . . . 'Look at her throw in that ball just like a man,' they would say, and they looked at me just like I was a freak. . . . I felt as though they ought to see that I didn't do the things they did because I didn't know how to and that I showed off on the football field . . . to show there was something I was good at."[3]

Although the attitudes that troubled Gibson have not been completely eliminated, the role of women in competitive sport has changed drastically. The growth of women's and girls' sports and the intensity and quality of their performances in the 1970s and 1980s were unprecedented. For example, in 1970–1971, 3.7 million boys and only 300,000 girls participated in interscholastic sports. By 1978–1979, after the passage of Title IX, an important law with significant implications for gender equity in athletics,[4] 2 million girls were participating in interscholastic athletics. A similar rate of increase in the participation of women in intercollegiate athletics took place during the same period.

Today in the United States women and girls continue to participate in organized athletics in significant numbers. By the late 1990s over 3.7 million boys and nearly 2.6 million girls participated in high school sports. The 2006–2007 survey of the National Federation of State High School Associations showed that the number of female participants in high school sports surpassed the 3 million mark for the first time. Over 4 million males participated as well.[5]

Although the rise in female participation in sport is dramatic, it has leveled off, and the gains for women are not evenly distributed. As one observer notes, "While Title IX benefited girls by increasing the opportunities to play sports, these benefits were disproportionately reaped by those at the top of the income distribution."[6]

Issues of equity in the distribution of its benefits aside, there is wide agreement that Title IX opened doors for women in sport that had long been closed to them. However, controversy continues over just how gender equity in athletics is to be understood and what principles should be employed in its enforcement. In particular, debate about how Title IX should be interpreted and applied to intercollegiate sports remains intense and reflects, if not different conceptions of gender equity, at least different explanations for and responses to the continuing gap between participation rates of males and females in sports.

Sorting Out the Issues

Title IX and Gender Equity

The changes described above were not easily achieved. *Sports Illustrated*, in a 1973 article, reported widespread indifference, even among educators, to women's athletics.[7] There is no doubt that before the recent increase in interest in women's athletics and the appearance of broader feminist concerns about gender equality, women's sports were separate and unequal. Only a tiny fraction of athletic funding was devoted to the needs of women students, who were excluded from participation in most varsity and intramural programs.

Such inequalities were sometimes defended on the grounds that relevant differences between men and women justified the differences in treatment. Women were held to be less interested in participating than were men or were less aggressive and, therefore, less in need of the outlet of intense athletic competition. Perhaps more often, inequalities between men and women in sports were not explicitly defended but just taken for granted as part of the then-normal cultural and social context.

Although, as we will see, biological differences may be relevant to the form gender equality takes in sports, they do not justify excluding women from sports or relegating women's sports to second-class status. First, the increased participation of girls and women in organized competitive sports is a most convincing refutation of the claim that they have little interest in taking part. Second, the claim that women are naturally less aggressive than men, even if it were true, is irrelevant to the right to participate and compete. After all, males who have less need to discharge aggression against other males are not excluded from participation.

Most importantly, as was argued in Chapters 2 and 3, claims about the value of athletic competition as well as the explanation of much of the fascination people have with sport lie much more in the idea of challenge and the pursuit of excellence than in any alleged discharge of aggression. Opponents respond to each other as persons within the rules of the sports contest. Males and females have an equal claim to participation because members of both sexes may seek the challenges competitive sport presents. Regardless of whether sport fulfills other social functions, such as allowing for the harmless discharge of aggressive impulses, their value does not lie primarily in such consequences.

What are the requirements of gender equity in athletic programs at the intercollegiate and interscholastic levels? Does equity simply require lack of discrimination? Should the coaches pick the best players, regardless of sex? Does sex equality require separate teams for women? If so, are such teams required in all sports or just those in which women are allegedly physiologically disadvantaged with respect to men? Are separate teams for physiologically disadvantaged men also required? Does equality require greater emphasis on competition in sports, such as gymnastics, where women may have physical advantages, or the introduction of new sports in which the sexes can compete equally?

We will begin our examination of these and related questions by considering the most important federal legislation addressing gender equality in sports. Title IX of the Education Amendments of 1972 prohibits sex discrimination in federally assisted education programs. The section of Title IX dealing with athletics states that "no person shall, on the basis of sex, be excluded from participation in, be denied the benefits of, be treated differently from another person or otherwise be discriminated against in any interscholastic, intercollegiate, club, or intramural athletic program offered by a recipient" (Section 86:41a). (Note that Title IX does not address discrimination based on sexual orientation, although, as we will see, there are other legal and moral grounds for condemning such a practice in sports.)

One interpretation of the above section of Title IX requires that athletic programs not make distinctions on the basis of sex. As long as no discrimination takes place, men and women have been treated by the same standards and so have no grounds to complain of inequity. In this view, sex equality in sports requires that we pay no attention to participants' sex.

The problem with this is that, if it were applied, far fewer women than at present would be competing in interscholastic or intercollegiate varsity contests in such sports as basketball, soccer, lacrosse, track and field, tennis, and golf. Although many women athletes in such sports have more ability than most men, it does appear that males have important physiological advantages, for example, in size and upper-body strength, that make a crucial difference at top levels of competition in many sports.

To avoid the virtual exclusion of women from varsity competition in such sports, particularly the so-called contact sports, Title IX departs from simple nondiscrimination by allowing institutions to sponsor separate teams for men and women. Title IX does not require that there be separate teams for each sex in each sport an institution offers, but it does stipulate that through an appropriate combination of mixed and single-sex teams, the opportunities for each sex be equivalent.

Our discussion so far suggests a distinction between two approaches to equality between the sexes in sport. According to the first, sex equality is equated with blindness to sex. Thus, a coeducational college that pays no attention to applicants' sex in deciding whom to admit has adopted the first approach. A second approach is to acknowledge sex differences in an attempt to ensure that members of each sex receive equivalent benefits.

These two approaches are, at best, not easily reconciled and, at worst, plainly inconsistent. The first requires that we ignore sex and assign no special significance to it; the second requires that we recognize sex differences when they are relevant to our practices. Title IX allows separate sports programs for each sex and so sometimes requires viewing sex as a relevant ground for making distinctions, but the requirement of being sex blind, that no one be treated differently with regard to sex for some purposes, also seems sometimes to be compelling—for example, with respect to voting rights.

Before turning to current controversies over the meaning and application of Title IX, let us examine the two approaches to equality between the sexes, sex blindness, and sex pluralism, in order to find the degree to which each approach is defensible before we apply these concepts to sport and athletics.

Ideals of Gender Equity

Like virtue, honesty, and truth, the principle that men and women are equals has few contemporary opponents, at least in public. However, shallow agreement on the surface may disguise deeper divisions over the nature of that equality. Just as equal opportunity can be understood in a variety of ways—as requiring simple nondiscrimination, conditions of background fairness, or equal life chances for representative persons from all major social groups—so too are there diverse and competing conceptions of sex equality. Thus, abstract support for a general ideal of sex equality from a variety of perspectives can obscure deep divisions on just how it is to be understood, what it implies in concrete contexts, and how it might best be achieved.

To those who identify sex equality with assimilation, a society has achieved sex equality when, as one writer put it, no more significance is attached to the sex of persons than is attached to eye color.[8] In this view sex equality is equated with almost total blindness to sex. In the assimilationist society, at least in its most uncompromising form, one's sex would play no role in the distribution of civil rights or economic benefits and, at most, would play a minimal role in personal and social relations. This assimilationist model of sex equality strongly resembles the integrationist ideal of racial equality. In particular it implies that "separate but equal" is as unacceptable in sex equality as it is in race. The implication for sport is that having separate athletic programs for men and women actually violates what equity and justice require.

Perhaps the principal argument for the assimilationist ideal is that the value of personal autonomy requires it. Although "autonomy" is far from the clearest notion employed by moral philosophers, it refers to our capacity to choose our actions and determine the course of our own lives. It has to do with self-determination rather than determination by others.

Defenders of the assimilationist ideal argue that it is justified by the moral requirement of respect for the autonomy of women because autonomy requires the withering away of gender roles. As Richard Wasserstrom, a distinguished advocate of the assimilationist ideal, argued, "Sex roles, and all that accompany them, necessarily impose limits—restrictions on what one can do or become. As such, they are . . . at least prima facie wrong."[9] Perhaps what Wasserstrom had in mind is that roles set up proper norms of behavior for those who fill them. Deviation from the norm exposes one to criticism from others. Social pressure enforces conformity. The effects of sex roles in sports was seen in a 1975 study, which reported that 90 percent of the respondents, selected from the general population, believed that participation in track and field would detract from a female's femininity, whereas only 2 percent thought participation in swimming, a more traditional sport for girls and women, would have the same effect.[10]

No society can exist without roles of any kind. But according to proponents of the assimilationist model of sex equality, sex roles are especially objectionable. Whether they arise from biological differences between men and women or from socialization and learning, they are imposed rather than chosen. As Wasserstrom maintained, "Involuntarily imposed restraints have been imposed on some of the most central factors concerning the way one will shape and live one's life."[11] Thus, some feminists argue that what are often called gender roles are largely socially constructed; there is no biological reason why society should assign members of each biological sex significantly different roles.[12]

The assimilationist conception of equality does seem particularly appropriate to many significant areas of life in our society. For example, in basic civil rights and liberties, justice and equity surely should be sex blind. Freedom of assembly, religion, or speech are rights of all persons equally regardless of their sex. Similarly, in employment or the distribution of important social benefits, making distinctions by sex normally is arbitrary and unfair.[13]

Should sex equality be identified across the board with blindness to sex, as the assimilationist model requires? Should it apply only to the public realm, or should it apply to individuals' personal lives as well? What, for example, are we to say of sexual attraction? If sex equality requires blindness to the sex of others, does it follow that people with relatively fixed sexual preferences, whether for members of the opposite sex or their own, are engaged in the social counterpart of invidious sex discrimination?[14] Might there not be other areas, including some in the public realm, such as athletic competition, in which the assimilationist model also breaks down? Accordingly, we might want to consider ideals of sex equality other than assimilationism. The identification of sex equality with sex blindness may not always capture our sense of what is just or reasonable. In particular, as we have seen earlier, equal treatment in the sense of identical treatment is not always a requirement of justice or fairness. Sometimes equality is to be understood as requiring equal respect and concern, which in turn requires us to acknowledge the significance of relevant differences among persons.

A second ideal of sex equality, which recognizes the significance of difference, might be called the pluralistic model. The pluralistic conception of equality is best illustrated by the tradition of religious tolerance in the United States. According to this tradition, religious equality does not require that we accord to religious differences only the significance presently attached to eye color; rather, a defensible conception of religious equality stipulates that no religion be placed in a position of dominance over others.

Unlike assimilationism, pluralism does not reject the ideal of "separate but equal" out of hand if separation is not coercively imposed by the dominant group and is justified by equal respect for all. Thus, it might allow separate but equal athletic programs for women. Although pluralists reject rigid gender roles, they concur that some significant biological differences between the sexes may exist and should be taken into account in an equitable manner in public policy.

Is pluralism or assimilationism the more defensible model of sex equality? Which approach has the most acceptable implications for sex equality in sports? We will consider these questions in the next section.

Gender Equity in Athletic Competition

Pluralism and Sport

Much of the controversy over sex equality in sport concerns whether men's and women's athletic programs are being treated equally in our schools, colleges, and universities. Is the women's program receiving its fair share of the budget? Does the women's basketball team enjoy the same kind of publicity as the men's team? Are there equivalent opportunities for men and women to play intramural sports? What does it mean for opportunities to be equivalent?

Such questions presuppose that separate sports programs for men and women are requirements of equity in sport or are at least permissible ways of achieving it. Which of the ideals we have considered, assimilationism or pluralism, is more defensible in sports?

The problem with assimilationism in sport is that sex blindness requires us to ignore what seem to be relevant sex-related differences in the average athletic ability of men and women. Generally, women are not as big, strong, or fast as men, although there is some evidence that over long distances females may show as much or more stamina than do males. It does appear that in the popular contact sports, such as football, lacrosse, and basketball, as well as in baseball, soccer, tennis, and golf, men's greater size, speed, and strength give them a significant physiological advantage over women. In short, if athletic competition were completely sex blind, women might be virtually absent from or at least significantly underrepresented in sport competition at the highest levels.

Some observers might argue that, contrary to the claims above, existing differences are largely the result of the past exclusion of women from many sports and that the differences would diminish or even vanish if boys and girls received equal encouragement and training in their athletic endeavors from an early age. That is, on this view, sex differences in athletics are largely the result of cultural practices that have unfairly excluded women from sport.[15]

Although it is true that the gaps in performance between men and women in many elite sports are shrinking and although elite women athletes outperform almost all men, women athletes have yet to show they can compete successfully against males at the same competitive level of performance in many sports. Thus, as talented as the top-ranked women's college basketball teams at Connecticut or Tennessee have been, size, strength, and speed differences alone make it difficult to see how they could compete successfully against the men's teams from their own institutions.

Thus, it seems difficult to deny that men have physiological advantages over women in most major sports. Separate competitions for each gender seem the best way in at least the immediate future of ensuring that women participate in athletics at elite levels of competition in those sports where males are physiologically advantaged. However, even if this argument does justify separate teams for males and females in intercollegiate or interscholastic competition, it may not do so in a less intense recreational league or intramural program. Moreover, in sports where one sex does not have significant physiological advantages over the other, sex blind competition may well be desirable or even required. (Mixed competitions, such as mixed doubles in tennis, are another possibility that needs to be considered.)

Finally, if particular women athletes wish to compete against men and are qualified to do so, they should not be prohibited from doing so based simply on generalizations that most women would not be competitive in such situations. A reasonable understanding of equal opportunity minimally would provide persons on an individual basis the chance to compete if qualified to do so and not prohibit them from doing so on grounds (such as sex) not related to their athletic qualifications.

Determining which sports the argument about physiological differences applies to may be largely an empirical matter. But is the pluralist argument acceptable even in sports played at high levels of competition and in which there are significant physiological differences between the sexes? We will consider two objections to the defense of pluralism based on physiological sex differences. The first is based on an appeal to assimilationism. The second maintains that separate sport programs provide women with the illusion of equality rather than the reality.

Evaluating Pluralism in Sports

To an advocate of the assimilationist ideal, sexual pluralism in sport may seem morally pernicious, as pluralism may only express and reinforce the traditional system of sex roles. In other words, "separate but equal" only masks a system that reinforces the inequality of women, just as racial segregation reinforced inequality between whites and blacks in the era of Jim Crow.

Such a rejoinder is implausible, however, for a variety of reasons. For one thing, the point of having separate athletic programs for women is to expand the options available to them. A proponent of pluralism in athletics can argue that separate athletic programs for men and women in sports in which physiological sex differences affect performance only increase opportunities for women rather than limiting them in the way that opportunities for African Americans were limited with racial segregation. In addition, women's participation at elite levels in previously male-dominated sports, such as basketball, surely breaks down stereotypes about what sports are appropriate for women.

A proponent of assimilationism might respond that if the ideal of sex blindness was adopted throughout society, it would not matter that few, if any, women played at the higher levels of athletic competition. This is because in the assimilationist society, when an individual's sex would be regarded as no more important than eye color is regarded in our society, it would not be important that nearly all the top athletes were male. At least it would not be regarded as any more important than the widely acknowledged fact that very few individuals under five feet ten inches in height have a chance to play professional basketball.

This response is open to two strong objections, however. The first is that, because we are not yet in the assimilationist society, it would be unfair to apply the assimilationist ideal only to sports, an area where it would particularly disadvantage women. It is one thing to say pluralism in sports is unnecessary in the assimilationist society but quite another to say it is unnecessary in ours.

This distinction between the ideal and the actual raises a fundamental point. Sometimes theorists believe they have succeeded when they present a defensible ideal conception of justice, equality, or liberty and that practical choices will attain the ideal. But this ignores the issue of whether and how it is morally permissible to reach the ideal.[16] For example, suppose a defensible ideal of equal opportunity required we abolish the family on the grounds that some families provide advantages to offspring that other families do not. It doesn't follow that individuals presently part of families can just ignore their duties to other family members on the grounds that in an ideal society the family might not exist. Indeed, if there were no way to adopt the ideal without seriously violating duties to members of presently existing families, that ideal may be morally impermissible for us to act upon.

A similar point may apply to the assimilationist ideal of sexual equality. Even if assimilationism is superior to pluralism as an ideal, it seems morally impermissible to introduce assimilationism in sport, where it would disadvantage women, before it is implemented elsewhere in society.

But even leaving aside implementation, it is far from clear that assimilationism is fair, just, and equitable in all contexts. In particular, competitive sports stand as a counterexample to the thesis that recognition of sex differences always involves coercive sex roles. On the contrary, the recognition of sex differences in sports frees women and girls from traditional gender restrictions and makes it possible for females to engage in highly competitive forms of athletics in a variety of major, traditionally male sports. In sport it seems to be assimilationism rather than pluralism that limits opportunities for women.

Unfair to Females? A Second Critique of Pluralism

Does pluralism in sport really work to the advantage of women? A critic might respond that if men really are better in certain sports, the women's teams in those sports necessarily will be thought of as inferior. Rather than liberate women, such teams will stigmatize women. As philosopher Betsy Postow has argued, "The number and prestige of sports in which men are naturally superior help perpetuate an image of general female inferiority which we have moral reason to undermine."[17] This perception of inferiority might be thought to account for the generally lower attendance at contests between women's teams as well as generally lower public recognition of the achievements of top women athletes than of top male athletes.

However, as we have already pointed out, if competitive sports were organized according to the assimilationist model, females would be almost absent at the top levels of competition. Is that preferable to pluralism? Is it fairer?

More importantly, we need to scrutinize the perception that women's sports are inferior versions of male sports. Perhaps, in spite of achievements of such female stars as Candace Parker, Annika Sorenstam, Sue Bird, Yani Tseng, and Venus and Serena Williams, much of the public still perceives such sports as inferior. But is that perception justified?

The claim that in the traditional major sports women's competition is inferior to that of men's at similar levels could mean one or more of the following:

1. Women's programs receive less financial and coaching support than men's programs.
2. Contests between women or between women's teams are less interesting and less exciting than contests between men or between men's teams are.
3. Men's teams will always beat women's teams in a particular sport if both play at roughly the same level of competition (e.g., intercollegiate athletics).

What are the implications of these different interpretations for our discussion of sex equality? If claim number one above is true, and women's programs receive less financial and coaching support than men's programs, this only shows that pluralism has not been fully implemented, not that it should be abandoned. The obvious remedy is to provide equivalent support for the women's programs.

Claim number three, however, is likely to be true. It is hardly likely that even a top women's intercollegiate basketball team will be able to beat an average male intercollegiate team. In fact, if claim number three were not true, there would be no need for separate women's sports teams in the first place. What does claim number three imply about pluralism in sports?

Many would argue that claim number three justifies claim number two. It is precisely because men's teams can beat women's teams at similar levels of competition that women's sports allegedly are inferior and uninteresting.

However, although much of the sporting public may accept such an inference, it is fallacious. Even if the men's team would usually beat the women's team, it doesn't follow that the men's contest would always be more exciting, more interesting, or of greater competitive intensity than the women's contest. It would be just as fallacious to argue that simply because the worst men's professional basketball team would always be able to beat the best boy's high school team, a contest between two mediocre professional teams would always be more exciting, more interesting, and more competitively intense than a championship game between two top high school teams.

If what is of major interest in a competitive sports contest is the challenge each competitor or team poses to the other and the skill, intensity, and character with which the participants meet the challenge, there is no reason why women's contests should be less exciting or less interesting than men's contests. This has long been known at the University of Connecticut and the University of Tennessee, where the championship women's basketball teams have huge followings. Tennis fans surely accept that top women stars such as the Williams sisters get as much attention as their male counterparts.

In sports such as tennis and golf as well as in some team sports such as basketball, one can plausibly argue that the women's game differs from the men's in ways that make it at least as good as a spectator sport. In tennis the power of male players' serves limits the extent of volleying, but the women's game is characterized more by clever use of ground strokes. In fact, fan interest in women's professional tennis is at least as high as in the men's game. Similarly, in golf women must have superb timing and coordination to compensate for their relative lack of strength in comparison to males. (In fact, top female players, such as Michelle Wie, hit drives nearly as long as most top male professionals. Some female professional golfers who are small in stature hit drives of 240 to 260 yards or more, and this may indicate that their swings are more efficient than those of a six-foot-two-inch male who drives 290 yards.) Why shouldn't it be just as exciting and interesting to watch the timing and tempo of a top female player, such as Annika Sorenstam or young phenomenon Lydia Ko as it is to watch the force male player applies?

In women's basketball the dunk or jam is virtually absent, and one-on-one moves may be somewhat less spectacular than in the men's game. However, the intelligent use of screens to get open shots, movement without the ball, and brilliant individual play are all there. It is simply a matter of appreciating different aspects of the game as well as the competitive intensity and character of the women playing it. Indeed, the Connecticut women's basketball program has for many years arguably played the best team-oriented basketball at the intercollegiate level, whether for men or women.

If women's sports can be as exciting and interesting as men's sports, in part because they are equally competitive and in part because subtly different qualities are being tested, it is hard to see why pluralism in sports necessarily stigmatizes women. Full appreciation of these sports may require better education of the general public, but it is hard to see why women should be denied the opportunity to compete simply because many fans are fascinated, perhaps unjustifiably so, by the power game males play. Although spectators may in the long run favor aspects of the men's game over the women's game, there is no reason why this *must* happen and much reason to believe that in some sports the women's and men's games, as is presently the case with professional tennis, may turn out to be equally appealing. If such a suggestion has force, it is not that women's sports are inferior but rather that more of us need to make the effort to appreciate the diverse qualities that are exhibited in athletic competition.

A Pluralist Proposal

Such considerations may have some appeal even to those who have been suspicious of "separate but equal" as a model of sex equality. However, some analysts may take this defense of a pluralist approach a step further. Why not place more emphasis on sports in which female abilities or qualities are especially advantageous? The suggestion here is that we redefine our catalog of major sports. The intuitive idea is that equal opportunity, even on the pluralist model, requires more than equal recognition of or appreciation for women's athletics; it also requires equal emphasis on sports in which women can be the top athletes and not merely the top women athletes.

Thus, Postow has recommended that we "increase the number and prestige of sports in which women have a natural statistical superiority to men or at least are not naturally inferior."[18] Jane English has given a concrete example of what Postow may have had in mind: "Perhaps the most extreme example of a sport favoring women's natural skills is the balance beam. Here, small size and flexibility and low center of gravity combine to give women the kind of natural hegemony that men enjoy in football."[19] In other words, our traditional catalog of major sports has a built-in bias toward athletic activities favoring men. The way to remedy this bias is not simply to introduce athletic programs that critics allege institutionalize female inferiority; rather, we should radically revise our conception of which sports are most worthy of support and attention.

The suggestion that we should learn to appreciate and develop sports that reward the physiological assets of women, just as we now tend to appreciate those that reward the physiological assets of men, does have merit. Properly understood, it does not require the abolition of women's programs in basketball, volleyball, soccer, tennis, and other traditional sports but instead the addition and increased support of other sports, such as gymnastics, in which women are physiologically advantaged (or at least physiologically equal).

Considerations of fairness and equity support this suggestion, but two competing considerations have to be kept in mind. First, individuals may continue to prefer traditional or currently more popular sports even after they are introduced to alternatives. The general public may continue to prefer watching and playing basketball and football to watching or participating in gymnastics and high diving. This may be as true for the majority of female athletes as much as anybody else, especially because traditional sports seem open to a wider variety of age groups and body types than are gymnastics.

Moreover, to require or compel individuals to attend or participate in certain kinds of sports and prohibit them from playing others would be a serious violation of individual liberty. It is one thing, for example, to require that schools introduce students in physical education classes to a wide variety of sports and athletic activities, many of which are not biased in favor of male physiology, but it is quite another to require that female athletes compete in such activities, even if they are more interested in playing basketball, soccer, lacrosse, tennis, or golf. It is possible that a broad program of public education could change individual preferences; however, such a program, if morally permissible, must appeal to people as autonomous moral agents and not dictate in advance which sports people are required to find more interesting or of greater worth.

Finally, it is important to remember that women's sports can be just as interesting and competitive as the men's version. Thus, the claim that pluralism in athletics promotes a stereotype of female inferiority is, at best, highly questionable.

Does Sex Equality Require Forgetting Sex?

The conception of sex equality as blindness to sex is most plausible in the realm of civil and political rights and in the economic marketplace. On this view, the right to vote, the right to freedom of speech, and the right to be free of discrimination in the marketplace should not be dependent upon one's sex.

But whereas assimilationism, or blindness to sex and gender differences, may be the favored conception of equality in many areas, such as civil rights, it is doubtful whether it is acceptable across the board in all areas of human concern. As our discussion of sports suggests, the assignment of significance to sex is not always a form of sexism.

We have not been shown, then, that separate athletic programs for men and women in those sports in which one sex is at a physiological disadvantage are morally suspect or illegitimate. Unlike the doctrine of "separate but equal" in the context of racial segregation, separate athletic programs do not stigmatize one group or the other, are not imposed against the will of either sex, and actually enhance the freedom and opportunity of the previously disadvantaged group. Sports seem to provide a model of a defensible pluralistic approach to sex equality. In sports and perhaps in other areas as well, sex equality does not require blindness to sex.

Legislating Equality: Title IX and Its Critics

What are the implications of the preceding discussion for policy? Much discussion focuses on Title IX of the Educational Amendments of 1972, the federal legislation that applies to gender equity in athletics in educational programs. Let us examine, first, the history of Title IX and then issues arising from the interpretation of Title IX advanced by the Office of Civil Rights in 1996 to see why this legislation, which has done so much to promote greater equality in athletics, is also the center of a controversy over how best to achieve gender equity in athletics.

The Development of Title IX

As we already have noted, women's participation in competitive athletics was significantly limited before the civil rights movement, the rise of feminism, and the passage of Title IX itself. In the early 1970s more than 4 million boys participated in high school athletics, compared to approximately 300,000 girls. Gross disparities in participation and expenditures on males and females also were the rule in intercollegiate athletics. James Michener, writing about the period before promulgation of Title IX, reported that "one day I saw the budget of . . . a state institution (a university), supported by tax funds, with a student body divided fifty-fifty between men and women. The athletic department had $3,900,000 to spend, and of this, women received exactly $31,000, a little less than eight-tenths of one percent. On the face of it, this was outrageous."[20] The passage of Title IX, along with other concurrent social trends, including the emphasis of the early feminist movement on equality for women, resulted in almost immediate jumps in participation by females in athletics and increases in expenditures by educational institutions on athletic programs for women and girls. By 1979, 2 million girls were participating in high school athletics, compared to about 300,000 before 1972. However, Title IX was never uncontroversial. In testimony before Congress even in the 1970s critics charged that it would lead to quotas for female athletes and argued that, at the very least, revenue-producing sports such as football should be exempted from its requirements. Proponents of the legislation responded that the new legislation was not designed as a quota system but as a way to level the playing field by providing women with opportunities in intercollegiate athletics equal to those enjoyed by men. These same controversies, as we shall see, continue today.

Perhaps part of the reason for the continuing controversy can be found in the history of Title IX. Although passed by Congress in 1972, it was only in the late 1990s that a consistent and relatively clear interpretation of the legislation emerged and began to be applied by the courts, although this interpretation has been the subject of bitter controversy.

Two court cases also explain the delay and much of the confusion about implementation. In *Grove City v. Bell*, decided in 1984, the Supreme Court ruled that Title IX applied only to programs directly receiving federal funds. On this interpretation, if College X's physics department received a federal grant, Title IX would apply only to the physics department and not to the college's athletics program. Because few, if any, athletic programs at high schools or colleges and universities receive federal grants, the Grove City case exempted them from legislative review under Title IX. This led Congress to pass the Civil Rights Restoration Act, which responded to the decision in *Grove City*, in 1988. This act made Title IX apply to an entire institution that received either direct or indirect federal aid. In the second case, *Franklin v. Gwinnett County Public Schools*, decided in 1992, a unanimous Supreme Court ruled that plaintiffs filing Title IX lawsuits were entitled to punitive damages if it had been found that the institution being sued intentionally took steps to avoid compliance with Title IX.[21] In effect, this decision put real teeth into the legislation—namely, the threat of having to pay damages for certain sorts of failures to comply.

Thus, disagreements about the scope and enforcement of Title IX help to explain delays in implementation. Even assuming goodwill on the part of educational institutions, it was unclear how to apply the legislation and what the remedy for failure to comply might be in different kinds of cases.

In 1990 the Office of Civil Rights (OCR) issued a manual for interpreting Title IX that, along with clarifications made in 1996, has become authoritative. The OCR interpretation included what has been called the "three-part test" that has become the center of controversy. Let us consider what Title IX, as it has evolved and as it has been interpreted by the Office of Civil Rights, actually requires.

What Does Title IX Require?

The OCR identifies three major areas of compliance with Title IX: athletic scholarships, accommodation of athletic interests and abilities, and other athletic benefits and awards. The first applies only to those institutions in Divisions I and II of the National Collegiate Athletic Association (NCAA) that award athletic scholarships. It requires roughly that male and female athletes receive proportional shares of available scholarships. The third requires that educational institutions treat male and female athletes equitably in the distribution of fields for practice, equipment, access to trainers, expense allowances, and the like. We will be concerned in our discussion primarily with the second area, accommodation of athletic abilities and interests, because it clearly is most fundamental.

Before turning to that, it will be useful to consider the general understanding of equity that seems to underlie Title IX. It might be natural to assume that Title IX requires identical treatment for men's and women's intercollegiate sports in the sense, say, of requiring identical expenditures on each. However, Title IX is better understood as requiring equivalent treatment rather than identical treatment. Consider an example from another area. Suppose that half the students in a particular school want to develop their musical abilities and half want to learn computer science. The school buys musical instruments adequate for instruction and provides for sufficient computers and faculty to allow the formation of a computer science program. But because computers cost more than musical instruments, the school spends several times the money it spends on the musicians on the students in the computer program. Even so, the opportunities are equal for both groups in the sense of being equivalent. All the students have an equal chance to pursue their interests. Another way of putting it, following the legal philosopher Ronald Dworkin, is to say that both groups of students have been treated with equal respect and concern.[22]

This example suggests that "equal expenditures" and "equal opportunities" are two distinct notions. The examples have clear analogies in the world of sports. For example, suppose equipment for men's teams in a particular sport is more expensive than equipment for the parallel women's team or that a more experienced coach of a women's team gets paid more than a rookie coach of a men's team at the same university. Such differences are allowable. Thus, the set of principles underlying Title IX seems to require equal respect and concern for each gender, understood as provision of equivalent opportunities rather than identical treatment.

Keeping the distinction between identical and equivalent opportunities in mind, let us turn to the OCR's three-part test for compliance. In particular, the OCR proposes that institutions can comply with Title IX in accommodating athletic abilities and interests by meeting any one requirement of the following three:

1. By providing opportunities for participation in the intercollegiate athletics program for students of each sex that are substantially proportionate to their respective enrollments in the student body as a whole.
2. If not, the institution can comply by showing a history and continuing practice of expansion of the intercollegiate athletics program responsive to developing interests and abilities of members of the underrepresented sex.
3. If not, the institution still can comply by showing that the interests and abilities of the underrepresented sex are "fully and effectively accommodated" by the existing program.

Legal compliance is established by satisfying any one of the three tests. An intercollegiate athletic program that fails one prong of the three-part test might still be in compliance with Title IX by satisfying another. The first is regarded as a "safe harbor" in the sense that a finding of proportionality will at the very least establish a strong and perhaps overwhelming presumption of compliance. However, failure to show proportionality (it is doubtful whether many institutions of higher education in the country, especially those with football programs with their huge rosters of players, now satisfy this requirement as strictly construed) is not sufficient to establish noncompliance if the other criteria are satisfied.

The three-part OCR test has some important similarities to what might be called a presumptive approach to gender equity. It presumes that both genders will be treated equally but acknowledges the possibility of allowable reasons for inequality. Representation of gender in proportion to its share of the overall student body will normally be taken as compelling evidence of equal treatment.

If proportionality cannot be satisfied, compliance with Title IX can be demonstrated by showing compliance with one of the other two prongs of the test. In applying the third prong by assessing whether the interests of the underrepresented gender have been "fully and effectively accommodated," the assumption is that each gender will be treated equally in the absence of justifying reasons for inequality. But justifying reasons are possible. For example, sometimes where there is interest in developing a new women's sport at an institution that does not satisfy the first two prongs, it is reasonable for the institution to expect that interest to continue for a sustained period of time and for the prospective participants to demonstrate sufficient ability before taking steps to support the new sports team.

What counts as a justifiable reason for inequality often will be controversial. Does the past success of the men's basketball team at a Division I institution justify them playing a more nationally prominent schedule than the less successful women's team? What if the athletic director promises to upgrade the women's schedule as soon as the team develops sufficiently to compete successfully at that level? Should a 98-pound female gymnast receive the same daily meal allowance as a 275-pound male lineman on the football team when the teams are on the road? Is it an inequity if the lineman is given a greater allowance because he needs more food?

Rather than pursuing the numerous questions that could be raised about what counts as justifiable reasons for inequality, which cannot all be explored here, we shall focus on the more useful task of examining fundamental issues raised by the OCR three-pronged test, particularly those concerning proportionality and the effective accommodation of interests. Because these areas are fundamental, exploring them may help shed some light on other important issues of gender equity that are likely to arise.

Proportionality

The idea that men and women should be represented in an educational institution's athletic program in proportion to their representation in the student body initially sounds plausible. After all, if participation in athletics provides significant benefits and opportunities and there is no reason to favor one gender in the distribution of these benefits and opportunities, then one would expect them to be made available to both genders equally. So if 60 percent of the student body is male and 40 percent female, in the absence of discrimination one would expect to find that about 60 percent of the institution's athletes were male and about 40 percent female.

But there are problems with this initial expectation. For one thing, there is about a three-to-two ratio of male to female participants in high school (interscholastic) athletics.[23] Given that there remains a disproportion in the representation of each gender in sports at the precollege level, is it reasonable to expect the proportion of women participating at the college level, which is significantly more demanding than at the high school level, to suddenly jump? If not, say the critics of the proportionality requirement, then it is unreasonable to place so much emphasis on proportional representation in the first place. Where will the additional female athletes needed to achieve proportionality come from?

This difficulty leads critics to raise a major objection to the proportionality requirement—namely, that regardless of the intentions of its proponents, proportionality functions to decrease opportunities for male athletes rather than increasing them for female athletes. That is because there are two ways to remedy the perceived underrepresentation of women. The first is to raise the proportion of women participating; the second is to reduce the proportion of men participating. In other words, by cutting men's sports, the institution could achieve proportionality and a "safe harbor" from further legal action without adding an additional opportunity for even one female athlete to participate.

In fact, critics of the proportionality requirement charge that numerous less-visible men's sport teams seem to have been cut at various institutions, quite possibly in part to achieve a more respectable-looking ratio of female to male athletes, including well over 150 wrestling programs and many men's tennis, gymnastics, swimming, and golf teams.[24] Accordingly, the requirement of proportionality may have the unintended consequence in American colleges and universities of decreasing the number of slots on athletic teams, possibly without significantly increasing opportunities to participate for women but mainly through decreasing them for men.

There are three important responses to this kind of criticism. The first is that Title IX does not require satisfaction of the proportionality requirement. Institutions can comply by satisfying one of the other two prongs of the OCR three-part test. The second is that Title IX does not require institutions to eliminate less visible men's programs but does allow them instead to shift resources from high-visibility and arguably bloated men's sports, particularly college football, to women's sports programs. The third is that it is not necessarily unjust to cut men's programs if men had previously enjoyed a disproportionate share of the resources. Nancy Hogshead-Makar of the Women's Sports Foundation argues that if a second child is born into a previously single-child family, the parents may need to reduce time spent with the first child to spend time with the new arrival. In such circumstances, no one claims an injustice has taken place; rather, equal concern is shown for each child. Similarly, Hogshead-Makar argues that perhaps reducing the men's program is necessary to show equal respect for "the new kid on the block," namely the women's sports program.[25]

Critics of proportionality might reply that, although these responses may blunt some of the force of the objection that proportionality reduces opportunities for men without raising them for women, each response also faces difficulties. The first response is that colleges and universities need not achieve proportionality but can satisfy one of the other two requirements OCR laid down. This approach surely is acceptable and is perhaps the fairest method of compliance, but it also raises some difficult questions. In particular, it is important to remember that questions of distributive justice in intercollegiate athletics arise at least at two levels: distribution of resources within the athletic program and distribution within the university generally. Thus, should colleges and universities be required to increase expenditure on athletics at a time when many academic needs are unmet because of lack of funding? Is it more important to add a women's team than to support faculty, provide financial aid to needy students, or make computer facilities more accessible to everyone in the institution? Expansion, then, may be an ideal solution in some contexts but may not be affordable or educationally warranted in others.

Proponents of the proportionality requirement, arguably with good reason, are unlikely to regard such a retort as fair or reasonable. After all, they can point out, men's athletic programs often are extremely costly. Why not reduce funds allocated to them in order to add women's teams rather than blaming women's sports for taking funds from academics and financial aid?

This reply, however, leads to another difficulty. We agree that it will sometimes be possible to shift some resources from football and perhaps from other high-budget men's sports to women's programs, particularly at the large Division I football powers. This may not be the case, however, for smaller colleges; indeed, the implications would be quite different at nonscholarship schools or those competing at the Division III level. In Division III schools transferring support from football to other sports might result in smaller rosters, which would mean that those young men at the bottom of the team's ability level could lose the opportunity to play. Because such athletes are playing primarily for love of the game, it is, at best, unfortunate that they would bear the brunt of compliance. Be that as it may, major college football teams could continue to play at an elite (Division I) level after, say, a 5 to 10 percent cut in the athletic scholarships they offer, perhaps with consequent increased participation by walk-on football players who compete for love of the game. Indeed, under present rules elite Division I institutions often have a greater number of scholarship players on their football roster than the number of players on the roster of a typical NFL team, so it is hard to believe some cuts in roster size would significantly reduce the quality of play in intercollegiate football. Nevertheless, the slogan "Cut big football budgets" is not necessarily an across-the-board solution to the problems proportionality raises, particularly at the schools that play football but do not offer athletic scholarships and do not have bloated budgets. At these schools cuts in rosters would affect walk-on players without necessarily adding opportunities for females.

In any case, we agree that compliance does not require meeting the proportionality requirement and that many, but not all, institutions might be able to comply by adding women's teams or diverting resources from high-budget men's teams to women's teams. We also find Hogshead-Makar's analogy of diverting resources within the family to be an important contribution to the debate. We point out, however, that in her example the second child gains from less resources devoted to the first, but the women's athletic program does not necessarily gain from simply eliminating men's teams to achieve proportionality.

What about the claim critics of proportionality sometimes make, that women simply are less interested in participating in athletics than men are? If so, it would be unreasonable to expect to find the proportion of women athletes at a given institution to be proportional to the representation of women in the student body as a whole. In other words, the argument that each gender should be proportionately represented in the university's intercollegiate athletic program presupposes that the members of each gender have an equal interest in participating. It is that very presupposition that critics of proportionality call into question.

Although such a criticism may prove to have some merit, it should not be accepted prematurely. As proponents of proportionality retort, females in America have traditionally been discouraged from participating in athletics and are only now beginning to overcome the socialization that has inhibited participation. Therefore, rates of participation are not adequate indicators of true interest. If colleges and universities provide additional women's sports, the participants will eventually come. We suggest caution in interpreting what may be the effects of adverse socialization of women about sports that may have discouraged many of them from participating as evidence of lack of interest under conditions of fair opportunity; indeed, the enormous growth of female participation in athletics after the passage of Title IX indicates the interest is there if opportunities to play are available and participation is encouraged. At the very least, there is an obligation to go beyond crude measures, such as how many women try out for teams, before we conclude that women have less interest in athletics than do men. For example, would more women try out if they were encouraged to do so, if a different range of sports was offered, or if the university recruited in a wider range of geographic areas?

What should we conclude about the debate over proportionality? First, both sides have points of some intellectual merit. The proponents of proportionality argue with plausibility that compliance with Title IX does not require satisfying the proportionality prong of the three-part test and that it is unfair to assume at this time that women have less interest in participating in sport than do men. Critics of proportionality have a point when they argue that however well intentioned the proponents may be, proportionality in practice is likely to result in further cuts in men's sports, possibly without the compensatory addition of sports for women.

In view of these conflicting arguments, it is natural to wonder whether compromise is possible. Although we doubt whether any compromise will be fully satisfactory, the following suggestions may help carry the debate between proponents and critics of proportionality closer to a common ground.

First, more emphasis should be placed on fully accommodating the interests of the underrepresented gender, usually women, as required by one of the other prongs of the three-part test, and less on proportionality. As suggested above, funds sometimes, and perhaps quite often at the Division I level, could be diverted from expensive men's programs without necessarily cutting sports or even slots on team rosters. For example, many teams could schedule more games locally or regionally and cut back on national travel. Similarly, recruiting restrictions could be tightened by cutting back the often large budgets devoted to attracting student athletes to the institution, most often for high-profile men's sports. (This might require all institutions in a conference to adopt common guidelines so no one institution would be placed at a competitive disadvantage.) Roster size of large men's teams, especially football, might be trimmed, thereby freeing up other resources for expanding the women's programs.

Second, expanding opportunities for women need not always mean the addition of varsity sports. In fact, in view of the nationwide disproportion of males to females in interscholastic varsity sports in the United States, the addition of extensive developmental programs for women, perhaps starting below the high school level, might promote women's lifetime involvement in athletics without necessarily leading to the addition of full-fledged varsities. Perhaps what would be more appropriate than the addition of varsity sports in some circumstances would be the addition of more lower-level recreational programs designed to involve large numbers of females in sports. The addition of a varsity team or two hardly fulfills such a role and surely is better justified for individuals who are already strongly interested in participating. Varsity sports demand commitment and competitive intensity and seem most appropriate for those who are already interested in athletic competition.

This does not mean institutions should be able to satisfy Title IX "on the cheap," say, by adding disorganized and underfunded intramural leagues. The suggestion is that genuine developmental opportunities, including expert coaching and opportunities to develop skills through training, be made available to significant numbers of women and girls. Although significant expense would be required, it should be less than the continual addition of varsity sports and may eventually increase women's overall interest in athletics.

Third, compliance with the proportionality requirement should be regarded as a last resort when it is achieved only by cutting men's sports. Institutions that attempt to comply by such means should have the burden of proof on them to show that less drastic means of compliance could not reasonably have been expected to work. Could travel schedules for men's teams have been reduced, recruiting budgets cut, or even slots trimmed from some rosters rather than actually eliminating a whole sport? Simply cutting men's sports does not result in increasing opportunities for women and should be an acceptable form of compliance only when it is a last resort to satisfy the law. (The case for cutting men's programs may be stronger, however, as suggested by Hogshead-Makar's analogy with the family, if resources from the programs that are eliminated are diverted to women's teams.)

Finally, in the competition for scarce resources it should not be forgotten that athletics help participants in meeting challenges, in developing dedication and commitment, in finding self-esteem, and in working for a common goal with people from different cultural, religious, and socioeconomic backgrounds, benefits that should be as available to women as to men. In short, athletics can have a significant educational component for all participants. We will explore this point more fully in later chapters, but it is important to ensure that sports are not assigned too low a priority when the allocation of resources is considered. Although fundamental academic needs normally should take priority over athletic needs, it is not so clear that less fundamental concerns also should always come first. For example, is the addition of significant athletic opportunities for women always less important than the addition of administrative positions or renovation projects?

Our discussion, though raising questions about proportionality, has not called for its elimination but instead has attempted to find some common ground between proportionality's critics and its proponents. Our proposals for compromise are simply a first attempt to reach a common ground between sides on the proportionality debate. Perhaps they suggest, however, that turning gender equity in sport into a zero-sum contest between men and women is far from the best strategy to pursue. Although transfer of resources from men's to women's athletics may well be called for, particularly in large Division I institutions when budgets for high-profile men's sports are out of line and when all three prongs of the test are unsatisfied, cutting less visible men's sports without adding new opportunities for women should be a last resort for achieving gender equity in intercollegiate sports.

Equivalent Opportunity and Revenue-Producing Sports

Although the public debate about proportionality has made Title IX seem more about the quantitative aspect of compliance, when seen as a whole the legislation is best understood as requiring *equivalent* rather than identical opportunities for each gender. Thus, Title IX does not require that total expenditures on men's and women's sports be identical and even allows for different expenditures in parallel sports if differences arise from such allowable factors as differences in costs of equipment for each group. Moreover, the notion of equivalent treatment seems more appropriate a standard for a broad theory of gender equity in athletics than does, say, an inflexible standard of identical distribution of resources to each gender.

But what makes opportunities equivalent? There is no easy answer to this question. Once the shift is made away from quantitative criteria that can be measured in dollars and cents, greater weight must be put on qualitative judgments, which, although they may not be "subjective," may well involve controversial and complex value judgments. A full examination of the issues that arise in evaluating whether opportunities are equivalent is not possible here. Factors that would clearly be relevant include the availability and quality of coaching, the availability of practice facilities, equal good-faith efforts in encouraging participation from members of each sex, and equal support from an institution's publicity officers in promoting women's sports as well as major men's sports.

However, the games that fans choose to attend or the publicity the external media decide to devote to particular teams and sports will often be beyond the control of the school or university. Moreover, it is appropriate that teams that are in contention for regional or national championships receive more attention than teams that are not, but colleges and universities normally should provide similar support for similarly successful teams regardless of gender.

Indeed, superior performance and a supportive institution can generate large, enthusiastic crowds and frequent appearances on national television for women's Division I teams, as demonstrated by the recent successes of the women's basketball teams at the University of Connecticut, Stanford University, and the University of Tennessee.

Are there instances in which the support provided for men's and women's programs should not be equivalent? Arguably, one kind of case might involve nationally recognized men's intercollegiate teams in such major sports as basketball and football. These sports are alleged to generate huge amounts of revenues and support for their home universities, income that supposedly helps support not only non-revenue-producing men's teams but also women's teams. Thus, national television networks pay over $1 billion for multiyear rights to televise the NCAA Men's Basketball Championship, and these revenues are distributed among NCAA member institutions to support such activities as participation in national championships by teams in lower-profile or lower-division sports. When men's teams can generate significant income and support, is it legitimate to provide them with such extras as national scheduling, a greater number of coaches, advantageous practice times, and extensive support in the area of public relations?

In considering this issue it should be noted that men's football and basketball often not only fail to produce a profit but also frequently operate deep in the red. Although figuring out just what revenues intercollegiate sports bring in can be complicated, the idea of a revenue-producing sport is more often myth than reality. Thus, "in 1997, fewer than half of the Division I programs (43 percent) reported 'profits' and that the average 'deficit' reported at the other programs was $2.8 million."[26] Although some high-visibility men's teams of several major colleges and universities do bring in enormous income, the argument for the special treatment of men's programs in major sports, based on their capacity to generate income, applies to fewer institutions than is often thought. As we will see in Chapter 6, relatively few athletic programs make a profit, and most are sustained, even at the elite Division I level, by subsidies from the home institution.

What about institutions where the men's programs in high-visibility sports do generate large amounts of revenue? Even though the argument for special treatment may have some force in such contexts, such a program should be implemented only when certain other conditions are also satisfied. These conditions should be based on justifiable requirements designed to ensure that the assignment of special status to men's teams in major sports does not block the emergence of women's athletics or deny them the chance to achieve "showcase" status of their own. If we do not accept such conditions of equity, we allow the utility major sports produce to override the claims of each person to equal respect and equal consideration. If we want to respect individuals and their rights, we cannot allow a concern for efficiency alone to override concern for persons and their entitlements.

What moral limitations might apply to institutions where large revenue-producing sports warrant special consideration? It is difficult to formulate an exhaustive list, but perhaps these guidelines can serve as a basis for discussion.

1. The revenues generated, over and above those covering expenses, either must go into the general university budget for the benefit of the entire university community or be distributed within the athletic program so that the women's sports programs (or perhaps lower-profile men's and women's sports) receive the greatest benefit.
2. The university must be making significant efforts to ensure that some equivalent number of women's sports have a reasonable opportunity to achieve the status of the showcase men's sports.

These criteria ensure that broad segments of the university community can benefit from the revenues the men's program generates, with emphasis on providing greater funding of the lesser-funded sports programs (or to support general academic concerns, such as providing financial aid for needy students), so arguably all members of the university could accept them from a position of impartial choice. That is, following the suggestion made in John Rawls's monumental work *A Theory of Justice*, inequalities can be just when they operate to improve the situation of the less advantaged.[27] Impartial members of the university community—for example, those who reason as if they did not know their position in the athletic program—would have every reason to favor a solution that would work to their benefit whether they participated on a high-profile men's sport or in the women's program. The same principles should also apply to high-profile women's programs, such as the Connecticut women's basketball team, when they generate significant revenues.

Discrimination and Sexual Orientation

We would be remiss in a chapter on gender equity and discrimination in athletics based on sex if we did not also discuss discrimination based on sexual orientation. Such discrimination has been prevalent is athletics, and it was only in 2013 that the first male athlete in a professional sport, NBA player Jason Collins, came out as gay. (Olympic diver Greg Louganis came out in 1994 but was not a professional athlete at the time.) In 2014 college football star Michael Sam announced he was gay and, at the time we are writing, appears likely to become the first openly gay player in the NFL. Although some prominent female athletes have been out about their sexual orientation for some time, tennis star Martina Navratilova being a prominent example, many male and female athletes have concealed their sexual orientation in order to avoid harassment and sometimes to even be recruited and compete at the college level.[28] Although a full exploration of the issues involving sexual orientation in sports would take us well beyond the confines of our discussion of gender equity, three points are important to note.

First, Title IX itself focuses on gender equity and does not directly address discrimination based on sexual orientation. However, there are a number of legal and institutional remedies for victims of such discrimination. For example, there are legal protections at the state level and in the code of educational institutions that prohibit harassment based on sexual orientation, as it creates an illegal hostile educational or working environment. Second, institutional codes as well as state law may prohibit discrimination based on sexual orientation.

But third and most important, such discrimination, in athletics as well as the work place, cannot be justified on moral grounds. In addition to more general moral arguments, such as the claim that such discrimination could not be endorsed from an impartial perspective such as illustrated by Rawl's veil of ignorance, the requirements of the mutual quest for excellence also forbid such discrimination as contrary to internal values of sport. What matters in athletics are such qualities as the skills of the participants, their dedication, and their ability to develop and grow. Athletes, as we have seen in Chapters 2 and 3, should want to compete against the best, regardless of such factors as the race, ethnicity, gender, religion, and sexual orientation of those involved. Good sports require no less.[29]

Concluding Comments

In this chapter we have argued for two main conclusions. First, we have maintained that sex equality is not always to be equated with blindness to sex. In particular, the ideal of sex equality as sexual assimilation (sex blindness) seems inappropriate as an ideal to apply across the board to the realm of sports, at least at present. Second, we have argued that the general emphasis of Title IX on equivalent opportunities for each sex in sports is justifiable. The operative principle should be equal concern and respect for all participants, recognizing that this may sometimes justify differences in actual treatment, sometimes including differences in expenditures between men's and women's athletic programs.

In addition, we have seen that the proportionality requirement has been criticized as too rigid a tool for achieving equity, because it can be satisfied by eliminating opportunities for men without increasing them for women. However, we have argued that the proportionality requirement should not be eliminated but rather used judiciously and, in particular, only as a last resort when it leads to eliminating sports for men without increasing opportunities for women. Title IX has helped transform organized athletics by creating opportunities for women to participate, surely one of the morally most positive and significant developments in our lifetimes.

Finally, our discussion also has raised broader concerns about the nature of sex equality and the evaluation of the assimilationist and pluralist models that go well beyond sport and athletics. Insofar as issues that arise in sport contribute to this broader discussion, they suggest that assimilationist ideals do not easily fit all areas of human life. Thus, one implication of our examination of questions of gender equity and sex equality in sport is that sex equality does not always require forgetting sex but sometimes demands showing equal respect for difference.

QUESTIONS FOR REVIEW

1. What is the difference between the assimilationist and pluralist ideals of equality? What reasons might support each ideal, and what criticisms might count against each ideal?
2. Explain the Office of Civil Rights' (OCR) three-part test for compliance with Title IX.
3. What are the criticisms of the proportionality requirement for compliance with Title IX? How might the requirement best be defended against these criticisms?
4. Explain the claim that the most popular sports are "male biased." What remedy for this bias have Betsy Postow and Jane English proposed? How would you assess their proposal?
5. If a men's college team would beat the women's team at the same school, does it follow that men's basketball is superior to women's basketball and, thus, more deserving of support? Can you defend your view against one criticism that might be brought against it?

Notes

1. Betty Spears, "Prologue: The Myth," in *Women in Sport: From Myth to Reality*, ed. Carol A. Ogelsby (Philadelphia: Lea and Febiger, 1978), 12.

2. *More Hurdles to Clear: Women and Girls in Competitive Athletics*, Clearinghouse Publication no. 63 (Washington, DC: US Commission on Civil Rights, 1980), 3. For a full account of the development of women's athletics in the United States, see Ellen W. Gerber, Jan Felshin, Pearl Berlin, and Waneen Wyrick, *The American Woman in Sport* (Reading, MA: Addison-Wesley, 1974).

3. Althea Gibson, *I Always Wanted to Be Somebody*, Perennial Library Edition (New York: Harper and Row, 1965), 42–43.

4. *More Hurdles to Clear*, 13, 22.

5. Annual Sports Participation Survey of the National Federation of High School Associations (1997–1998), available online at www. Balliwick.lib.uiowa.edu/ge. The data from 2006–2007 can be found at www.nfhs.org/custom/participation_figures/default.aspx.

6. Betsy Stevenson, "Title IX and the Evolution of High School Sports," http://wharton sportsbiz.org/documents/research/TitleIXandtheEvolutionofHighSchoolSports-11–07 .pdf.

7. "Sport Is Unfair to Women," *Sports Illustrated*, May 28, 1973.

8. Richard Wasserstrom, "On Racism and Sexism," in *Today's Moral Problems*, ed. Richard Wasserstrom (New York: Macmillan, 1979), 96–97.

9. Ibid., 10.

10. Eldon E. Snyder and Elmer A. Spreitzer, *Social Aspects of Sport* (Englewood Cliffs, NJ: Prentice-Hall, 1978), 158.

11. Wasserstrom, "On Racism and Sexism," 104.

12. Whereas we acknowledge that the line between what is biological and what is social may be difficult to draw, in the rest of this chapter "gender equity" and "gender equality" will be used most often to refer to specific legal and moral issues Title IX raises in our own cultural context, whereas "sex equality" will be used primarily to refer to broader philosophical issues of equality and justice between the sexes.

13. Pregnancy leaves seem a relevant exception, however, and may show that the assimilationist model should not extend to all areas of economic life or even that it requires severe modification.

14. For a critique of the identification of sex equality with sex blindness in areas other than sports and athletics, see Bernard Boxill, "Sexual Blindness and Sexual Equality," *Social Theory and Practice* 6, no. 3 (1980): 281–298.

15. For such an argument, see Claudio Tamburrini, *The Hand of God: Essays in the Philosophy of Sports* (Gotesborg, Sweden: Acta Universitatis Gothoburgenis, 2000), 104ff.

16. This idea was suggested by an unpublished paper by Randy Carter, "Are Cosmic Justice Worlds Morally Possible?"

17. Betsy Postow, "Women and Masculine Sports," *Journal of the Philosophy of Sport* 7, no. 1 (October 1980): 54; Jane English, "Sex Equality in Sports," *Philosophy and Public Affairs* 7, no. 3 (Spring 1978): 275.

18. Postow, "Women and Masculine Sports," 54.

19. Jane English, "Sex Equality in Sports," 275.

20. James Michener, *Sports in America* (New York: Random House, 1976), 20.

21. See *Grove City College v. Bell*, 465 U.S. 555 1045 S. Ct. 1211 (1984) and *Franklin v. Gwinnett County Public Schools*, 112 S. Ct. 1028 (1992).

22. Ronald Dworkin, *Taking Rights Seriously* (Cambridge, MA: Harvard University Press, 1987), 227–229, where he develops his conception of fundamental rights.

23. Thus, according to the Annual Sports Participation Survey of the National Federation of High School Associations, in 1997–1998 there were roughly 3,763,000 male participants in high school sports and 2,570,000 female participants. Although the total of female participants had grown since 1993, the disproportion in participation remained basically similar, as noted in footnote above. Reports on participation rates can be found online at www.Balliwick.lib.uiowa.edu/ge.

24. For a critique of the effects of the proportionality requirement on men's sports, see Jessica Gavora, *Tilting the Playing Field: Schools, Sports, Sex and Title IX* (San Francisco: Encounter Books, 2001).

25. Nancy Hogshead-Makar, "The Ethics of Title IX and Gender Equity for Coaches: Selected Topics" in *The Ethics of Coaching Sports: Moral, Social, and Legal Issues*, ed. Robert L. Simon (Boulder, CO: Westview Press, 2013), 200–201.

26. James L. Shulman and William G. Bowen, *The Game of Life: College Sports and Educational Values* (Princeton, NJ: Princeton University Press, 2001), 245. See also Daniel Fulks, *Revenues and Expenses of Division I and Division II Intercollegiate Athletic Programs: Financial Trends and Relationships—1997* (Indianapolis, IN: NCAA, 1998) for a study based on figures provided by the NCAA.

27. The operative concept here is Rawls's veil of ignorance, a major part of his argument in *A Theory of Justice*. Rawls suggested that just principles are those that would be accepted by rational persons reasoning as if behind a veil of ignorance that obscured from them their personal position in society, their own talents and abilities, and even their values. This would ensure not only that they could not favor their own position but also that arbitrary contingencies, such as initial distributions of natural talents, would not unduly influence the choice of principles of justice. John Rawls, *A Theory of Justice* (Cambridge, MA: Harvard University Press, 1971).

28. For example, the documentary film *Training Rules* presents allegations of discrimination against lesbians during the late 1980s through the 1990s in Penn State's women basketball program under coach Rene Portland. For more information about this film and its allegations, go to www.trainingrules.com.

29. We are grateful to Nancy Hogshead-Makar for correspondence on the legal remedies for discrimination based on sexual orientation, but we alone are responsible for any errors in the text or for any misunderstanding of the information she provided.

Sports on Campus

INTERCOLLEGIATE SPORTS AND THEIR CRITICS

On the surface and to the casual observer, intercollegiate athletics may appear to be a healthy segment of the American sporting scene. The NCAA men's basketball Division I championship is one of the most popular sporting events in the United States and attracts attention throughout the world. Big-time college football has long held the national limelight, and programs such as those at Notre Dame, Florida, and Alabama have national as well as regional followings. In the 2002–2003 season the popular University of Connecticut women's basketball team set a record for consecutive wins by a women's team and, in the 2009–2010 season, set a new record for both men's and women's basketball for consecutive wins. In 2013 this outstanding women's basketball program won another national championship in a string of such accomplishments. The team has contributed significantly to the growing attention given to women's college basketball.

College athletics have provided sports fans with many thrilling moments over the years. These moments include Michael Jordan's shot that gave North Carolina the NCAA basketball championship over Georgetown in 1982, when Jordan was still relatively unknown, and the last-minute win by Ohio State over Miami in the 2003 Fiesta Bowl in a game that decided the national championship. Even more recently the success in 2007 of the previously unheralded University of Hawaii's football team thrilled fans of college sports across the country. Exciting comebacks by Auburn's football team during the 2013 season attracted the attention of fans of the sport everywhere.

But exciting contests and superb athletes are not the whole story in college sports. There is an ethically questionable side to intercollegiate athletics, particularly at the elite Division I level and especially in the high-profile men's sports of football and basketball. Critics of intercollegiate athletics cite the scandals that continually seem to surface and ask whether intercollegiate athletics actually harms the academic and educational functions of the university.

Public criticism of intercollegiate athletics in the United States goes back at least to 1905, when President Theodore Roosevelt summoned the presidents and football coaches of Harvard, Yale, and Princeton to the White House in an attempt to reduce the extreme level of violence then prevalent in the game. In our own day criticism has focused on the scandal-plagued programs of the large Division I institutions, which offer athletic scholarships and tend to dominate intercollegiate sports. Such scandals have involved academic fraud, the alleged coddling of athletes who have behaved outrageously, and cheating in the effort to recruit the most talented high school athletic stars. In contrast, intercollegiate athletics at the level of the Ivy League, many liberal arts colleges, and other institutions in Division III of the NCAA as well as academically highly respected but also athletically elite Division I universities such as Duke and Stanford are still thought of as strong examples of what college sports at their best should be. But, as we will see, even that view has come under fire.

Only a few months after North Carolina's victory over Georgetown in 1982, the game that brought Michael Jordan to national attention, another national basketball power, the University of San Francisco (USF), which in the past had been represented by such great players as Bill Russell and K. C. Jones, announced that it had dropped intercollegiate basketball to preserve its "integrity and reputation." According to the Reverend John LoSchiavo, then-president of USF, people at the university (presumably in the athletic program) felt they had to break NCAA rules in an attempt to remain competitive in big-time intercollegiate athletics.[1]

This fear was far from unfounded in view of what seems to be an epidemic of scandals at the elite level of Division I. For example, in one of the most serious of abuses involving academics, an NCAA investigation of the University of Minnesota men's basketball program found that from 1994 to 1998 a secretary in the athletics academic counseling office, who was also employed as a tutor for the team, was involved in preparing about four hundred pieces of course work, including providing substantive material for papers, for student athletes in the program. The head coach of the basketball team, Clem Haskins, was found to be "knowledgeable about and complicit in the academic fraud" involved. According to the NCAA investigation, "the violations were significant, widespread, and intentional. More than that, their nature—academic fraud—undermined the bedrock foundation of a university and . . . damaged the academic integrity of the institution."[2]

Unfortunately such cases of academic fraud involving athletes are not just onetime events. In 2007, for example, more than twenty Florida State University football players had to miss the Gaylord Hotels Music City Bowl game against the University of Kentucky because of their alleged involvement in academic fraud involving an Internet course in which they were enrolled. Even more recently a significant number of students, including numerous athletes at the University of North Carolina, were found to have enrolled and received grades in fictitious courses listed but not actually given by some members of an academic department. This was especially embarrassing for UNC, an institution that had, with reason, long prided itself on its "clean" athletic program. An expose published in *Sports Illustrated* in the fall of 2013 alleged that some players in the highly ranked Oklahoma State football program received payments from alumni and assistant coaches and, in some cases, were also involved in academic fraud.[3]

Although it did not involve any cheating or rule breaking, let alone academic fraud, the child abuse scandal at Penn State, involving former assistant football coach Jerry Sandusky, rocked the world of college sports to its core. The 2012 report by Louis Freeh, former director of the FBI, alleged that high Penn State officials, ranging from the president to renowned football coach Joe Paterno, "showed total and consistent disregard . . . for the safety and welfare of Sandusky's child victims."[4] The NCAA then imposed unprecedented penalties on Penn State, including a $60 million fine (to be used to benefit the victims of child abuse), vacating Penn State victories from 1998 to 2011, and reducing the number of scholarships the football program would be permitted to offer. (We note that although Sandusky's behavior was morally horrendous and Penn State officials seem to have, at the very least, dropped the ball, the NCAA conducted no independent investigation regarding the role the senior Penn State officials and coach Paterno played in the affair. The criminal trial of these administrators has, at the time of this writing, not taken place. We also note that some of the penalties the NCAA imposed, such as taking away the victories of players who had nothing to do with the scandal, may have been excessive.[5])

Other problems have plagued college athletics as well. These range from low graduation rates for male athletes in major sports at many Division I institutions to the kind of not only embarrassing but also dangerous misbehavior and sometimes criminal activity of academically marginal athletes in some big-time intercollegiate programs. Although there are many fine athletes and coaches in major college sports, a concern for winning, along with the status and income that go with it, too often has taken priority over the university's academic mission. Thus, the 2002 NCAA Men's Championship basketball game featured a win by the University of Maryland over the University of Oklahoma. But according to NCAA statistics, fewer than one in five of the scholarship athletes at both programs were able to meet graduation requirements. Out of the seven classes at the University of Oklahoma the NCAA reported on, those arriving as freshmen from 1989 to 1995, not even one player graduated.[6]

It would be a mistake to think, however, that the problems with intercollegiate athletics are limited to isolated instances of athletes' outrageous behavior, recruiting violations, and academic fraud; many critics believe the problem lies deeper. The moral questions that can be raised about intercollegiate athletics go well beyond an examination of NCAA rules violations—we can ask questions about the rules themselves. For example, should colleges and universities be allowed to give athletic scholarships at all? Does the NCAA permit teams to play too many games, to the academic detriment of the athletes? For example, how can athletes benefit from classes or pursue a rigorous and demanding major if they participate on a baseball or softball team that plays more than fifty games a season or requires athletes to spend extended periods of time off campus playing a basketball schedule against ranked teams all across the country?

At an even more fundamental level we can question whether intercollegiate sports even belong on campus in the first place. After all, shouldn't colleges be educational institutions rather than minor leagues for professional sports? Is the academic mission of the university compatible with a commitment to intercollegiate athletics? Is commitment to excellence in athletics in conflict with commitment to academic excellence?

These questions suggest what might be called the Incompatibility Thesis. This thesis states that intercollegiate sports are incompatible with the academic functions of colleges and universities. The strong version of this thesis asserts that the incompatibility is between academic values and *any* serious form of intercollegiate athletics. A weaker version holds that the incompatibility lies only between academic values and elite Division I athletic programs, those that offer athletic scholarships and whose teams, particularly in high-profile sports, regularly compete for national rankings.

This chapter is an examination of the Incompatibility Thesis and, more broadly, of the value, if any, of intercollegiate athletics. Its central question is what place an athletic program should have on a college or university campus. We shall be concerned not only with the proper role of athletics on campus but with the very nature and mission of the university.

The Role of Sports in the University—The Case for Incompatibility

Why should a university support an intercollegiate athletic program? After all, some distinguished institutions, including the University of Chicago, Emory University, and the California Institute of Technology, have well-deserved reputations for academic excellence yet at various times in their history have not supported a full intercollegiate athletic program or, in some cases, have not had any such program at all. In much of the world, including Europe, athletes play on club teams not associated with universities, and the system seems to work quite well.

Is there any reason for thinking that intercollegiate athletics programs should be eliminated? The question here is almost certainly too broad, as it is important to remember that college athletics includes many sorts of programs, ranging from those of Division III schools (such institutions do not offer athletic scholarships, for the most part they compete regionally rather than nationally, and they emphasize athletics less than schools in Divisions I and II do) right up to the athletic giants such as Michigan, Oklahoma, Texas, and Notre Dame.

Keeping the diversity of intercollegiate athletics in mind, we will begin our inquiry into its value by considering an ideal but important model of what the university should be in our attempt to ascertain just what academic values ought to be regarded as fundamental. By assessing this model and seeing its relationship to various forms that intercollegiate athletics can take, we may be able to offer a judicious assessment of the proper role, if any, of intercollegiate athletics.

The University as a Refuge of Scholarship

Why have the college or university at all? What would be lacking in an educational system that devoted the elementary and high school years to imparting basic skills in reading, writing, mathematics, and the sciences? After high school, students would either seek employment or go on to specialized professional training. Does a college education serve a function that such a system would fail to satisfy? Particularly, what is the value of education in the liberal arts, as distinguished from training directly for a profession or vocation?

Traditionally, the role of education in the liberal arts has been thought to fill an important gap that is ignored by merely professional training and that is not fully approachable by those still mastering basic skills. Education in the liberal arts exposes students to "the best that has been thought and said" in their own and other cultures. By reflecting critically and analytically on the significant works, including artistic achievements, that the best minds have produced throughout human history, students should become better able to acquire a broad perspective on the human situation, learn to analyze difficult problems critically, and appreciate excellence in the arts, humanities, and sciences. And although there is often controversy about what works should be studied and what counts as "best," debates over that issue can themselves have enormous educational value.

Similar rhetoric can be found in the catalogs of most colleges and universities, for behind the language lies an institution that, though evolving, traces its heritage from ancient Greece, through the medieval universities of Europe, to the modern colleges and universities of our own time. The most important function of these institutions, it can be argued, is to transmit the best of human intellectual achievement, to subject different viewpoints to critical analysis, and to add to human knowledge through research.

Although today's huge "multi-universities" have many functions, including provision of professional training in medicine, business, education, nursing, and law, it can be argued that the most important function of the university still is to transmit, examine, and extend the realm of human knowledge. This function often places the university, or at least some of its members, in an adversarial relationship with the rest of society because the university's function commits it to the often critical examination of popular ideas of a given time and culture. If that function were not performed, many bad ideas would not be subjected to criticism, and even good ideas would be less appreciated or understood because their advocates would never have to modify or defend them in the face of objection.[7]

Critical inquiry, then, is a major function of colleges and universities. It is fundamental to a democratic society because it gives people the information and skills they need to function as citizens. And by exposing ideas to critical scrutiny, it allows for the kind of correction of errors and checks on power that are lacking in tyrannies and dictatorships.

Accordingly, let us consider critical inquiry as a normative claim about what the principal function of the university should be. Can a case be made for the inclusion of an intercollegiate sports program in the university conceived not as a business or as a training ground for tomorrow's professionals but as a center of scholarship, critical thought, and training for citizenship in the democratic state? Are intercollegiate athletics at least compatible with the major educational mission of the university? Can athletics actually contribute to or enhance that mission?

A Defense of the Incompatibility Thesis

Why are athletic programs thought to be incompatible with academic values, particularly the kind of education involved in critical inquiry in the arts, sciences, social sciences, and humanities? Some of the points already touched on support the Incompatibility Thesis, especially when applied to elite Division I athletics.

First, the enormous pressures to win, often generated by the need to keep jobs, produce revenues, and promote the institution's visibility, all too often generate cheating. The academic fraud we have seen at Minnesota, Florida State, and other institutions testifies to the strength of these pressures and to the values associated with victory at all costs.

Second, even if we ignore the abuses in some major intercollegiate athletic programs, there seems to be a basic contradiction between the aims of education and the aims of athletics; thus, the time students spend on the athletic fields is time spent away from their studies. Likewise, athletes either uninterested in academic work or unprepared to do it undermine the academic mission of many institutions.

Finally, many of the values associated with athletics, such as obedience to coaches' orders, seem at odds with the kind of inquiring and questioning minds professors attempt to develop in the classroom; indeed, some critics see athletics as a mindless activity in which only physical skills are developed. Thus, to many college and university faculty, athletics are at best a necessary evil, perhaps useful in allowing students to let off steam but in basic conflict with educational values.

The Corruption of Intercollegiate Sports

In many athletically prominent colleges and universities sports have become big business. Many see the television revenues and the visibility and support accompanying success in the major "visibility sports," such as men's football and basketball, as undermining the educational ideal of sport. To gain visibility and the revenues and support that go with it, a program must be successful. But success in this context means winning, and so the temptation is to do whatever is necessary to win. For example, coaches who teach their athletes effectively and who recruit only academically qualified players may not be as valuable to an institution interested in athletic success as a coach who wins, who can handle the media, and whose scruples about recruiting are less strict. Corners get cut. Other schools feel they too must cut even more corners just to be competitive, and soon serious abuses become far too common.

Violations of NCAA rules and the misbehavior of athletes who are only marginally qualified as students get much of the publicity. However, perhaps the most significant form of abuse goes deeper: if the purpose of participation becomes winning for the sake of external goods, such as visibility and financial support, won't players come to be viewed as mere means to that end rather than as students to be educated? Indeed, to keep players eligible, athletic programs could view education as an obstacle that must be overcome; many players could be inadequately educated and perhaps never graduate. Former star Minnesota Viking lineman Alan Page has described a meeting of eight defensive linemen to go over the team's playbook:

> We had each spent four years in colleges with decent reputations . . . and I remember that two of us could read the playbook, two others had some trouble with it but managed, and four of my teammates couldn't read it at all. . . . The problem seems to be that these athletes—and there are many more like them, blacks and whites—were never expected to learn to read and write. They floated through up to this point because they were talented athletes.[8]

Various reforms made by the NCAA over the past twenty-five years, especially under the leadership of Myles Brand, who served as president of the NCAA from 2003 to 2009, may have contributed to some improvement since Page was a player. The overall graduation rate for student athletes at NCAA institutions is higher than for students at large. Graduation rates for African American athletes also are higher than for African American students who are not athletes. However, serious problems remain, particularly in the high-visibility sports of men's football and basketball. Although highly regarded institutions such as Stanford and Duke report high graduation rates even in those sports, some other programs remain seriously deficient.

For example, for students entering college in 1995–1996, the overall graduation rate was 58 percent. The graduation rate for all athletes was 60 percent and for all male athletes 54 percent. However, male basketball players graduated only at a 43 percent rate, and African American basketball players fared even more poorly, graduating at a 35 percent rate (although that rate was comparable to the overall graduation rate for black male students). Some individual institutions did far worse: the University of Oklahoma and the University of Nevada at Las Vegas graduated no male basketball players, and Florida State and the University of Cincinnati graduated no male African American basketball players. In fact, forty-two institutions failed to graduate *any* black male basketball players between 1991–1992 and 1994–1995.[9]

More recent figures for the cohort of athletes entering college in 2005 show improved graduation rates for NCAA athletes generally and was 70 percent for football players at the top football schools at the elite Football Bowl Series level of competition for 2012, the highest rate yet seen. Notre Dame's football players graduated at a rate of 97 percent. However, the picture was not so rosy everywhere. The University of Connecticut's men's basketball graduation was 11 percent, and the program was rules ineligible for postseason play in 2012 under recent NCAA legislation promulgated under the leadership of the organization's late president Myles Brand. Athletic powerhouse Oklahoma had only a graduation rate of 47 percent for its football players.[10] So although we have seen some welcome progress in graduation rates for athletes in high-visibility men's programs, there is good reason for continuing concern as well. (Also, keep in mind that the NCAA's recent method of calculating graduation rates excludes transfers and other students who depart from the institution while in good academic standing, arguably inflating the graduation success rate perhaps significantly.)

Thus, perhaps the morally most damaging charge brought against major intercollegiate athletics is that it exploits the participating athlete. Such athletes are ostensibly offered scholarships to play their sport in return for an education, but often, critics claim, the athlete is expected to give everything on the field, sometimes to the huge financial benefit of the university, and little or no time or effort is taken to ensure success in the classroom. (Moreover, scholarship athletes who do not produce on the field may lose their scholarships and receive neither an education nor the ability to play at a high level of intercollegiate sport.)

For example, football at major universities and often at smaller schools as well is virtually a year-round sport. Practice starts in late summer. The season can extend into December and even further if postseason competition in the major bowls is involved. The season itself may be followed by an off-season "informal" weight-training program; this goes through winter and may, in turn, be followed by spring practice. Not only does the time devoted to practice leave athletes little time for the nonathletic aspects of university life; it also affects academic achievement and, as we discussed earlier, may well encourage academic fraud.

Finally, it is often argued that in Division I, highly visible men's football and basketball programs generate revenue for the university that may support nonrevenue-producing sports, including women's teams, and that they even generate excess funds that can be used for educational purposes. But although many of these programs do produce revenue through gate receipts, television exposure, and licensing fees on logos, they also have enormous expenditures. Think of the costs of offering more than fifty football scholarships, recruiting the players, and building facilities—such as adding skyboxes to football stadiums to the tune of millions of dollars—to say nothing of travel expenses and highly paid coaches, and it becomes clear why only a handful of athletic programs, even in Division I, actually turn a profit. Even highly successful football programs that make money one year may go deeply into debt shortly afterward.

Thus, according to research conducted and published by the NCAA, only twenty-three athletic programs among their athletically elite Football Bowl Series institutions made a profit for the 2012 fiscal year. Yet "Between 50 and 60 percent of football and men's basketball programs reported net . . . surpluses for each of the nine years (covered in the report)."[11] Institutions are forced to subsidize those athletic programs that lose money, thereby transferring money to athletics that could have been used for academics.

In addition, spending per athlete is increasing faster in many conferences than spending per student at large, and some figures are quite disturbing. According to research conducted by the prestigious Knight Commission on Higher Education, spending per student in the Atlantic Coast Conference in 2010 was just over $15,000 per student-at-large but over $103,000 per athlete, and the ratio was even higher on conferences such as the SEC and the Big Ten. Even in Division I institutions with no football program, expenditures per athlete were more than three times higher than for other students.[12] Although some differentials are acceptable (for example, more is probably spent on undergraduate engineering students than on philosophy majors, in part due to the costs of the technology involved in training the former) the degree of differential surely is disturbing.

The Problems of the Black Athlete

The problems discussed above, especially those involving the alleged exploitation of athletes, may apply particularly to the black athlete. Although African Americans constitute about 12 percent of the population of the United States, they make up well over a third of college football and basketball players, about 40 percent of professional football players and about two-thirds of professional basketball players. Disproportionate representation is even greater in the major intercollegiate programs and at the very top levels of major professional sports, where black players often dominate all-star teams.

One plausible explanation for the high representation of black athletes in many sports is discrimination and lack of opportunity in inner-city areas. If African Americans, for example, perceive many doors as closed to them because of discrimination, sport may seem the best escape route from poverty and the ghetto. The effects of discrimination and the focus of the mass media on athletes may also lead to a dearth of nonathletic role models in the black community, a gap filled by successful black athletes. Or such alternate role models may exist but may be less appreciated than is warranted because of the attention focused on such African American superstars as Michael Jordan, Shaquille O'Neal, and Kobe Bryant. As a result, success in athletics may come to be more highly valued in the black community than it is in the white community. Thus, blacks become disproportionately involved in athletics, especially such sports as basketball, track, football, and baseball, all of which normally do not require large investments in equipment and for which inexpensive facilities are widely available in urban areas. Although some may suspect that genetic differences contribute to the disproportionate representation of black athletes in some sports, the kinds of environmental factors pointed to above surely are especially influential. Which natural talents are expressed in action depends in great part on the environmental stimuli to which agents are exposed and the choices they make within that context.[13]

If it is true that sports are more often viewed as the path of choice to upward mobility in the black community than in the white community, we might worry whether black athletes are more vulnerable to the dangers of big-time college athletics, particularly the failure to get a rigorous education, than are whites. For example, many African American youngsters, particularly from less affluent segments of the black community, might tend to see sports as the major and perhaps only avenue to success open to them and may, therefore, be more likely than white students to neglect their studies. The hope of obtaining an athletic scholarship and playing professional sports may prevent them from developing the educational tools that make for success in other areas. Once in college, black athletes in football and basketball may overestimate their chances of making the professional leagues or not even be concerned about graduation because they hope or expect a professional team will draft them. Although athletic scholarships are available for many athletes, including underprivileged blacks and whites, the odds of obtaining them are not high. Unfortunately, there is some evidence that suggests African American youngsters have a greater tendency than whites to overestimate their chances of playing college and professional sports and so may assign a higher priority to athletic than academic success.[14] Some writers even argue that athletics in the United States, often considered in popular thought as a road to equal opportunity for African Americans, have been harmful to them.[15] Although such a thesis may be overstated, for many of those who neglect educational opportunities, athletic talent may be far more likely to lead down a dead-end street than to the pot of gold at the end of the rainbow professional sports seemingly provide.

A Summary: The Case Against Major Intercollegiate Athletics

To review, the criticisms of "big-time" intercollegiate athletics arise from the change of emphasis from athletics as an educationally valuable activity complementing the normal academic curriculum to athletics as a source of revenue, support, and high visibility. These benefits—revenue, support, and visibility—depend upon winning, which in turn depends largely on recruiting the best athletes. The pressure to win can become so intense that coaches and athletes as well as university administrations (often under pressure from influential alumni boosters) make decisions that reflect athletic rather than educational priorities. At their worst, the pressures lead to recruiting violations, misbehavior, academic fraud, and even crime and other abuses, all of which have too often dominated our daily newspapers' sports pages.

If the ideal of the university is that of an institution concerned with the discovery and preservation of truth and the recognition of human excellence, isn't that ideal compromised by sacrificing the education of athletes for athletic victories and even more so by outright cheating? Even though it is true that the modern university has become what has been called a "social service station," fulfilling a variety of social needs, its most important function is still to formulate, test, teach, and evaluate achievement in the arts, sciences, humanities, and professions. How can the university claim to represent such fundamental values when it subverts them in its own practice?

Reasonable people may doubt, then, whether intercollegiate sports should be played at the level of national competition and intensity found in the major football and basketball conferences of our nation. Many would argue that the only reputable intercollegiate athletic programs are those resembling the Division III or Ivy League levels, where no athletic scholarships are given, athletes are expected to be students, and competition is normally regional rather than national. Perhaps this level of intercollegiate competition is the only kind compatible with respect for the athlete as a person, with respect for the educational value of athletic competition, and with respect for the integrity of the university.

A Defense of College Athletics

Perhaps, however, the above critique is overstated. After all, even if there are major problems in some high-profile programs at athletically elite universities, the majority of programs, even in Division I, are not highly visible. Many high-profile programs at major universities, such as Duke, Stanford, and Notre Dame, are not prone to scandal, and athletes in those programs have high graduation rates. Moreover, the vast majority of college athletes play with no desire to become professionals, and the majority of athletic programs compete at the Division II and Division III levels of the NCAA. So, proponents argue, in many cases athletic programs at colleges and universities not only do not undermine the academic mission of the university but sometimes may actually reinforce it. Let us consider the case for such a view in more detail.

College Athletics and Entertainment

Millions of sport fans enjoy high-profile college contests such as those that occur in football bowl games, the men's NCAA Division I basketball championship, and, increasingly, the women's championship. In effect, proponents of big-time college sports argue that even if relatively few intercollegiate athletic programs make an overall profit, they still produce enormous amounts of benefits—what utilitarian philosophers call "utility"—for society. And especially in the case of large state universities, they may engender support among not only residents of the state but also legislators, who provide funding through the political process.

Proponents of such a view might also argue that the critics of high-profile intercollegiate athletics conceive of the mission of the university too narrowly. If the mission of the university is instead conceived broadly, to encompass more than purely academic and intellectual concerns, why couldn't it plausibly be extended to cover the provision of various public services, including the provision of entertainment to the student body and the wider community that intercollegiate athletics can provide? According to proponents of this view, it is clear that the university already in fact does provide entertainment for the community in a variety of areas including theater, music, and other performing arts, such as dance, as well as through programming on college-sponsored radio and television stations. Intercollegiate athletics are simply another way in which academic institutions can and do provide this good to their students and staff as well as to the population at large.

Thus, Peter French, who is critical of other arguments in defense of intercollegiate athletics, pointed out in his 2004 book, *Ethics and College Sports: Ethics, Sports, and the University*, that the mission statements of many universities, especially large state institutions, include explicit mention of service to the community, often including reference to serving the economic and cultural needs of the population. Similarly, some mission statements of athletic departments, sanctioned by their universities, specifically include entertainment among the functions of their programs. Developing this line of thought, French maintained that the honest and potentially successful defense of intercollegiate athletics, especially including the elite sports, is that they are the way, or at least one way and probably the most visible and successful way, the university responds to its public service obligations in the area of public entertainment. In fact, they likely touch the lives of more members of the public in a positive and effective way than any other service the university may extend in that direction.[16]

Accordingly, once we abandon the assumption that the mission of the university should be purely academic, encompassing only teaching and scholarship in recognized academic disciplines to the exclusion of anything else, the inclusion of athletics can be seen in a new light. The sponsorship of intercollegiate athletics can then be defended as fulfilling other legitimate functions of the university. As French put it, "The tension in the university, particularly within the faculty, that sets the academic and athletic side of the campus at odds is caused by the general failure to appreciate the multiple missions of a contemporary university and on the part of the academic faculty typically to think that only their function is the 'real' mission of the university."[17]

How should such a position be evaluated? First, even if correct, this position applies with the most force to highly visible sports, such as men's football and basketball and perhaps women's basketball at large, athletically elite universities, particularly state institutions. So even if French's argument does have force, that force is greatest when applied to high-profile sports at athletically elite levels of the NCAA and loses strength (although probably not to the vanishing point) when applied to different sorts of institutions or to lower-profile sports.

A second criticism is that even if the university does have an obligation to provide entertainment, the kind of entertainment athletics provide differs in kind from the other kinds of entertainment the university legitimately provides, such as concerts and art exhibits. Programs in the arts, as French recognizes, arguably have a much more direct link to the academic mission of colleges and universities than do intercollegiate athletics. These can be defended as extensions of academics, whereas, at least according to the critics, athletics cannot.

Is this second criticism decisive? We think not, for at least two reasons. First, as we have seen, the issue of what activities of the university are fundamental is itself a contested issue. To assume that only entertainment closely linked to academic programs is legitimate is to beg the question about what functions universities should fulfill. More importantly, however, the objection begs the question in a more basic way. If the presumed divide between athletics and academics is nowhere near as deep as the critics assume and there is or can be a significant degree of coherence and mutual support between the two, at least at some kinds of institutions, then intercollegiate athletics do not differ from university-sponsored entertainment in other areas, such as the arts, to the degree the critics assume. We will explore this point more fully in later sections of this chapter.

That leads to the third criticism of the entertainment defense, namely, that athletic programs involve abuses of academic ethics that other activities of the university, including artistic performances, normally do not involve. Given the scandals, including cases of academic fraud, that have plagued high-profile athletic programs at elite Division I schools, this criticism clearly is true. The low graduation rates, particularly of minority athletes, at some institutions clearly are unacceptable. Moreover, if the admissions standards for athletes differ so drastically from those for other students that a significant number of athletes are unprepared for college-level work and if, as a result, their academic course load is so diluted as to be educationally vacuous, then the charge of abuse is also warranted.

However, such abuses occur mainly in high-profile sports at some institutions and are not reason enough to regard all forms of intercollegiate athletics, even at the Division I level, as involving abuses of academic values. Moreover, the NCAA has taken some meaningful steps to raise graduation rates and ensure that athletes are taking a core of serious academic courses. For example, Division I athletic programs with poor graduation rates will have the number of athletic scholarships they can offer reduced. Presumably this will provide an incentive to coaches to make sure athletes graduate, and the coaches will then encourage athletes to study and help them develop strategies that will lead to success. Even if incentives also exist to circumvent such rules, perhaps by diluting the academic content of the courses that athletes take, the stricter rules should help by setting the bar higher than it is at present. In addition, penalties might deter violations, but faculties of each institution as well as the NCAA have a responsibility to ensure that courses offered on their campus are serious and have significant academic content and rigor.

A broader concern applies even to elite athletic programs that do encourage athletes to pursue their education and graduate. The intensity of competition, the missed class time involved in playing a national schedule, the extended length of seasons, and off-season training schedules may demand such a heavy time commitment that the pursuit of educational goals is severely compromised. Thus, revenue may be generated when high-profile teams earn national ranking, but that requires playing a national schedule and gaining attractive time slots on television and traveling to games in distant locations influence game scheduling more than the requirements of class attendance. These factors raise a plethora of questions for those who would defend elite, high-profile intercollegiate sports as presently constituted.

French's defense of elite, high-profile intercollegiate sports as forms of entertainment universities legitimately provide does, however, have some force. It is at least arguable, as he suggested, that provision of entertainment is one of the legitimate functions of colleges and universities, particularly large public institutions. However, such activity is legitimate only if it does not undermine the athletes' chances to receive an education, does not subvert academic norms (as would be the case with academic fraud), and, more broadly, does not involve a kind of disdain for the academic mission of the university, which might come to be regarded as an obstacle to athletic participation rather than as essential to the student athlete's intellectual and personal development.

The entertainment argument also suggests, however, that both sides in this debate may have erred by relying on a dubious common assumption. That assumption is that athletics and academics are two sharply distinct kinds of activities. As we will see in the next two sections, that assumption itself is open to serious challenge.

Can Athletics Enhance Academics?

At most, the argument so far shows that athletics at the level of major intercollegiate sports, given appropriate and effective regulation, can provide benefits such as a sense of community, fun, visibility, and perhaps revenue for some highly successful, high-profile programs. Skeptics may question whether regulations can be effective, given the many incentives to win, and claim that the argument shows athletics to be a necessary evil, at best, but that response may well be too bleak. Most athletes in elite Division I programs graduate, often at higher rates than other students. Female athletes do particularly well, but many athletes, even in high-visibility men's programs, also graduate at high rates at some institutions whose athletic programs have achieved national prominence.[18] Although graduation rates are not always an indication of the rigor of the programs in which athletes are enrolled, greater faculty control would surely enhance the quality of education athletes at high-profile institutions receive.

But even if this limited defense of elite Division I athletics has force, an even stronger kind of argument should also be considered. This argument claims not merely that, under suitable conditions, big-time athletics and academics can be minimally compatible and, thus, should be accepted for their utilitarian benefits but that intercollegiate athletics in the right circumstances can enhance or contribute to the academic mission of colleges and universities.

Athletics and the Performing Arts

An argument supporting such a view was advanced by philosopher Myles Brand, former president of Indiana University and, as noted earlier, president of the NCAA from 2003 until his death in 2009. Brand, like French, believed that the critics of intercollegiate athletics took too narrow a view of what colleges and universities should be about. But where French has argued for a pluralistic view of the mission of the university, including purposes beyond the purely academic, Brand argued for a broader notion of what counts as academic in the first place.

Brand started from what he called a "seemingly small point," namely, that "when the educational experience of student-athletes is compared with those studying the performing arts such as music, dance, and theater as well as the studio arts, it is difficult to find substantive differences."[19] Thus, like student athletes, student musicians practice for many hours, often more than are required of them, and perform in events that are often college sponsored and at which audience members may be charged an admission fee. Performance and practices often are intense. In addition, there is competition for places in the performing groups, just as there is for becoming a player on a sports team. Some preference may be given in the university admissions process to talented students in the arts, and some of these students may have aspirations for professional careers; although, as is the case with student athletes in the NCAA, almost all go on to careers in other areas of endeavor. According to Brand, "these similarities point to a convergence of educational experiences between student-athletes and others . . . but the activities of the student-athletes alone are not considered to be academic, or to be in conflict with academics."[20] Is there any plausible justification for this distinction?

Brand's reply was that there is no such justification. The distinction is arbitrary, perhaps expressing a prejudice many academics hold against the body and against physical rather than intellectual activity. Brand concluded, then, that intercollegiate athletics fall within the domain of the academic, at least if performances in the arts do so as well.

Brand's position raises serious questions, not least of which is the question of how sharp the line between the academic and the nonacademic really is. Pondering this question, some critics might maintain that the goal of elite intercollegiate athletics seems to be to win and to generate the revenue winning produces, not to express artistic or intellectual values, as is the case with performances in music, dance, and theater. Thus, these critics would say the line between academic and nonacademic is quite sharp and that athletics is clearly nonacademic, whereas theater and music are clearly academic activities.

Although this criticism does not lack force, it does seem overdrawn. First of all, the overwhelming majority of intercollegiate athletic contests do not involve high-profile sports and are not intended to be revenue producing. Second, although artists normally may not aim at "winning," they do aim at excellence in performance. Similarly, although the cult of winning may have gotten out of hand in many areas of sport, intercollegiate athletes often can be seen as aiming at excellence as well, with winning the natural by-product of top performance, just as acclaim or awards can be the by-product of outstanding achievement by an artist or actor. So there might be a difference, as Brand's critics argue, between performance in athletics and performance in the arts, but perhaps it is not as sharp a distinction as the critics suggest.

Brand's critics also might argue that music and dance are embedded in a long tradition of intellectual achievement. Performance in these areas takes place in a context of artistic thought and often expresses or illustrates important themes of human existence or basic human values. Moreover, as one of Robert L. Simon's students, a very talented musician, pointed out, an artistic performance may involve mastering a work; the performer needs to, for example, learn a musical composition, analyze different interpretations of it, understand its underlying logic or theme, and study its history and that of the tradition to which it belongs.[21]

However, athletics also can be studied as taking place within a tradition and a history. Moreover, athletic competition can express or illustrate important values, such as dedication, excellence, and perseverance in the face of adversity. Brand's case would be stronger, however, if intercollegiate athletes not only participated in sports but also studied their history, their social significance, and the ethical dilemmas that arise within them, just as many artists not only perform but are students of art as well. In other words, Brand's argument would apply most fully when intercollegiate athletes not only participate in sports but also study them within an academic framework, just as students in the arts often take courses in, say, the history of music, art, or theater.

In addition, Brand's argument raises the question of just which skills should be regarded as within the proper domain of a university or college education. If we include not only dance recitals and musical performances but also basketball and soccer games, what about skillful performance in activities ranging from poker to cooking or from gardening to playing Monopoly? Must we become so inclusive that no exercise of skill can be excluded from the realm of the academic? Moreover, should we view those exercises of skill that do seem to be closely related to the academic enterprise, *possibly* including athletics, to be offered for academic credit, or should they be viewed as adjuncts that reinforce a more traditional academic education but, as Elaine of *Seinfeld* might express it, are not "credit worthy"?

Brand's argument, then, though controversial, does raise issues worthy of further consideration. In particular, is it arbitrary to include musical and dance performances within the realm of the academic but then exclude athletic performance? Perhaps the university should recognize in its academic program, either through credit or through cocurricular recognition, contributions to the community that exhibit a variety of mental and physical skills, including those exhibited in dance, music, photography, and athletics. Rather than pursuing this issue in greater depth, however, let us consider another approach that maintains that athletics and academics are or can be compatible, perhaps even mutually reinforcing, precisely because of the cognitive skills employed in each enterprise.

Athletics, Education, and Cognitive Skills

Consider again the model of athletic competition as a mutual quest for excellence through challenge as developed in Chapters 2 and 3. Arguably, such competition has several features that make it a desirable supplement to a broad liberal arts education. On this model athletic competition can be thought of as a test through which competitors commit their minds and bodies to the pursuit of excellence. To meet such a test, they must learn to analyze and overcome weakness, to work hard to improve, to understand their own strengths and weaknesses, and to react intelligently and skillfully to situations that arise in the contest. In the sports contest they must use judgment, make decisions that are open to reflective criticism, apply standards of assessment, critically analyze play, and exhibit perseverance and coolness under pressure. During a season athletes can learn and grow by understanding their physical and psychological weaknesses and by trying to improve.

Many of these same traits are also required for successful study in the humanities and sciences. An important part of education is learning to know and understand oneself, and that kind of self-knowledge is one of the most valuable kinds of knowledge that can emerge from participation in sports. In addition, athletes must learn to think critically about their own performance and that of their teammates and opponents, to learn from the criticism of others, to focus on the task before them in the contest and avoid distraction, and to appreciate standards of excellence even when the standards are met better by opponents than by themselves. These skills are similar and arguably may reinforce similar critical skills and the ability to appreciate achievement in the classroom.

If this point is valid, then academics and intercollegiate athletics, when properly conducted, can be and often are mutually reinforcing. This mutual reinforcement can occur in at least three ways. First, athletes' acquisition of the kinds of skills specified above can help promote the acquisition of parallel skills in the classroom. Athletes who learn to accept and integrate criticism of their athletic performance may be primed to accept and apply criticism of their writing or logical analysis as well. Second, athletes' exhibition of skills to spectators may illustrate the value of such skills to a wider audience. Thus, a team that overcomes ideological differences to perform well can illustrate the value of teamwork, whereas a team dominated by selfish individuals who care mainly about their own statistics can illustrate what happens when egoism predominates. Third, the values implicit in sport can serve as grounds for criticism in academic performance as well. Thus, a professor might chastise an athlete for not working as hard on drills in a language course as the athlete does on the field, or an athlete can point out to a professor that he should not be stereotyped as an unintellectual "jock" because participation in sport has taught him to think outside the box about strategies and, by extension, other topics, thereby increasing his problem-solving skills. These three aspects of mutual reinforcement can be thought of as causal, illustrative, and justificatory.[22]

In calling for the best that is within each participant, a good athletic program can provide educational experiences that are unusually intense and unusually valuable and that reinforce and help develop many of the same traits that promote learning elsewhere. But even leaving aside such consequences, the good sports contest is a crucible in which important learning takes place and involves the discipline, understanding, and analysis that are related to learning in other parts of the curriculum.[23]

Critics might object that even if these points are correct, they do not show that intercollegiate athletics is a necessary or unique part of an educational curriculum.[24] After all, if the same values are directly promoted, taught, and exemplified in the classroom, the additional indirect reinforcement athletics provide is at best marginal and at worst distracts students from more academic pursuits in which the most important aspects of education are dealt with. At most, critics might argue, intramural programs may well be warranted, but not the kind of intense activity found in varsity intercollegiate athletics.

This sort of critical rejoinder is not decisive. Although the critics surely are right to argue that athletics do not play a unique educational role, sports may still be in a relationship of significant mutual reinforcement with academics. As philosopher Paul Weiss pointed out, students, particularly undergraduates, are novices in the academic disciplines they study. At best, the more advanced undergraduates may become apprentices by assisting professors in research, but they rarely have the chance to be at the cutting edge of achievement in a discipline until later in their careers. Athletics, along with the performing arts, are perhaps the only areas in most colleges and universities where students can achieve and demonstrate excellence—and not just as apprentice learners but also in performances that rank among the best at a high level of comparative judgment.[25]

Perhaps more importantly, appreciation of achievement in athletics is widespread, far more so than understanding of achievement in mathematics, physics, philosophy, or other specialized disciplines. Because of this, athletics can and should serve as a kind of common denominator that allows people from vastly different backgrounds, cultures, social classes, and academic interests to experience together the lessons of striving to meet challenges. These experiences not only can be educationally valuable to the participants but also can inspire, teach, and inform other members of the wider university community who also enjoy the competition. Moreover, because athletic contests are accessible to and attract the interest of wide segments of the population, they can be a unifying force in an intellectual community that is often split along ideological, ethnic, religious, socioeconomic, and disciplinary lines. Although this function is perhaps distinct from universities' primary educational functions, it makes intercollegiate athletics an important aspect of academic communities. Sport, in short, helps to create bonds that allow communication to persist when it might otherwise break down because of differences within the university.

Moreover, as noted above, sport can illustrate important values and express critical standards that apply elsewhere. Social scientist Michael Putnam, author of the widely discussed study *Bowling Alone,* has provided data indicating (to his own disappointment) that the greater the ethnic and racial diversity within a neighborhood, the more trust among residents tends to be diminished. However, further work by such writers as James Q. Wilson maintains that sports teams counter this general rule because in sport, participants from diverse ethnic, racial, ideological, and socioeconomic backgrounds work together for a common cause. As a result, team members form bonds despite their differences. Athletic teams may be ahead of much of the rest of society in this respect, setting a standard for the rest of society to emulate.[26]

Accordingly, because of the intensity and high level of the competition, intercollegiate athletics can serve as a common medium through which large and diverse segments of the academic community can demonstrate and appreciate excellent performance and the struggle to meet challenges. Michael Oriad, a professor of English at Oregon State University, captured the effects of his institution's basketball program and its then-coach, Ralph Miller, when he wrote,

> My colleagues and I recognize the most important functions of the university to be teaching, research, and service. . . . But on Friday or Saturday night from December through March, we cannot conceive of a finer place to be than in Gill Coliseum watching what the locals have termed the Orange Express. . . . Most of us never appreciated the art of passing until we saw how O.S.U. executes it. . . . It is a particular kind of excellence that our basketball team exhibits and that most appeals to us. Ralph Miller speaks the truth when he calls himself not a coach but a teacher, and we teachers in other disciplines appreciate what his pupils have learned to do.[27]

Our discussion suggests, then, that even if, contrary to Brand's suggestion, intercollegiate athletics are not strictly part of an education in the way the classroom experience is, they add a desirable educational component to the university and can even reinforce central academic values. Of course, our account has been highly intellectual and is not meant to deny that intercollegiate athletics can provide other benefits to the academic community as well. These benefits include opportunities for relaxation, to make new friends and meet different kinds of people, to promote a sense of community on campus, and, as Peter French has argued, to entertain local, regional, and sometimes national audiences.

In all fairness to critics of intercollegiate sports, this model of athletics does not easily fit the major intercollegiate athletic programs found at the athletic pinnacle of Division I. The institutions that come closest to meeting it most probably are schools like those in the Ivy League; perhaps other major universities that award athletic scholarships but have strong academic reputations, such as Duke, Notre Dame, and Stanford; and many of the institutions in Division III (the largest division within the NCAA), where athletic scholarships are not awarded, athletes take the same courses as other students, and athletics is regarded as complementary to the educational program.

Our discussion suggests, then, that an important case can be made for the thesis that where athletes have a legitimate chance to get a good education and academic values are honored, intercollegiate athletics can reinforce those values in a variety of ways. Athletics and academics need not be incompatible; instead, they can and should be mutually reinforcing. Where athletically elite Division I institutions fail to meet proper standards and promote coherence of academic and athletic goals, the values implicit in mutual coherence provide grounds for criticism of their policies and practices.

However, although it may be comforting to think of intercollegiate athletics at some schools (such as members of the Ivy League and Division III of the NCAA) as pure and pristine, at least compared to the kind of problems that have plagued big-time intercollegiate athletics, some recent criticism has called even that assumption into question. This criticism goes directly to the heart of the claim that athletics can enhance academics and have a significant educational role to play at many institutions of higher education.

Do Intercollegiate Athletics Fail the Game of Life?

In their book *The Game of Life: College Sports and Educational Values*, James L. Shulman and William G. Bowen, officers of the prestigious Mellon Foundation (Bowen is also a former president of Princeton University), use material from an extensive database comparing the academic performance of athletes and students at large as well as their careers after college. They conclude that intercollegiate athletics is at least as harmful at the Ivy League universities and highly selective liberal arts colleges than they are at large universities with high-profile athletic programs.[28]

Critics point out that at smaller, more academically selective schools, athletes constitute a high percentage of the student body, as much as 30 to 40 percent.[29] In the late 1950s athletes at the schools Shulman and Bowen studied performed well academically, often better than their peers. This, the authors of *The Game of Life* maintain, is no longer so. Furthermore, they suggest that if athletes are given too great an admissions advantage and perform much worse academically than their classmates, they can drag down the academic atmosphere of the whole institution. Shulman and Bowen propose that a "culture of athletics," a kind of "jock culture," exacerbates this problem. This culture, they point out, apart from its consequences, may be inherently in conflict with academic values.

Although the highly selective schools in the book's database may not be typical of the majority of institutions of higher education, these schools have an importance larger than their numbers would indicate. Not only are they widely regarded as academic standard-bearers, but they also appear to have resisted the temptations inherent in major intercollegiate sports. Many observers will conclude that if intercollegiate sports are harmful even in such a context, nowhere in higher education can they be a positive educational and ethical influence.

Much of the argument of *The Game of Life* rests on statistical comparisons between athletes and nonathletes in terms of academic performance while in school and achievements after graduation. Because the argument is based on an exhaustive analysis of a major database, it cannot fully be analyzed here; however, we can look at some of the questions about methodology that go well beyond one particular study.

Although it may seem methodologically sound to compare the academic performance of athletes to those of nonathletes at colleges and universities, we need to be careful about the conclusions we draw from such a comparison. Suppose the athletes do worse than students at large. Does this mean the academic stature of the student body could be raised if we stopped giving admissions preferences to talented athletes who applied?[30]

Not necessarily. Much depends on how much preference is given and on who would have been accepted if athletic talent was not taken into positive consideration in the admissions process. If schools are comparing academically less-qualified athletes not to potential academic superstars but to applicants who are academically weaker, then the applicants who would have replaced the athletes might not have done all that well either.

To assess the effect of athletics on the academic stature of the student body, we also would need to consider another issue, one not given significant attention in *The Game of Life*, namely, the extent to which a competitive athletic program might attract athletes, as well as nonathletes who are fans of intercollegiate athletics, who are outstanding students and who want to participate in intercollegiate athletics at a respectable level of competition. This was brought home to Robert L. Simon in the spring of 2001 when an excellent student in his seminar, who was also a top player on Hamilton College's women's basketball and softball teams, remarked after he had summarized *The Game of Life* for the class that "I would never have come here if I hadn't been a recruited athlete." Thus, in evaluating the effect of athletics on academics, one must consider not only weaker students who would not have been admitted if they had not been athletes but also top students who would have attended other institutions if they had not been attracted by the opportunities to participate in athletics or to be a spectator at athletic competitions at the school where they matriculated.

Finally, it is important to remember that the academic performance of many, perhaps most, athletes does not differ significantly from the performance of other students, as suggested by data in *The Game of Life* itself. In fact, Shulman and Bowen's data suggest that female athletes do as well academically as other students, on average, and that—again, on average—the academic performance of male athletes in many sports does not differ much from that of other students. The widest divergence from the performance of the overall student body probably is in male high-profile sports, where the population of student athletes is also more socioeconomically diverse than the student body as a whole.

This raises the issue of whether the recruitment of athletes might contribute to the diversity of an institution's student body. We have already seen, for example, that African Americans are disproportionately represented on the major sports teams of athletically elite Division I schools. In their analysis in *The Game of Life* Shulman and Bowen find a much more modest contribution at the schools in their sample, presumably because less weight is given to athletics in recruiting at those schools than in big-time college athletics and because the majority of student athletes at such schools play lower-profile sports, such as golf, lacrosse, tennis, and crew, that historically have not always attracted or been open to minority participation.

However, by considering diversity among all athletes, the study may have underemphasized how high-profile men's sports can contribute to diversity.

In particular, male student athletes in high-profile sports such as football do disproportionately tend to come from socioeconomic backgrounds that gave them fewer advantages in life than other students enjoyed. Sometimes those very same high-profile men's sports are the ones in which the academic performance of the student athletes is least satisfactory. But if athletes in high-profile sports tend to do less well than others academically, this may be due to a complex combination of factors, including their somewhat different educational backgrounds, their cultural attitudes, and the amount of time serious commitment to intercollegiate athletics requires.

Our discussion suggests that measuring the effect of athletic recruitment at academically selective schools is a complex matter. Because Shulman and Bowen may not have given adequate attention to some of these complexities, the quantitative analysis underlying *The Game of Life*, although raising issues of concern, arguably is not always compelling. But rather than focusing simply on quantitative analysis, important as it is, let us turn to more philosophical criticisms of the claim that athletics and academics can be mutually reinforcing.

The "Culture of Athletics" and Academics

At a large state university athletes may constitute a small percentage of students simply because the institution is so large. As we have seen, that may not be true at smaller Division III schools, such as liberal arts colleges, or even at Ivy League colleges. If athletes' values and attitudes are different from other students' values and attitudes and inimical to the educational mission of the institution, then a critical mass of athletes can negatively affect the educational atmosphere of an institution apart from their academic performance as individuals. In other words, "jock culture" and academic culture, the argument goes, may be in conflict.

Thus, Shulman and Bowen identified a cluster of traits characterizing a culture of athletics. Although they did not precisely define this culture, they noted that athletes have a tendency to socialize mainly with other athletes, to pursue different majors from those pursued by the rest of the student population, and, for male athletes especially, to focus more on financial success after college than do other students. They claim that youngsters' early specialization into particular sports, recruiting policies that reward such specialization, and athletes' consequent estrangement from the academic missions of their institutions fosters this culture of athletics.

Although the idea that a culture of athletics adversely affects athletes' academic performance may be plausible as a partial explanation, it is questionable whether it is the whole story or even the most significant part of the story. This kind of explanation suggests that athletes, even at highly selective and academically demanding institutions, lack a true commitment to academic success. But surely the picture may be more complex than this conclusion implies.

Institutional factors built into selective colleges and universities may also play a significant role, as might cultural factors having little to do with athletics. For example, athletes whose parents did not go to college or who attended different sorts of institutions may be unaccustomed to interaction with faculty, particularly during their freshman year.[31] These are the very students who might be most in need of academic support from professors, but they may not know how to go about getting it.[32] Even worse, if too many faculty members exhibit outright disdain for intercollegiate athletics or, more likely, are indifferent to athletes, players may sense this and be more reluctant than other students are to seek help from those faculty members. Again, because review sessions or outside lectures may be scheduled during practice or game times, athletes may be more likely than others are to miss them. Moreover, the amount of time and energy that goes into athletic training may be more demanding than many other kinds of extracurricular commitments. It is unclear, then, just how much "jock culture," assuming it exists, affects academic performance and whether it has a greater or lesser effect than other explanatory factors.

Should the culture of athletics be viewed primarily negatively, as in *The Game of Life*, or is a more positive assessment plausible? For example, is there an ideal distribution of students across concentrations, let alone of values or career goals, that institutions should seek to foster? If not, why should we regard the culture of athletics as negatively as the critics suggest?

Thus, *The Game of Life* suggests that athletes, both male and female, increasingly tend to have more conservative values than their peers. But surely the different values attributed to some athletes can be a contribution to diversity on campus, at least if "diversity" is not understood in a narrow and partisan way. If so, athletic recruiting not only can contribute a degree of socioeconomic diversity to a campus, as suggested above, but can contribute to a potentially intellectually fruitful mix of values within the academic community as well.

Athletics and Educational Values

Let us return more directly to what might be called the academic defense against the Incompatibility Thesis. According to this defense, athletics, properly structured, are not only compatible with academic values but may enhance and reinforce them. This point was defended earlier when it was argued that an athletic contest, conceived of as a mutual quest for excellence through challenge, is educational or has educational components closely related to academic virtues. Let us analyze this point from another direction.

Surely, a major part of intellectual inquiry is a willingness to question what often is taken for granted, including one's own cherished beliefs. We often find that our own students, at least when they are new to philosophy, are quite good at articulating their own views but less than satisfactory at anticipating serious objections to their own positions and meeting the challenges that a thoughtful critic would present. Similar behavior on the athletic field can lead to the serious underestimation of an opponent or overestimation of one's own ability, misjudgments that are often made all too visible to participants and spectators alike through exposure in competitive contests.

This indicates that the kind of intellectual honesty and respect for truth so crucial for intellectual inquiry are closely related to similar virtues necessary for athletic success and personal improvement in sport. Participation in competitive athletics can require intellectual honesty and a concern for truth, including accuracy about one's own values and talents, in ways parallel to academic inquiry.

Thus, participation in competitive athletics conducted within a defensible educational and ethical set of requirements can be educational in its own right. And although there need not always be a causal relationship between the development of these virtues in one context (say, in athletics) and in the other (say, academics), there also is no reason why these qualities should not be mutually reinforcing, given the proper emphasis from coaches and professors. Even where the connection is not causal, as noted earlier, athletics, when properly conducted, may illustrate and exhibit the importance of such values as intellectual honesty and critical reflection on performance and provide standards for criticizing those who might reject such values. Perhaps if both coaches and academic faculty alike made a greater attempt to emphasize the common values central to both academics and athletics, athletics and academics might, in the right circumstances, be mutually reinforcing rather than antithetical to each other.

Our discussion so far has associated the academic mission of undergraduate education with the promotion of critical inquiry, which involves understanding major achievements in different fields, mastery of critical tools needed to assess them, and the ability to apply those tools in evaluating and assessing major positions in a variety of fields and disciplines. This does not mean, however, that colleges and universities should have as their primary role the replication of more and more professors. It is important and even essential that students develop enthusiasm for some intellectual pursuit or activity, but it does not follow that the goal of undergraduate education is simply to produce scholars.

Surely one additional major goal is to train people to function as intelligent and committed citizens in a democracy. If so, many of the skills learned in sport and developed through competition (and expressed to spectators through scheduled contests) can contribute to that objective. These would include learning teamwork skills, including how to cooperate with those very different from oneself in pursuit of a common enterprise; learning to appreciate achievement (including that of opponents); and learning to view opponents as persons who contribute to one's own development. Our democracy might be much healthier if many of the attitudes the ethical athlete would have toward a worthy opponent, as outlined in Chapters 2 and 3, were also applied toward those who engage in reasonable debate within the democratic process.

Finally, let us suggest, however tentatively, a contribution that competitive athletics make to liberal arts colleges that is too often ignored. The contribution we have in mind is *ethical*. Competitive sport is, by its very nature, a value-laden activity. If carried out properly, such sports involve fair play, respect for opponents, and understanding and appreciation of and even reverence for the traditions, practices, and values central to one's sport. Sport at its best is an unalienated activity participants engage in for its own sake as well as for whatever external rewards participation may promote. As many scholars of sport have argued, concern for external rewards crowds out the love of the game, often corrupts sport's internal values, and lead to many of the excesses of commercialized big-time sport in the United States.

However, the kinds of institutions that are best equipped to promote harmony between athletics and academics, such as many of the institutions studied in *The Game of Life*, are just the ones where the participants play primarily for love of the game and where commercialization is minimal. Although it remains controversial whether participation in athletics at these institutions actually makes the participants more ethical than they would be otherwise, whether in sport or in unrelated activities, competitive sport arguably can express or illustrate these values to a wider community. Thus, competitive sport at such institutions exemplifies the pursuit of an activity for its own sake and illustrates the attempt to meet challenges simply for the sake of testing oneself and learning from the test. As such, it stands in contrast to a crude sort of utilitarianism approach that asks what everything is good for in terms of immediate payoffs or to a view that rejects achievement and standards of excellence as arbitrary or mere matters of opinion. Of course, other activities, especially in the arts, also do the same. The suggestion here is not that athletics are unique in the way suggested but only that their role in illustrating, expressing, and possibly reinforcing important values is significant and should not be ignored. The French philosopher Albert Camus was making an important point of general educational relevance when he remarked that the only context in which he really learned ethics was sport.[33]

Concluding Comments

The principal thesis of this chapter has been that although academic values and intercollegiate athletics may often be in conflict, especially at the athletically elite colleges and universities that pursue national recognition at the top of Division I, this conflict is far from inevitable. Athletics can too often be the tail that wags the academic dog, as was indicated by one university president who, when seeking funds before a state legislature, was said to have stated, "We need to build a university our football team can be proud of." But athletics, properly integrated into the academic community, can also fill important and valuable functions. In the proper context intercollegiate athletics can even enhance and reinforce the institution's academic mission.

This academic defense is probably best realized within the framework of institutions that do not offer athletic scholarships and tend to integrate athletics into the overall academic community. This does not mean that athletic programs, even at colleges and universities that most exemplify the model of the mutual quest for excellence—let alone those of many Division I athletic powerhouses—are fine just as they are. However, our discussion suggests that harsh criticism of intercollegiate athletics, though justifiable in some specific instances, may be far too bleak when applied across the board and regardless of context. The role of athletics in academia can and should continue to be subject to critical scrutiny, but at the same time we should not ignore athletics' positive contribution to many college and university communities as well as the educational experiences athletics provide in their own right.

QUESTIONS FOR REVIEW

1. What do you take to be the major educational mission of the university? Explain the view that intercollegiate athletics undermines or subverts the educational mission of the university. Do you agree? How would you support your view?
2. Do you agree that coaches teach students to simply obey authority, whereas professors teach students to think critically? More broadly, do intercollegiate athletics promote values opposing those presupposed in the classroom?
3. Explain and assess the defenses of intercollegiate athletics proposed by Peter French and then by Myles Brand.
4. On what grounds do the authors argue that intercollegiate athletics, properly conducted, support and reinforce important educational values central to academics at colleges and universities? How would you assess their position?

5. Do you support intercollegiate athletics in its current state, or would you recommend eliminating it or reforming it? If you are in favor of reform, what specific reforms would you suggest?

Notes

1. Rev. John LoSchiavo, "Trying to Save a University's Priceless Assets," *New York Times*, August 1, 1982, S2.

2. NCAA Infractions Report on the University of Minnesota, October 24, 2000, 2, http://fs.ncaa.org/Docs/NCAANewsArchive/2000/division+i/infractions%2Bcase_%2Buniversity%2Bof%2Bminnesota,%2Btwin%2Bcities%2B-%2B11-6-00.html.

3. See George Dohrmann and Thayer Evans, "The Money: Payments, Bonuses and Sham Jobs," *Sports Illustrated* 119, no. 11 (September 16, 2013): 34–41.

4. *Report of the Special Investigative Counsel Regarding the Actions of Pennsylvania State University Related to the Child Sexual Abuse Committed by Gerald A. Sandusky*, 14, www.thefreehreportonpsu.com/REPORT_FINAL_071212.pdf.

5. Likewise, we also note that while Paterno's role in the affair is morally questionable, he may well have had no motive for participating in a cover-up, as many sources on the Penn State campus confirm that for several years there was, to say the least, no love lost between Paterno and Sandusky and that the football program might well have been best served by exposing the wrong-doing.

6. Reports on graduation rates are issued annually by the NCAA and are broken down into various categories. The information in the text is from Steve Wieberg, "Off Court, Top Teams Fall Short," *USA Today*, October 18, 2002, 1c. Data collected by the NCAA on graduation rates, costs of intercollegiate athletics, and other areas of interest can be found at www.ncaa.org and then selecting "Research."

7. John Stuart Mill is famous for defending freedom of thought and discussion in his *On Liberty* (1859) by arguing that such freedom gives us the opportunity to correct our ideas when they are false and strengthen them and, therefore, appreciate them more fully when they are true.

8. Quoted in Ira Berkow, "College Factories and Their Output," *New York Times*, January 18, 1983, D25.

9. See, for example, the discussion in James L. Shulman and William G. Bowen, *The Game of Life: College Sports and Educational Values* (Princeton, NJ: Princeton University Press, 2001), esp. xv–xxiv.

10. The NCAA's reports on graduation rates can be found at www.ncaa.org and then selecting "Research." For a summary of recent data, including figures provided in the text, see Earl Christianson, "D1's Men's Basketball, FBS Football Graduation Rates Highest Ever," *NCAA News*, October 25, 2012. For another useful summary of the full report, see George Schroeder, "Notre Dame, SEC Also Win in the Classroom," *USA Today Sports*, October 25, 2012, www.usatoday.com/story/sports/ncaaf/2012/10/25/ncaa-graduation-rates-notre-dame-sec-college-football/1656329/. Keep in mind, however, that, as we point out in the text, the NCAA's method of calculating graduation rates may, to some degree, inflate the success of its member institutions in graduating their athletes.

11. "NCAA Revenues and Expenses of Division I Athletic Programs," 2004–2012, 13, www.ncaapublications.com/productdownloads/D12011REVEXP.pdf.

12. "Restoring the Balance: Dollars, Values and the Future of College Sports," The Knight Commission, 2010, www.knightcommission.org/restoringthebalance.

13. See Harry Edwards, *Sociology of Sport* (Homeward, IL: Dorsey Press, 1973), esp. 198, for a critique of genetic explanations for the disproportionate participation of African American athletes in many sports.

14. A Louis Harris Poll released in 1990 reported that 55 percent of black high school athletes expected to play ball in college, and 43 percent said they could make it in professional sports. Only 39 percent of whites thought they would play in college, and just 16 percent thought they would compete at the professional level. In reality only about 3 percent of high school athletes make it in college sports, and only 1 in 10,000 go on to compete at the professional level. This poll was reported in *NCAA News* 27, no. 41 (November 19, 1990): 16. On the positive side, the survey also reported that participation in sport may help reduce racial barriers, as 70 percent of the responding athletes said they had become friends with team members from another racial or ethnic group. Moreover, 74 percent of black athletes, a higher percentage than for whites, claimed that participation in sport helped to keep them away from drugs.

15. See, in particular, John Hoberman, *Darwin's Athletes: How Sports Has Damaged Black America and Preserved the Myth of Race* (New York: Houghton Mifflin, 1998).

16. Peter French, *Ethics and College Sports: Ethics, Sports, and the University* (Lanham, MD: Rowman and Littlefield, 2004), 115.

17. Ibid., 116.

18. For example, NCAA graduation statistics for the 1987–1992 period show 68 percent of female athletes graduating, compared to a roughly 58 percent graduation rate for other female students. Male athletes, even in high-profile sports, graduate at very high rates at such Division I scholarship institutions as Notre Dame and Stanford.

19. Myles Brand, "The Role and Value of Intercollegiate Athletics in Universities," *Journal of the Philosophy of Sport* 33, no. 1 (2007): 10.

20. Ibid., 11.

21. We owe this point to Robert L. Simon's former student Sarah Wissel.

22. Robert L. Simon argues more fully for these points in his paper "Does Athletics Undermine Academics? Examining Some Issues," *Journal of Intercollegiate Sport* 1, no. 1 (2008): 40–58.

23. For criticism of the claim of uniqueness for athletics, including cogent objections to some of the comments advanced in earlier publications by Robert L. Simon, see J. S. Russell, "Broad Internalism and the Moral Foundation of Sport," in *Ethics in Sport*, ed. William J. Morgan (Champaign, IL: Human Kinetics Press, 2007), 51–66.

24. For such a view, see Leslie P. Francis, "Title IX: Equality for Women's Sports?" in *Philosophic Inquiry in Sport*, ed. William J. Morgan and Klaus V. Meier (Champaign, IL: Human Kinetics Press, 1995), 305–315. Francis defended Title IX as necessary to provide fairness in an ethically suspect practice, intercollegiate athletics, but suggested that replacing intercollegiate athletics with intramurals would, in many contexts, be desirable. See, especially, p. 312 of her article.

25. Paul Weiss, *Sport: A Philosophic Inquiry* (Carbondale: Southern Illinois University Press, 1969), 10–13.

26. J. Q. Wilson, "Bowling with Others," *Commentary* 124 (2007): 31.

27. Michael Oriad, "At Oregon State, Basketball Is Pleasing, Not Alarming," *New York Times*, March 8, 1981, S2.

28. Shulman and Bowen, *The Game of Life*. Shulman and Bowen drew from an extensive database involving cohorts of graduates from the institutions they studied from the years 1951, 1976, and 1989 as well as from some recent but less complete studies from the 1990s.

These institutions included academically respected Division I universities such as Duke and Penn State, the Ivy League schools, selective women's colleges such as Smith, and small, coed, selective liberal arts colleges such as Williams, Swarthmore, Denison, and Robert L. Simon's own institution, Hamilton. The same database was the basis for another widely discussed book, *The Shape of the River*, in which Bowen and former Harvard president Derek Bok defended affirmative action programs in the colleges and universities they studied. See William G. Bowen and Derek Bok, *The Shape of the River: Long-Term Consequences of Considering Race in College and University Admissions* (Princeton, NJ: Princeton University Press, 2000).

29. For a critical discussion of *The Game of Life* that focuses primarily on methodology, see Hal Scott, "What Game Are They Playing?" *Journal of College and University Law* 28, no. 3 (2002): 719–755. Material in the text is drawn from Robert L. Simon's own review of *The Game of Life* in the *Journal of the Philosophy of Sport* 29, no. 1 (2002): 87–95.

30. The failure to explore this issue is especially surprising. In *The Shape of the River*, a study of the effects of affirmative action based on material from the same database as that discussed in *The Game of Life*, Bowen and Bok did consider such a comparison, although admittedly not in depth. Their tentative conclusion was that students admitted under considerations of affirmative action were not displacing other applicants with vastly superior qualifications but rather were competing for spots with less qualified candidates (pp. 37–38). Although their discussion of this issue was quite brief, their tentative conclusion certainly was suggestive. For if it also is true to a significant extent that preferred athletes generally are displacing other applicants who are relatively weak academically, then it is far from clear that the effects of admitting athletes on the academic climate is as great as *The Game of Life* suggests.

31. For example, according to data from *The Game of Life*, in the 1989 cohort at coed liberal arts colleges only 59 percent of the high-profile athletes had fathers with bachelor's degrees, compared to 82 percent of students at large, and at the Division 1A private universities only 53 percent of the athletes had fathers with bachelor's degrees, compared to 78 percent of the students at large (see Shulman and Bowen, *Game of Life*, 51).

32. Shulman and Bowen found that athletes with faculty mentors outperformed other athletes academically, but are there institutional obstacles to the development of such a relationship (see *Game of Life*, 71–74)? If so, athletes' underperformance might be in significant part a result of experiences of indifference or rejection (as well as other institutional factors that might need to be considered) rather than being due largely to lack of academic commitment on their own part.

33. Albert Camus, "The Wager of Our Generation," in *Resistance, Rebellion, and Death*, trans. Justin O'Brien (New York: Vintage Books, 1960), 242.

=7=

The Commercialization of Sport

MARKETING AND CORRUPTION IN COMPETITIVE ATHLETICS

A t its very best, competitive sport can express a quest for human excellence, exhibit beauty, and create excitement and drama that fascinate millions of people throughout the world. But is its popularity its Achilles's heel? High-profile sporting events, top athletes, and dramatic athletic contests, at least in popular sports, are in demand. People want to see such events, sometimes identify with sports stars, and show tremendous loyalty to the teams or individuals with whom they identify. But because elite sports are in demand, they become something people will pay to see. In other words, sports have become more than a mutual quest for excellence: market forces have transformed them into a commodity. Good sports, as well as frequently mediocre and even bad sports, sell!

Top professional athletes and coaches in popular sports make many millions of dollars in a season, often many, many times more than teachers, college presidents, oncologists, to say nothing of the president of the United States. Professional sports franchises can be worth hundreds of millions of dollars or more. Even at the level of college sports in the United States, high-profile Division I football and basketball are often defended based on the supposed revenue they generate. High-profile athletes provide entertainment and, like other entertainers, can have a huge impact on fans of all ages. Sport dominates the mass media, and television rights to major events, such as the NCAA Men's Basketball Championships, sell for billions. It is no coincidence that sport is now referred to as another "industry" and fans are portrayed as "consumers."

Sport, then, is not only engaged in by athletes at various levels of play; elite sports, including major professional sports, also have become commercial institutions, with governing bodies and business with other than sporting interests.

Has this commercialization of sport been for good or ill? What sort of ethical problems does it raise? Has sport, as many critics have charged, been corrupted by its role in the world of commerce and markets? Has it become just another commodity, something to be bought and sold, and has this commercialization not only robbed it of its defining character but also damaged the internal values that make sport a significant area of achievement and endeavor?

In this chapter we will examine selected issues arising from the commercialization of sport. In particular, we will explore claims that the commercialization of sport has led to its corruption, then look at specific issues raised by attempts to "market" sports to a mass audience.

The Corruption Thesis: The Corruption of Sport by Commerce

A persistent theme in the writings of many critics of modern sport is that today the marketplace has corrupted sport.[1] What does this claim mean? The term "corruption" refers to decay, a falling off from an original and perhaps noble purpose. We can understand corruption to mean that the values internal to sport, such as those of fair competition, sportsmanship, and perhaps the mutual quest for excellence, are being or already have been undermined by the growing commercialization of sport.

One area of concern is the relationship between the mass marketing of sports and participation by masses of people. Critics have argued that the emphasis on elite athletes and the marketing of elite sports contests, along with coverage by mass media, have had a harmful effect on the ordinary person's participation in sports. For example, in his provocative and readable book *Sports in America*, James Michener warned that "we place an undue emphasis on the gifted athletes fifteen to twenty-two, a preposterous emphasis on a few professionals aged twenty-three to thirty-five, and never enough on the mass of our population aged twenty-three to seventy-five."[2] Michener's book was published in 1976; since then the number of physically active people in the United States has declined. The situation is nothing short of extremely alarming. According to the Centers for Disease Control and Prevention, in 2011 only 20.6 percent of adults eighteen years of age and over "met the Physical Activity Guidelines for both aerobic and muscle-strengthening physical activity."[3]

Perhaps the greatest concern is that the commercialization of sport actually corrupts the sport itself. For example, rule changes can be introduced that make the game more entertaining for the mass of fans who do not understand the nuances of the game. These changes can make the game more marketable, but they also can take away from the subtlety of the game or the skill needed to play it. For example, the introduction of the designated hitter into Major League Baseball may have made the game more exciting to fans who wanted more action and more frequent home runs, but, arguably, it minimized subtle strategic decisions, such as whether to have someone pinch-hit for a pitcher or have the pitcher sacrifice through a bunt, and it may also have contributed to the cheapening of the home run.

Perhaps an even better example is the kind of loose officiating that observers claim has become commonplace in the National Basketball Association. Critics charge that NBA officiating allows stars to score more points but also allows them to get away with what ordinarily would be rule violations, such as traveling with the ball, thus minimizing skills but maximizing sales.

Commercialization can affect sporting contests in other ways too. For example, "TV time-outs," designed to stop play to allow commercials to show on televised broadcasts, disrupt the flow of many games, particularly in professional and college basketball, and can even affect outcomes by allowing less well-conditioned teams to recover during the many additional breaks in the action. This kind of intrusion can conflict with the best overall interpretation of a given sport, affecting its aesthetic dimension as well as diminishing the importance of some skills or physical conditioning. Television also seems to dictate the scheduling of many high-visibility college sports events, often without regard to either participating athletes' academic obligations or whether the timing of the game will allow for peak performance. This suggests that many times key decisions appear to be made based mainly on commercial interests instead of on the internal values of sport and the interpretation that best portray them.

Indeed, the role of money in sport can cut very deeply, especially in professional sports, because the wealthiest teams often find it easier to win. As some critics of sport have concluded, "Commodification is pathological when it leads to the violation of the . . . meanings of the central culture of the game."[4] Isn't the entire ethic of competition undermined when the richest teams can buy the best players and, in effect, field a vastly superior team before the game has even begun? Although the success of the New York Yankees over decades has led to the phenomenon of Yankee hating, especially virulent in Boston and dramatized in the 1950s hit musical *Damn Yankees*, it seems more understandable in recent years when the Yankees, as one of the wealthiest franchises in Major League Baseball, can simply outbid other teams for the best players.

Similarly, the desire for profits can lead sports franchises to seek special legal status that exempt them from antitrust laws. This in turn can lead sport franchises to operate as monopolies. The desire for profits is also seen in relocating teams and expanding leagues. For instance, Major League Soccer (MLS) started play with ten teams in 1996. Since then it has expanded several times into new markets, reaching Canada in 2006. MLS will count twenty teams in 2015, and its goal is to have twenty-four teams by 2020.[5]

Other developments such as the establishment of longer and longer seasons can also be understood as the product of increasing interest in financial gain. Some observers believe that the trend to prolong seasons devalues regular season games, puts undue emphasis on postseason play, and sacrifices the accurate measurement and determination of athletic excellence to promote values such as excitement, entertainment, and drama. In other words, for these observers the playoff system deemphasizes the internal goods of sport.[6] Another and perhaps even more troubling example of the corrupting danger of money in sport is the recent New Orleans Saints' bounty system, in which some of its defensive players were paid bonuses out of a slush fund for deliberately injuring opponents.

The influence of money can also change the relationship between fans and players. As professional sports become more and more commercially oriented, players can be viewed as commodities to be bought, sold, and traded from team to team. As a result, they may be seen less as persons and more as products and viewed as defective if they do not produce high performance on the field. As the income available to sports stars surpasses that of the average fan many times over, fans may become alienated from players, who may be viewed (sometimes, but far from always, with justification) as spoiled, inaccessible, and remote. Because professional teams aim at making a profit, tickets may be priced beyond the means of traditional fan bases, thereby creating even more alienation. Many fans have indeed been priced out of the sports market altogether.

As sports become more entertaining but perhaps less nuanced, they may draw new fans to the game who lack knowledge and respect for its defining internal values, traditions, and ethos. These less-educated fans may contribute to a steamroller effect in which their sport is changed more and more frequently to become ever more entertaining but at the price of important principles that make the game challenging and traditions that have been part of its history. Thus, baseball authorities may have been reluctant to enact strict rules for testing players for performance-enhancing drugs because such drug use may lead to stronger players and more home runs. Home runs are exciting, and so more home runs may be thought to attract more fans, but, as we suggested earlier, in the long run drug use may cheapen the value of the home run, lessen the challenge of the game, and make comparisons to the performances of stars of the past impossible.

These remarks suggest what might be called the Corruption Thesis. This thesis states that the commercialization of sport, the transformation of elite sport into a product that can be bought and sold, corrupts sport. This is because the kinds of values that broad internalists (see Chapter 2) would regard as central to sport can conflict with the market value of sport. As William J. Morgan has argued, commercialization installs market values, such as the pursuit of money and fame, "as the proper ends of sporting practices thereby depriving their practitioners of any reason, let alone a compelling one, to value or engage the particular competitive challenges they present, the select athletic skills they call upon, and the human qualities and virtues they excite."[7]

Athletic excellence, according to Morgan and other proponents of the Corruption Thesis, thus becomes only an instrument to achieving external goods of sport such as fame, power, and wealth. The importance of internal goods, those skills and excellences created by the practice that are intelligible only by references to its rules and the challenges they present, is diminished or regarded as only instrumental to more important extrinsic rewards. What is entertaining is what sells, but it might not necessarily be good sport.

Morgan illustrated this point in his 2006 book, *Why Sports Morally Matter*, by describing a change in attitudes he has observed in his students over the years in a class he teaches on ethics and sport. In the past his students were able to relate to ideas of sportsmanship and respect for the internal values of sports, such as appreciation for the challenge of the game, its constitutive skills, traditions, and core values. Today, however, more students seem to regard sports as simply means to external ends and the rules as something to be manipulated for one's own advantage.[8]

In an attempt to combat the more recent cynicism toward the internal values of sport, Morgan told his class about the famous 1967 international championship tennis match between Hungarian Istvan Gulyas and the Czech star Jan Kukal. At a key point in the match Kukal collapsed on the court with severe cramps. Although Gulyas was entitled to the win if Kukal could not resume play within a required time period, Gulyas persuaded the officials to give Kukal the extra time he needed for recovery. Kukal not only recovered but eventually won the match!

Morgan expected his students to admire Gulyas's unselfishness and sportsmanship. (Remember the quotation cited in Chapter 2 when David Duval stated that if he was playing Tiger Woods for a major golf championship, he would want Tiger to be playing his best so that a victory over him would be truly significant.) Morgan was shocked to find out, however, that his students not only did not endorse Gulyas's generous action but actually condemned it. On his view, this was because the students had not accepted the basic internal values of competition in sport (or, in terms of this book, the idea of sport as a mutual quest for excellence) but instead viewed sport through an egoistic— that is, self-interested and self-serving—lens.

"Because the students' only apparent vocabulary for evaluating actions in sports was in terms of their positive (benefits) or negative (costs) effects on the aims and desires of the individuals who play them," Morgan wrote, "Gulyas's strategic misuse of the rules was mistakenly branded as a moral failure."[9] Although we have not noticed such a dramatic change in our own students' moral attitudes toward sport, perhaps because we teach at institutions that compete in Division III of the NCAA rather than at an athletically elite Division I sports power, there is little doubt that many participants and fans alike have adopted the purely instrumental attitude toward sports that concerns Morgan.

The dismissal of Gulyas's unselfish and sportsmanlike behavior as detrimental to his interest reminds us of the criticism to markets recently advanced by Michael J. Sandel in his book *What Money Can't Buy: The Moral Limits of Markets*.[10] Sandel argues that one of the reasons why people should worry about living in a society in which everything has been transformed into a commodity concerns corruption. Markets, as we have seen, can have a corrosive tendency, mainly in the way we look at and relate to the things up for sale. For Sandel, "That's because markets don't only allocate goods; they also express and promote certain attitudes towards the goods being exchanged."[11] Many times "market values crowd out nonmarket norms worth caring about."[12] This seems to be what happened to Morgan's students along with the legion of sports coaches, athletes, and fans who would agree with them: winning, and the concomitant external goods it usually brings about, are perceived as more valuable than the internal values on which sport rests. This change of attitude, the argument goes, degrades, defiles, or simply corrupts sport. As Sandel maintains, "Markets are not mere mechanisms; they embody certain values."[13] The adoption of these values leads to an attitudinal change, and this, in turn, changes the meaning of social practices, including sport.

Consider one of Sandel's many sports case studies in his book to exemplify how the markets can change the meaning of social practices: naming rights for stadiums. Sports teams have been sources of pride for communities. Their stadiums embody that pride and serve as places for gathering and communion, places to forge a common identity. Although Sandel admits that "It would be an exaggeration to say that naming rights and corporate sponsorship have ruined the experience of rooting for the home team," he affirms that "changing the name of a civic landmark changes its meaning."[14] The public character of sports stadiums could impart lessons in civics (even if only obliquely), inspire social commingling, and remind us all of our commonalities. However, "As stadiums become less like landmarks and more like billboards, their public character fades,"[15] not to mention that ticket prices crowd the less affluent out and luxury boxes are a financial windfall and at the same time a vivid reminder of social inequality. All this represents the antithesis of sports stadiums as relevant civic institutions.

According to the Corruption Thesis, many of the effects of the commercialization of sport cited above, such as the disruption of the flow of televised basketball games by TV time-outs, are simply symptoms of an underlying corruption of sport. According to this general account, because of the undue influence of the economic market on sports, they have been reduced or are in danger of being reduced to a commodity, a means for satisfying our other desires, such as the desire for fame and fortune, rather than remaining valuable activities in their own right with their own ethic of a mutually acceptable challenge and pursuit of excellence through competition.

Is the Corruption Thesis defensible? Has commercialization spoiled sport, as the remarks above suggest, or is there another side to the story? For example, has the mass marketing of sport broadened its appeal and made elite sport accessible to millions of spectators through greater coverage in the media? Let us consider the commercialization-of-sport critique in more detail.

Examining the Corruption Thesis

Participation and Elite Sport

Let us begin with the line of criticism Michener suggested, that we are a nation of spectators rather than participants. Critics of American sport point out that millions of us spend our weekends glued to the television screen, watching football, baseball, basketball, and golf rather than playing a sport ourselves. Moreover, most of us watch sport in relative isolation, as networks such as ESPN bring more and more major games into our homes rather than, say, in the communal setting of a local high school game. Critics see the time devoted to observing sports rather than participating in them as unfortunate not only because of ill effects on the health of those who only sit and watch but also because spectators miss out on the other basic benefits of participation. According to this view, the true result of the "star" system is to drive people from participation on the playing field to the grandstand or, more often, the living room couch, instead.

There is no doubt that many Americans do need to adopt a healthier lifestyle that includes a sound diet and exercise. In 2009–2010 more than one-third of adults and almost 17 percent of children and adolescents in the United States were obese.[16] It is well known that "obesity-related conditions include heart disease, stroke, type 2 diabetes and certain types of cancer."[17] The Centers for Disease Control and Prevention state that obesity "is common, serious and costly."[18] But does emphasis on elite athletes and major sports competitions actually lower participation in sports? After all, there can be many other reasons why people don't exercise, ranging from lack of time to lack of inclination.

In fact, the thesis that emphasis on top athletes reduces participation by the many rests on at least two hidden assumptions, neither of which is clearly correct. First, it is assumed that watching sports tends to preclude participation: spectators tend not to play precisely because they are spectators. But the truth or falsehood of this assumption is hardly obvious. On the contrary, many fans, particularly youngsters, may be motivated to try to emulate the moves of the successful athletes they see on television. What schoolyard basketball player has not tried to copy the moves of Michael Jordan or LeBron James? Spectators may promote participation rather than lower it because they often observe top players' techniques and apply them to their own games. As social critic Christopher Lasch has noted, "It is by watching those who have mastered a sport . . . that we derive standards against which to measure ourselves."[19]

What about the fan who is a spectator only? Here we must be careful not to jump to the conclusion that such individuals are not participants simply because they are fans. Perhaps they wouldn't be participants even if they weren't fans. Maybe they enjoy watching skilled performers but would not be motivated to play themselves even if there were no top athletes to watch. Or perhaps there are inadequate facilities for participation in their area, as is true for many golfers in metropolitan areas. Accordingly, the simple assumption that emphasis on big-time sports and on the skills of an athletic elite reduces mass participation is open to serious question; indeed, the growth in women's participation in athletics since the passage of Title IX indicates that increasing the presentation of elite events in the mass media does not necessarily reduce participation.

Moreover, participation in some outdoor recreational activities is increasing, and this supports the same conclusion. For example, one major survey indicated that the number of people participating in walking as a form of recreation grew from about 93 million in 1982 to over 133 million in 1994–1995. There was a 14 percent increase in those running or jogging and a 16 percent increase in those swimming during the same period. According to a 2009 study over 170 million Americans were participants in physical recreational activities, although some were only occasionally involved.[20] A report on participation in physical activity published in 2012 has a somewhat optimistic yet realistic subtitle that summarized the nation's situation: "Physical Activity: Slight Progress for Some but More Work to be Done."[21] Although the population also grew during this period and perhaps even more people would have participated had they not been glued to the couch watching games on television, data suggest that the effect of elite sport on participation may be much more complex than critics have postulated.

A second assumption about the relationship between participation in sports and watching them is open to even more serious question. According to a moderate version of this second assumption, being a participant in sports is of greater value than being a spectator. Playing is better than watching. In its most extreme form this assumption characterizes watching sporting events as a passive, almost slothful activity that requires minimal intellectual and emotional capacities. The stereotype of the beer-drinking, overweight football fan who spends the whole weekend in front of the television set watching games expresses the disdain in which mere fans are sometimes held.

In rebuttal one might point out that none of us can participate in everything. Most of us are spectators of some practice or other; theater, music, cinema, and dance come immediately to mind. After all, we don't sneer at spectators, commonly known as audiences, at the ballet or a play, even though few members of the audience are also dancers, actors, or musicians.

Moreover, spectators of sports, like audiences in other areas, are often called upon to exercise critical judgment and apply standards of excellence. It is not uncommon at all to hear spectators discussing with a high degree of sophistication about whether a team, sometimes their own, deserved to win. Merit, excellence, and the internal values of sports occupy a prominent place in these discussions. As Lasch has pointed out, "Far from destroying the value of sports, the attendance of spectators makes them complete. Indeed, one of the virtues of contemporary sports lies in their resistance to the erosion of standards and their capacity to appeal to a knowledgeable audience."[22]

Consider, for example, a fine double play executed at a crucial point in a pressure-packed baseball game. An observer unacquainted with baseball might appreciate the grace and fluidity of the players' movements; however, such a spectator could not see the movements as examples of excellence at baseball. To such an uninformed spectator, a botched double play would be indistinguishable from a well-executed one, as the failure of the fielder to, say, pivot properly while throwing from second base to first base would be unappreciated.

Thus, it is unclear that watching games is of less value than playing in them, just as it is unclear that appreciating a ballet is less valuable than dancing in it. Indeed, audiences and performers often feed off each other, and superb

performers in the arts as well as in sports find that spectators' reactions enhance their performances.

Even if there is less value in watching than in participating, it is far from
clear that the intelligent observation of sports or of other human activities in
which excellence is demonstrated is without any sort of value at all. Spectators
at sporting events can be rude, ignorant, or passive, but so can audiences of
other kinds. And truly appreciating a competitive athletic contest requires intelligence, observation, and the critical application of standards of excellence.

Some authors even go further than that and argue that watching sport has
the potential to improve people. For instance, Stephen Mumford has recently
maintained that watching sport might allow spectators to reflect about moral
issues and form conceptions about what is morally good or bad, about what constitutes acceptable or unacceptable behavior. He even contends that watching
sport might positively influence people's moral habits.[23] "Sport contrives scenarios for us to watch," Mumford advances, "that we might liken to a contest of
the virtues. When we see the virtues in action, we are able to see their successes
and follow their examples."[24] That is, these virtues can be then carried over to
all sorts of different scenarios in our lives, within and outside sports. We could
add that even when contests go awry and turn into a battle of vices, there is
still the potential for spectators to reflect upon what went wrong, why, and how
that could be avoided. In short, watching sport has educative value. It offers an
opportunity to understand moral life better.

A critic might respond that although such points have force, they are an
intellectualized account of what it is to be a sports fan. Spectators don't just
appreciate good performances; they also root for their teams to win. Indeed,
the atmosphere at an important college basketball game often far more resembles the atmosphere at a revival meeting than that of a seminar on excellence
in sport. As the critics of commercialization have argued, mass audiences have
become less appreciative of excellence and more interested in partying and
being entertained. More and more fans see themselves as consumers out to get
their money's worth and have fun, and this perhaps explains the increase in
their boorish behavior.

Loyalty to our favorite teams and players and expressing emotion in support of them surely play a major role in sport. And why shouldn't they? In
many other areas of life, too, we develop special relationships with the people
and things we care about. This, however, does not imply blind loyalty and
accepting anything our favorite teams and players do. Paraphrasing a popular
saying, "My favorite team or player, right or wrong" is unacceptable. Loyalty
and emotion should not get out of hand. The behavior of fans who go on ram-
pages, destroying property and threatening life, should not be tolerated. Even

when overt violence is absent, the partisan, hostile character of crowds at many sporting events threatens to intimidate visiting players and referees alike.

Thus, it is true that commercialization, along with excessive partisanship, may often attract mass audiences unfamiliar with the nuances of the game and just out for a good time. When combined with the easy availability of alcohol at many contests, the combination may just be a recipe for trouble. Nevertheless, perhaps spectators would act this way even in the absence of mass media and the kind of commercialization we have today, as they may have done, say, at the gladiatorial games in ancient Rome.

Although the critical perspective toward sport that was attributed to fans is only part of the story, and undoubtedly idealized at that, it does serve as a moral and intellectual constraint on the emotionalism generated by excessively provincial fan loyalty, ignorance of the traditions and nuances of the sport, or just plain bad behavior. A moral requirement of good sportsmanship for fans is that they retain their critical perspective. Even though we need not be ashamed of caring about our team's fate and wanting them to win, when we care so much that we become unable to appreciate good play by the opposition, we are not only showing disrespect for the opposing players as persons but also undermining the very justification for athletic competition. If competition in sport should be conceived of as a mutual quest for excellence, then spectators should retain enough detachment to appreciate who best meets the challenge. Otherwise, sport is reduced to a mere means for satisfying our own egos rather than constituting an arena in which spectators and athletes alike can learn and grow by understanding and meeting ever-increasing challenges to their athletic and critical skills.

Fans, then, should be what philosopher Nicholas Dixon calls "moderate partisans," combining loyalty to their team with allegiance to the core internal values of the sport rather than either "total partisans" who care only for their team or "total purists" who are devoted only to excellence but are without loyalty to or affiliation with others.[25] Mumford, however, defends sporting purists, arguing that they wish to see the best version of their sport flourish and that such devotion can rise beyond the limitations of particular allegiances so they emerge more passionate and perhaps even more knowledgeable about their sport than the partisan.[26]

Finally, we must not forget the positive side to commercialization. Commercialization and the mass media have made athletic contests available to large audiences all over the world and, arguably, have made sport more open by making it more accessible to all. The trick is to enjoy this benefit while minimizing the deleterious effects of mass consumption. More will be said about how this might be accomplished later in the chapter.

Our discussion suggests that, first, it is unclear whether emphasis on elite sport in the mass media lowers participation. Second, watching athletic contests may have its own kind of value and also serve educational purposes. Sporting audiences, no less than other audiences, are called upon to appreciate excellence and to apply critical standards of judgment. Emotional bonds to favorite teams and players, when constrained by the norms of respect for persons and appreciation of excellence, can enrich our existence and motivate us to do our best.

The Internal Goods of Sports

We have considered the claim that too much emphasis has been placed on the star athlete and too little on participation by the many. It may remain controversial just how much emphasis is too much, but some important distinctions have emerged from our discussion among the kinds of goods that sport can promote. Michener and others who worry about lack of participation in sport seem focused on what might be regarded as the *basic benefits* of involvement with sport.[27] These benefits involve, for example, better health through exercise, the fun of recreation, and the joy of competition. Presumably, they are available to all participants, not just elite players. The basic benefits are to be contrasted with what have been called the *scarce benefits*, or goods of sport— namely, fame and wealth. By their very nature these are available only to elite stars at the highest levels of athletic competition. Those who worry that we have overemphasized elite athletes' performance fear that the majority of people will lose out on the basic benefits by becoming passive observers of the elite's pursuit of fame and fortune. Those worried about commercialization fear that emphasis on the scarce benefits will corrupt sport.

Our discussion suggests that emphasis on the basic and the scarce benefits of sport alone sets up far too narrow a framework for discussion. In philosophy the questions we ask may determine the answers we consider. In restricting ourselves only to questions about scarce and basic benefits, we may have cut ourselves off from considering the relationships that exist between outstanding performances by the few, on the one hand, and the enjoyment and appreciation of the many, on the other.

In particular, scarce and basic benefits are external to sport; that is, each logically can be conceived and obtained apart from sport itself. They are what we call "external goods." Those who have no understanding of our relationship to sport can understand and obtain goods such as health, fun, fame, and wealth.

In addition to such external goods, we noted in Chapter 3 that there are also values and principles that are *internal* to sport. Often these identify goods of sport that are distinct from both basic and scarce benefits. Goods are internal to a practice or activity when they cannot be understood or enjoyed independently of that practice or activity. For example, the concept of a "home run" is unintelligible apart from the practice and rules of baseball; the elegance of a winning combination in chess cannot be understood or enjoyed without an understanding of the rules and strategy that characterize the game of chess.[28]

The distinction between the internal and external goods of sport is central to our concerns in this chapter because the conformity to standards of excellence implicit in various sports creates shared internal goods available to the whole community. Spectators appreciate and share in the enjoyment of the internal goods top performers create at all levels of athletic competition. Although often ignored by those who fear overemphasis on an athletic elite, skilled participants in sport are as capable of creating internal goods, shared by large numbers of people, as are skilled participants in, say, dance or theater. As argued in the previous section, audiences who can appreciate these goods are no more passive than those who appreciate the arts and humanities.

Thus, when it comes to an evaluation of the Corruption Thesis and the degree to which sport has become commercialized, we need to look at positive as well as negative aspects of commercialization. Perhaps, as argued above, the alleged conflict between benefits for an elite and benefits for large numbers of others has been overstated, and critics of the current sporting scene have not given the attention it deserves to top athletes' role in creating internal goods that unprecedented numbers of observers can appreciate and enjoy.

Does Commercialization Undermine Internal Values?

One of the principal arguments in favor of the Corruption Thesis is that the transformation of elite sport into a commodity is in conflict with the internal goods that define sport and make it so valuable. This is largely because sport needs to be entertaining if it is to sell. But for it to be entertaining to mass audiences, it needs to enjoy mass appeal. Therefore, in many cases sport becomes cruder, perhaps more violent, and certainly less nuanced. Players come to value external goals over internal ones, and thus sport is further corrupted. For example, because many professional basketball players' salaries are based more on scoring averages than on fitting into a team, the offense on a basketball team must ensure that a star player gets his quota of shots. More generally the players come to see their sport as a business, and personal profit becomes more important than the good of the game. Many young stars are too immature to handle their wealth and celebrity status, and stories of star athletes' self-destructive and criminal behavior have become far too common.

Although even the casual observer of contemporary sport will acknowledge that this critique has much force, it is not the whole story. For one thing, as just noted above, the mass media's presentation of major sporting events has allowed millions of spectators to observe top athletes at the highest levels of competition, something that might well have never been possible without commercialization. Of equal importance, not all changes in the rules of sport have been for the worse, even when one of the reasons for the change was to make the sport more appealing to the masses.

For example, the introduction of the shot clock and the three-point field goal in basketball did make the game more entertaining, but, arguably, they also made it better and more challenging. The three-point shot helped open the court for fast, fluid play; gave teams more options on both defense and offense, thereby making the game more nuanced; and produced more chances for comebacks and exciting finishes. Similarly, the shot clock made the game more entertaining by limiting the extent to which teams with a lead could stall rather than attempt shots, but it also made it faster by bringing out top players' tremendous athleticism.

Remember, also, that some advocates of the Corruption Thesis have maintained that the playoff system, primarily supported by sports organizations because it brings in money, is not the ideal method of measuring and determining athletic excellence and that the lengthier regular season is much more representative of how good teams are.[29] Proponents of the playoff system contend that goals such as entertainment, excitement, and drama are worthy of consideration in sport and legitimize such choice to organize athletic competition. The playoff system, though, has a heavy price. Stephen Finn, who defends it, admits that "I would rather have a season with a playoff system because it increases the enjoyment of sport while still being a good, although not the best, indicator of athletic excellence."[30] So, for Finn, playoffs may bring about dramatic and enthralling moments to be enjoyed by fans and participants alike that justify some loss of accuracy in determining which team is the best.[31]

Although playoffs may be commercially successful, it is not clear that we have to choose a competitive format that devalues the mutual quest for excellence and the accurate measurement and determination of athletic superiority. Also, it is questionable whether the playoff system promotes entertainment, excitement, and drama. As Cesar R. Torres and Peter F. Hager have shown through the case of rugby union, "The play-off system does not necessarily fulfill its promise of more entertaining, attractive, and joyful games."[32] The playoff system, by virtue of its structure and purpose, tends to focus on outcomes more than on the internal values of sport. Another problem with the playoff system is that it renders these values and the pursuit of excellence as contingent to external values. Should it not be the other way around? "Pursuing, measuring, and comparing athletic excellence [should] take precedence over the unqualified desire for a flick of . . . excitement."[33]

It should not escape us that all over the world the season long system is not only commercially viable but at times also extremely successful. Consider, for example, the national soccer leagues in Europe, Asia, and South America. The pursuit of athletic excellence as well as the accurate measure and determination of athletic superiority is compatible with commercial viability and success.

If the arguments against the playoff system and those in favor of the season long tournament are credible, we could argue that the former is both a second not so good choice to structure athletic competition that seriously risks devaluing the internal goods of sport as well as its core purpose and is mainly used to create postseason opportunities for increased profit. (However, it also should be considered that teams who improve after a bad start or the recovery of injured players might lose out in the regular season but, because they are riding a hot streak at the season's end, demonstrate athletic superiority in a playoff system.)

Commercialization and the Individual Athlete

What about the effects of commercialization on individual athletes? Critics of commercialization argue plausibly that the big money available to top athletes has had a corrupting effect on many young players (although it has also lifted many athletes out of poverty). It also is true that many players have become athletic nomads, going from team to team as market forces dictate, through trades and free agency agreements. This may well have had a deleterious effect on fan-player relationships, as professional players are far less likely to be viewed as members of a shared community. Rather, they are too often seen as mere products or resources whose function is to provide wins; they quickly lose fans' support and may even open themselves to abuse when they fail.

An example of this change involves a comparison of fan reaction to Gil Hodges's failure in the 1952 World Series and Bill Buckner's famous error in the 1986 series. Hodges, later to become a World Series winner as manager of the New York Mets, was, in 1952, a star slugger and top fielding first baseman for the National League champions, the Brooklyn Dodgers. The Dodgers had led the way in breaking the color line in Major League Baseball in the late 1940s, and Jackie Robinson, the first African American to play Major League Baseball, was a star of the 1952 team, along with Roy Campanella, Pee Wee Reese, and Duke Snider. The team was beloved in Brooklyn and, indeed, gave Brooklyn much of its identity. The series was against the archenemy, the cross-town New York Yankees, a team with its own stars, including Mickey Mantle, Yogi Berra, and Phil Rizzuto. Feelings ran high in Brooklyn, which had never won a World Series and loved its team.

The Dodgers lost in a thrilling series that ran seven games. Throughout the series Hodges time after time failed to get a hit. However, as his hitless streak continued, fan support for him became more and more vocal. The fans suffered with him rather than regarding him as a failed product to be treated with derision and disgust. The Dodgers might well have won if Hodges had gotten just a few key hits, but he went hitless throughout the series. Nevertheless, the Dodger faithful fan support for Hodges throughout the off-season was overwhelming. Hodges responded by having an outstanding season for Brooklyn in 1953, when the Dodgers ran away from the rest of the league to win the pennant once again.

Contrast this with the treatment given to Red Sox player Bill Buckner after his crucial error in game six of the 1986 World Series contributed to Boston's loss of the series to the New York Mets. The Red Sox led in the ninth inning of the sixth game. One more out would have given them a victory in the World Series. A ground ball was hit toward first base that would have ended the game if fielded cleanly. Although the grounder was not routine, it should not have presented extraordinary difficulty to a Major Leaguer; however, Buckner, first baseman for the Red Sox, failed to field the ball. The batter for the Mets was safe on first base, and the Mets went on to win the game and, the next day, the series.

Although Buckner lived in Boston, fans reviled him during the off-season. The harassment became so great that Buckner felt he had to move from the area and leave the Boston team. In effect, Buckner was driven out of Boston by the fans' reaction to his error. In contrast, Hodges had been supported by his fans in spite of his failure in the 1952 World Series, and he remained a star for many years. What accounts for the difference in treatment?

Although the reasons are complex, some critics of contemporary sport might argue that the growing commercialization of the game since Hodges's time as a player was a contributing factor. True, a long series of their team's perceived failures frustrated Red Sox fans, but the Dodgers had never won a World Series before 1952. Dodger fans were also frustrated, but they still treated Hodges with compassion. Indeed, it is plausible that, because fans in 1986 were not as close to players as in 1952, they tended to regard them more as high-priced products than as fellow members of a sports community. Players were expected to produce rather than being respected as individuals.

In addition, some would argue that the Buckner example is just one instance of a disturbing trend toward fans' increasingly abusive behavior, which in turn is at least partially the result of the increasing commercialization of sport and the consequent split, alienating fans not only from players but from the traditions and principles of the game as well.

A more recent example involves baseball player Alex Rodriguez. Controversy has marred his career due to his exorbitant contracts and his use of illegal performance-enhancing substances. Both could allegedly be related to the commercialization of sport and the pursuit of external goods. Although Rodriguez has impressive statistics, fans have criticized him as being a greedy player mostly concerned with securing lucrative contracts. After becoming a free agent at the end of the 2000 season he signed a ten-year contract with the Texas Rangers worth $252 million, which was at the time a record deal. However, after just a few years Rodriguez joined the New York Yankees. Fans of the Seattle Mariners, his first team, and of the Texas Rangers were disappointed to see him leave their clubs and express their sentiments, even to this day, when Rodriguez plays in those cities. In addition to the jeers, fans frequently waved fake money to show their displeasure. As of late, despite an overall strong performance with the Yankees over the years, Rodriguez has also drawn criticism in New York.

Although the force of any explanatory hypothesis for these cases is empirical rather than purely philosophical, the claim that the commercialization of sport and its marketing as a product have frequently been harmful has the ring of plausibility, but it too can be overstated. Commercialization may have had a corrupting effect on many athletes, but it does not seem to have affected others' love of the game. Many great professional and top amateur athletes and coaches retain a tremendous work ethic and are exemplars of respect for their games. Michael Jordan, Annika Sorenstam, Grant Hill, Derek Jeter, Lionel Messi, and Billie Jean King are among the many who come immediately to mind.

And although the behavior of spectators and players alike has deteriorated in many respects in recent years, it is doubtful whether all the blame can be placed on the commercialization of sport. What of the general decline in ethical standards throughout society? These, in turn, may be due to strains on the family, inadequacies in the educational system, declining economic security, alcohol and drug abuse, and a variety of complex factors that go well outside the world of sport. Indeed, it is not in the interest of professional teams, sports organizations, or top athletes to encourage abusive behavior among fans or in society at large.

How, then, are we to assess the Corruption Thesis? First, is it simply a matter of adding up the benefits and harms commercialization causes in a kind of utilitarian cost-benefit analysis? Do the benefits produced outweigh the bad effects, or does the bad outweigh the good? Or does commercialization violate some fundamental moral principle so that it is wrong, at least if carried too far, regardless of the results of the utilitarian calculus?

Our own discussion suggests that the transformation of elite sport into a commodity does present real dangers to an ethic of sport. We also have argued that there are compensating benefits and that the criticism of commercialization may sometimes be exaggerated. Rather than engage in a purely consequential analysis of the effects of commercialization, it may be more profitable to ask what moral principles should apply to professional and elite sports in our society. In any event, commercialization is so entrenched that it has probably become a permanent feature of the sporting scene, one with positive as well as negative aspects. Let us consider, then, whether there is an ethical framework that would regulate the effects of economic markets in sport so we could enjoy the benefits of commercialization while also maintaining respect for the internal values of sport. Perhaps we can arrive at such a framework by considering ethical issues that arise in the business of sport.

The Ethical Responsibilities of Business and Sports Management

Business and Social Responsibility

What ethical principles should constrain the commercialization of sport? On whom do the responsibilities for applying these principles fall?

The second question is crucial. Part of the process of commercialization has been the transformation of many professional sports franchises into corporations, some with international connections in recruiting players and marketing products. Equipment companies, such as Nike, are transnational corporations as well and exert enormous influence on the world of sport. We also need to consider the role of sports regulatory organizations, such as the National Football League, the Professional Golfers Association, and Major League Baseball, which, through officials such as the commissioner of baseball, are supposed to serve as a check on corporate interests that might be harmful to the game.

Some might think the answer is relatively easy to determine, at least as far as corporations are concerned. Professional sports franchises, they might say, are the same as other business organizations in fundamental ways. Their role is to make a profit, and to expect them to do otherwise is to ask them to disregard their obligations to stockholders or to, in effect, requisition private owners' money for public purposes without their consent. As the economist Milton Friedman, winner of the Nobel Prize and defender of the free market, once put it, "There is one and only one social responsibility of business—to use its resources and engage in activities designed to increase its profits as long as it stays within the rules of the game, which is to say, engages in open and free competition, without deception and fraud."[34]

Friedman's view is open to criticism, however; in a way it is similar to the claim that the only moral responsibility of the athlete is to try to win within the rules. As we have seen, athletes may well have other moral responsibilities, such as respecting the principles presupposed by their sport, showing appropriate respect for their sport, and carrying out both negative and positive obligations to bring about good competitive contests. Can similar points be brought against the thesis that the only social responsibility of business is to make profits?

To begin, consider what arguments might support Friedman's view. A utilitarian might say that the economy simply works best if business aims at profits, for this promotes the most efficient allocation of resources. Second, where corporations are concerned, one might argue that the managers have a moral responsibility to use the stockholders' funds in the way the investors themselves intended, which surely is to get the best financial return possible. Wouldn't the allocation of funds for other purposes, including the pursuit of moral goals, in effect be taking from the investors without their consent or, as some Kantians might argue, treating the investors as mere means or instruments for the achievement of social goods? Wouldn't this be stealing? Rule utilitarians could argue for a similar conclusion by maintaining that the investment would be discouraged and the economy harmed if investors could not be sure their money would be used for its intended purpose of making the company more profitable. Accordingly, don't professional sports teams, equipment companies, and other sports-related businesses have exactly the duty Friedman specifies—to make as much of a profit as the market allows?

These arguments, although important, are not decisive. Even if a totally free market could be achieved and did promote economic efficiency, economic efficiency is not always the only value at stake in morally evaluating social policy. The most efficient system, for example, may not be the most just. Friedman's own analysis conceded this point by acknowledging that profits may be pursued subject to the constraint of other values—namely, nondeception and avoidance of fraud. But why should those be the only values corporations take into account? What about, for example, workers' safety, the safety of products, and concern for the environment? To put this in a different way, we can argue, paraphrasing Sandel, that a most relevant objection to market reasoning asks why we should only maximize economic efficiency without regard for the moral worth of doing so.[35]

Such concerns undermine the claim that corporations' only obligation is to make a profit. However, what of the argument that for managers to appropriate investments to secure ethical goals is to divert money from the purpose stockholders intended when investing, which is to make a profit, and is, in effect, stealing from them? But this claim assumes the very point at issue—namely, that it is correct to regard making a profit as a business's only obligation. If businesses have other obligations, such as promoting workers' safety and not committing injustices, and stockholders have good reason to be aware of those obligations, then the balancing of profits against appropriate ethical constraints is an obligation of business, not an improper distraction from its true goals.

Although the issue here is complex, several writers have suggested that the relationship between business, particularly corporations, and society is contractual, or at least based on a kind of reciprocity. The terms on which a corporation can exist, what legally counts as a corporation, and its various privileges and powers are defined by society through the legal system. In short, society grants business a certain sphere of legitimate activity but has a right to expect it to honor certain duties in return. The political scientist Robert A. Dahl expressed this sort of view: "Today it is absurd to regard the corporation simply as an enterprise established for the sole purpose of allowing profit making. We the citizens give them special rights, powers, and privileges . . . and benefits on the understanding that their activities will fulfill purposes. . . . Every corporation should be thought of as a social enterprise whose existence and decisions can be justified only insofar as they serve public or social purposes."[36] As Norman E. Bowie also commented, "The corporation must not only benefit those who create it, it must benefit those who permit it (namely society as a whole)."[37]

The point here is that large corporations don't operate in a social vacuum; rather, the legal and political order often lays down the constraints under which corporations can operate. Even more, it provides benefits that enable them to prosper through tax codes and provision of other forms of public support. Thus, sport stadiums in which professional teams play may be funded in part by the public. Because corporations are not purely private entities and because they benefit from public support in a variety of ways, reciprocity requires that they also pay appropriate attention to broad values of central concern to the public in the democratic state. As one prominent approach to business ethics put it, corporations have responsibilities to "stakeholders," those whom corporate actions might seriously harm, as well as stockholders.[38]

But doesn't this view itself start from the questionable assumption that society has a right to dictate the terms on which those who have legitimately acquired wealth may invest it? After all, isn't it the stockholder's or owner's money? On what grounds can society regulate what they do with it?

These questions reflect a position in political philosophy often referred to as "libertarianism." Libertarians believe that the fundamental human right is the right not to be interfered with by others, particularly not to be used for the purposes of others. In their view, at least in an extreme form, the appropriation of property without consent is an unjust interference with personal freedom. Thus, libertarians would regard any income tax used for redistributive purposes, such as provision of education, health care, or basic welfare benefits for the poor, as a gross violation of our most fundamental right.[39]

However, if it is conceded that society does have a right to regulate the economy to an appropriate extent, as happens in Western democracies, including the United States, the contractual analysis of business responsibilities seems defensible. Regulation can be seen as defensible to the extent that it enhances social welfare and recognizes nonlibertarian basic rights, such as the right to public education, compatible with a reasonable and significant degree of economic freedom.

Although a full exploration of libertarianism and its critics would take us too far afield, further reflection may well support the modern welfare state's rejection of libertarianism and its endorsement of a broader set of economic as well as liberty rights.[40] The same reasons that may lead us to defend the right to the kind of personal liberty that libertarians rightly defend and to embody versions of it in our basic constitution may also support broader welfare rights to basic necessities. For example, libertarian rights to personal liberty seem important because we justifiably view persons as centers of autonomy entitled to make their own choices about how they should live. But welfare rights are also important to preserving autonomy and choice. How autonomous can one be without food, shelter, education, or health care? How much control over one's life would one have then? Libertarianism can be reasonably rejected, then, as arbitrarily regarding only liberty rights to freedom from interference as fundamental while rejecting all welfare rights, even though some form of welfare rights seem as necessary to securing our control over our destinies as liberty itself.

We can approach this point from the ideal social contract we considered when assessing the use of performance-enhancing drugs in Chapter 4. Reasonable and impartial people (following John Rawls's idea of choosing the principles of society as if in ignorance of one's position in it as well as of personal characteristics that might contribute to personal success or failure) arguably would reject a society organized entirely around the freedom of market transactions, because they would (being impartial) need to consider people with disabilities, the poor, the frail elderly, children in need of education and health care, and (especially relevant for our purposes) the commitments of many to social practices regarded as having value over and above their value as commodities, such as the practice of sport.[41]

Accordingly, although libertarians are right to emphasize liberty and the preservation of freedom that protects us from exploitation by society, it is reasonable to think that limitations on the economic market designed to preserve fundamental values and rights are also justifiable. This implies, to return to the social responsibilities of corporations, that business is not entitled to do anything it pleases to increase profits but that it can be constrained to operate according to reasonable principles designed to protect fundamental rights and values. Stockholders, therefore, have no right to expect that corporations in which they invest may do anything to increase profit, no matter how ethically repugnant, such as disregard the safety of workers or consumers. Rather, business, including corporate entities in businesses connected to sport, such as professional teams, can and should be expected to pursue profits within reasonable ethical constraints.

Moral Responsibilities of Business to Sport

But although we might agree that business has some ethical obligations, such as not deliberately marketing unsafe or defective products, what are the obligations of businesses closely connected with sport? In particular, what moral constraints, if any, apply to major league professional sports teams?

According to one view, sports teams may have the same obligations as other businesses with respect to safety and the environment but have no special obligation to preserve and protect important principles of sport. If making sport more entertaining sells, then, because they are in business, sports teams ought to do it. What sells is what pleases fans; making sport more entertaining and, therefore, more profitable increases overall utility by making fans happy and also by increasing financial returns for owners and players alike.

But should professional sport be regarded as only a form of entertainment and should it maximize the satisfaction of preferences irrespective of their moral worth? Focusing only on what sells and never on the competitiveness or the internal goods and the standards of excellence of the game, may not even be in the best financial interests of owners and players. Suppose, for example, that newer football fans wanted to see more and more violence in the game. To sell more tickets, professional football eliminated rules that protected vulnerable players such as quarterbacks and punt returners, moving toward and even beyond the so-called Extreme Football League experiment of the late 1990s. The result would likely be a rash of injuries to star players, followed by less exciting contests, and then, probably, fewer sales. Pro football might come to be regarded as more like professional wrestling, a form of unsophisticated entertainment rather than a thrilling sport, and fans might turn their attention from it to sports perceived to be truer to the idea of competitive challenge. (In fact, Extreme Football did not sell.) Similarly, if professional basketball players became more and more focused on great individual moves that looked good on televised highlight films and less and less on fundamentals and team play, fans would likely lose interest in the professional game and turn to college basketball instead.

Thus, it may be to the *mutual advantage* of sports teams in a common league or sport to agree to arrangements that limit their freedom to tamper too much with the best interpretation of the game, one that highlights competitiveness, its internal goods, and standards of excellence. Leagues may create an official bureaucracy, such as the Office of the Commissioner of Baseball or the PGA Tour, that has the explicit function of protecting the good of the sport. Although it is important for such officials to be truly independent of owners and players, each of whom may become too focused on short-term financial gain, such independence may be difficult to achieve. However, the creation of official regulatory institutions, which have as at least part of their mission the preservation of the integrity, or best interpretation, and competitiveness of the game, is a structural mechanism for preserving some of the values of sport as a mutual quest for excellence even in the professional arena.

This argument from mutual advantage suggests that it is in each team's overall interest to set limits on the pursuit of profits. If all teams engaged in the unlimited pursuit of profit, sport might become so diminished by commercialization that it attracted less and less interest, and so everyone would lose.

Mutual advantage aside, would it be morally wrong on other grounds for the sports industry to turn a sport into merely a form of entertainment, even though that would severely diminish the key principles of skill, competition, and excellence central to the game? In fact, it is doubtful whether the moral obligations of business can be reduced to considerations of mutual advantage alone. What if one team was so dominant that it was not to its advantage to cooperate in setting limits? Or what if one group—say, traditional sports fans concerned about preserving the integrity of the game—was so weak that it was not in the interest of more powerful companies and firms to negotiate with them? Considerations of mutual advantage, in many areas, seem to conflict with rather than exhaust the demands of fairness and other fundamental moral principles.[42] We should keep in mind that, as argued above, the commercialization of sport has the risk of changing its character, meaning, and defining values.

Let us apply this idea to concrete examples. Suppose that Major League Baseball introduced a much livelier ball than the one used at present, leading to home runs becoming routine. Further, say it became common for teams to score twenty runs in a game, but for some reason many fans found this entertaining and bought more tickets. What would have been lost, however, would be the balanced contest between pitcher and hitter that has always been central to the game. Or, even worse, suppose professional basketball games came to have scripted endings, just as professional wrestling matches are now said to have. Games would become less like contests and more and more like dramatic plays that followed exciting and entertaining scripts. Thrilling comebacks, last-minute shots, and comical mistakes might help to fill arenas, but they would all be choreographed in advance, the outcome decided by the writers of the day's "play" rather than by the play of the game.

What, if anything, would be wrong about such scenarios? After all, the owners would profit, as would the players (perhaps better referred to in the last example as "actors"), and masses of fans would enjoy the entertainment provided. The "purists" who objected that true sport no longer existed would be powerless and ignored. Such changes might be to the mutual advantage of many, but would they be justifiable ethically?

It is probably true that if sport were transformed in such a manner, it would not remain interesting to many people. Good sport is entertaining because it demonstrates human skills and virtues in meeting difficult challenges to mind and body alike rather than mimicking such values by following a script. To the extent that professional wrestling or partially scripted exhibition games, such as those of the talented Harlem Globetrotters, are popular, it is because they are parasitic on genuine competitive sport, in which the outcome of the game depends on the effort, skills, and excellence of players and coaches. In other words, it is activity governed by the underlying principles of sport as a mutual quest for excellence that make sport of interest in the first place. (That is why it is to the mutual advantage of members of the sports industry to preserve those values rather than allowing them to diminish or disappear.)

More importantly, something of great value would be lost if sport were transformed solely to a commercially viable form of entertainment at the cost of losing its basic character—namely, the value of sport as a mutual quest for excellence through challenge. Although professional sports do not exactly fit this model, and in many ways (sometimes justifiably) try to appeal to mass audiences, their appeal has value precisely because it reflects the underlying principles of sport, not only entertainment.

Another way of making this point begins by asking who would be harmed if commercialization were allowed to transform sport too radically in the direction of pure commercial entertainment, thereby changing its character, meaning, and defining values. Surely it would be members of the broader sports community: players, officials, and fans who were devoted to the principles of the sport and respected the best interpretation of the game. If sport, as argued in earlier chapters of this book, embodies and expresses values of enduring significance, such as the importance of dedication in overcoming challenge or the value of internal goods and standards of excellence, then the broader community would lose as well.

If it is justifiable to regard corruption in the goods and values of sport as wrong, or, more simply, if it is wrong to corrupt goods and values of such fundamental importance, there is an argument for concluding that the sports industry is more than just a marketer of sport; it can also be regarded as having a fiduciary relationship to sport. This means the industry has some responsibility for preserving both the best interpretation of sport and respect for its central values. This may not only be in the best interests of the industry, as indicated by the argument from mutual advantage, but may also extend beyond self-interest to the protection of what is of deep value as well. What is at stake is a commendable form of life.

An Ethical Compromise to Avoid the Corruption of Sport: The Case of Technology in Sport

The growth of technology and its application to sport have raised a host of ethical issues. One such issue is the potential conflict between the marketing of technologically advanced equipment and what is appropriate and desirable for the game. Consider, for example, the growing concerns in the golf community of whether technological advances in club design might reduce the challenges the game puts forward, particularly by making existing golf courses too easy because of the greater distance the newer clubs allow golfers to hit the ball. In this regard the United States Golf Association (USGA) has adopted rules to keep technology under control. Another example is the controversy over full-body suits in swimming, whose use prompted a rash of world records a few years ago. These high-tech swimsuits, now banned by the Fédération Internationale de Natation (FINA), the international governing body of aquatic sports, improved buoyancy and, arguably, diminished the role of core swimming skills.

In the ensuing debate equipment companies as well as governing bodies and their respective supporters in the sporting community have made points of some merit. The equipment companies surely are correct to point out that technological advances are part of sport, have often made sport more exciting, and can benefit recreational as well as elite players by bringing the game within the grasp of ordinary participants. But surely governing bodies of sports are also correct to say that equipment companies should not be the judge of when technological advances cease to be good for the game or even harm it by reducing its challenges and internal goods and that a line sometimes may need to be drawn, even if not always in a perfect place.

The challenge of where to draw the line is significant. Preserving the integrity or the best interpretation of the challenges of a sport is only one consideration that needs to be taken into account. Safety may be another. Thus, the use of aluminum rather than the traditional wood bats in baseball has raised concerns because the velocity with which the ball rebounds from such bats is so high that pitchers' safety is threatened: a ball hit sharply right back at the pitcher's mound may come so quickly that the pitcher has no defense against being hit and, perhaps, suffering a serious injury. Cost is another factor. In golf, courses may simply be lengthened to mitigate the impact of "hot" clubs and balls. But longer courses are more expensive to build and maintain, and extra costs may be passed on to participants. This could make the game less accessible to many players, thereby reducing their numbers and actually hurting the equipment companies in the long run by reducing the size of their market. (Remember the argument from mutual advantage discussed above.) In addition, the prohibitive cost of high-tech equipment could provide a competitive advantage unrelated to athletic ability to only the wealthiest athletes or teams.

Although there often will be no perfect place to draw the line deciding when technologically advanced equipment is and is not permissible, all these factors suggest that it is best to have a line drawn rather than have none at all. Otherwise, we might find ourselves in the sporting analog of what Thomas Hobbes, a great sixteenth-century British philosopher, called "the state of nature" (in which the absence of a central authority leads to no enforceable common standards left to soften rivalry and restrain our baser impulses), where the unconstrained pursuit of commercial interests is all too likely to undermine the good of the sport.

Hobbes's own solution to the problem of the state of nature was to argue that all power should be conceded to a sovereign who would make the rules for all. But, as proponents of democracy have long argued, such a solution has grave dangers of its own: sovereigns may rule arbitrarily and need not focus on their subjects' best interests.

In sport a more desirable solution would be for governing bodies to have control of where the line on technology is set but to operate in an open manner that takes into account the interests of the constituents of the sporting community, including fans, equipment companies, sports teams, recreational and elite athletes, and the principles of the game itself as well as its best interpretation. When there are disagreements, different points of view need to be expressed and heard by the governing authorities. Finally, the sports governing bodies, such as the USGA in golf or FINA in swimming, need to make decisions constrained by concern for the basic values underlying their sport and the more general constraints set by the value and nature of competition in sport.

These authorities will not always make the best possible decisions; however, as in drawing a line with respect to performance-enhancing drugs, decisions must be reasonable and nonarbitrary, must be based on dialogue among different constituencies of the sport, and must give due weight to underlying principles of sport that apply to the situation as well as to the internal goods and standards of excellence of sport.

This suggests that business concerns should be aligned with, if not the best, at least reasonable interpretations of sport. Great increases in the entertainment value of a sport and its interest to a wide audience may sometimes justify modifications in the rules, but they should not alter the basic structure, internal goods, and standards of excellence—that is, the meaning—of sport. (Perhaps the introduction of the designated-hitter rule in baseball might be such a modification.) How the balance is to be struck when interests or values conflict may depend heavily on contextual factors specific to each sport. Nevertheless, our discussion supports the view that sports organizations properly exercise a fiduciary responsibility to preserve the integrity of competitive sport.

Reassessing the Corruption Thesis

We began this chapter by considering the Corruption Thesis. We have taken this thesis to be making an empirical claim about causality—namely, that as sport becomes more and more commercialized, market forces tend to subvert the central principles of an ethic of good competition and replace it with what sells, what has entertainment but not necessarily sporting value. What does our discussion suggest about the truth of the Corruption Thesis?

First, the growing commercialization of sport does sometimes represent a threat to its integrity. The argument of earlier chapters suggests that sport does have an internal morality of its own that is centered around principles presupposed by a mutual quest for excellence through challenge. Moreover, commercialization can threaten the internal principles or values of sport. For example, rule changes designed to make the sport more entertaining to relatively unsophisticated mass audiences can reduce the significance of skills central to a sport as well as its standards of excellence. Or a professional sport can be structured so the wealthiest teams can dominate competition season after season. The pursuit of wealth can lead teams as well as individual athletes to sever their roots with local or regional communities in an attempt to reach larger audiences but at the price of creating alienation and disaffection in the serious sports community. And, as Morgan has argued, commercialization can change the social meaning of sport, replacing the values of achievement, excellence, and good competition with a focus on the external rewards of winning games and setting records. Sandel, who believes markets can change the meaning of social institutions, would most probably agree.

Nevertheless, our discussion also suggests that commercialization is not always harmful and that proper governance of elite, commercially viable sports has the potential to reduce significantly the conflict between commercialization and the integrity of competitive sport. This type of governance should be concerned with articulating, advancing, and defending a vision of sport that honors its unique structure as well as the principles and values underlying it.

For one thing, commercialization allows the internal goods elite athletes create to be available to enormous numbers of people. Elite sport, including professional sports, has the potential to play a positive social role in this regard by exhibiting and expressing standards of excellence, achievement, and commitment. Second, commercialization can lead to improvements in many sports. New equipment that improves play without undermining the central challenges of the game, such as the sand wedge in golf or well-designed running shoes in track, might be introduced, for example, or rule changes, such as the three-point shot in basketball or the rule that prohibits goalies in soccer from using their hands on balls intentionally kicked back to them by teammates, might be instituted. Such changes might both improve the game and make it more entertaining to mass audiences. In these cases the entertainment value emerges directly from the internal values of sport.

But commercialized sport can play a predominately positive social role only if it operates within ethical boundaries that set parameters for the pursuit of profit. Thus, a second point our discussion suggests is that the sports industry has a fiduciary moral responsibility toward the practices with which it is involved. This requires that governance of elite sports, especially professional sports, should reflect more than commercial interests concerned with generating wealth from the game. Governance should also give voice to and reflect the concerns of those whose allegiance is to the basic principles of competitive sport. If the argument of this chapter has force, this is not only because the sports industry stands to lose if sport is cheapened beyond repair (the argument from mutual advantage) but also because impartial reasoning suggests that the values and goods central to good sporting competition are of sufficient weight to set moral limits on the pursuit of profit.

QUESTIONS FOR REVIEW

1. What is the basic tenet of the Corruption Thesis?
2. Is there a need to protect sport from market values? Why?
3. Explain and exemplify the internal and external goods of sport.

4. What are the main responsibilities of the sports industry?

5. Can you think of an example in which market values advanced the values internal to sport and the mutual quest for excellence through challenge?

Notes

1. William J. Morgan, *Leftist Theories of Sport: A Critique and Reconstruction* (Chicago: University of Illinois Press, 1994), esp. ch. 3; and William J. Morgan, *Why Sports Morally Matter* (New York: Routledge, 2006).

2. James Michener, *Sports in America* (New York: Random House, 1976), 17.

3. Centers for Disease Control and Prevention, "Exercise or Physical Activity," www.cdc .gov/nchs/fastats/exercise.htm.

4. Adrian Walsh and Richard Giulianotti, "This Sporting Mammon: A Normative Critique of the Commodification of Sport," *Journal of the Philosophy of Sport* 28, no. 1 (April 2002): 53–77, 62.

5. Evan Hilbert, "Major League Soccer Plans to Expand to 24 Teams by 2020," *CBSSports.com*, August 1, 2013, www.cbssports.com/general/eye-on-sports/22971267 /major-league-soccer-plans-to-expand-to-24-teams-by-2020.

6. See Nicholas Dixon, "On Winning and Athletic Superiority," *Journal of the Philosophy of Sport* 26, no. 1 (May 1999): 10–26; Cesar R. Torres and Peter F. Hager, "The Desirability of the Season Long Tournament: A Response to Finn," *Journal of the Philosophy of Sport* 38, no. 1 (May 2011): 39–59; and Morgan, *Why Sports Morally Matter*, 28.

7. Morgan, *Leftist Theories of Sport*, 147.

8. Morgan, *Why Sports Morally Matter*, x–xiv.

9. Ibid., xiii.

10. Michael J. Sandel, *What Money Can't Buy: The Moral Limits of Markets* (New York: Farrar, Straus and Giroux, 2013).

11. Ibid., 9.

12. Ibid., 113.

13. Ibid.

14. Ibid., 172.

15. Ibid., 173.

16. Cynthia L. Ogden, Margaret D. Carroll, Brian K. Kit, and Katherine M. Flegal, "Prevalence of Obesity in the United States, 2009–2010," *NCHS Data Brief* 82 (2012): 1–7.

17. Centers for Disease Control and Prevention, "Adult Obesity Facts," www.cdc.gov/obesity /data/adult.html.

18. Ibid.

19. Christopher Lasch, "The Degradation of Sport," in *Philosophic Inquiry in Sport*, ed. William J. Morgan and Klaus V. Meier (Champaign, IL: Human Kinetics Press, 1988), 407.

20. US Department of Agriculture, US Forest Service, Nationwide Recreation Survey, 1982–1983, and 1994–1995 National Survey on Recreation and the Environment, in Alison S. Wellner, *Americans at Play: Demographics of Outdoor Recreation and Travel* (Ithaca, NY: New Strategist Publications, 1997), 3. Participation rates vary according to various demographic factors, such as age, so caution must be used in evaluating the figures. Wellner provides a helpful discussion.

21. Physical Activity Council, *2012 Participation Report: The Physical Activity Council's Annual Study Tracking Sports, Fitness and Recreation Participation in the USA* (Physical Activity Council, 2012).

22. This point also is made by Lasch, "Degradation of Sport," 405–407.

23. Stephen Mumford, *Watching Sport: Aesthetics, Ethics and Emotion* (London: Routledge, 2012), 87–98.

24. Ibid., 87.

25. Nicholas Dixon supports what he calls "moderate partisanship" in his paper "The Ethics of Supporting Sports Teams," *Journal of Applied Philosophy* 18, no. 2 (2001): 149–158.

26. Mumford, *Watching Sport*, 9–18.

27. The distinction between scarce and basic benefits was, to the best of my knowledge, introduced into discussions in the philosophy of sport by Jane English in her article "Sex Equality in Sports," *Philosophy and Public Affairs* 7, no. 3 (Spring 1978): 269–277.

28. Here we are indebted to the work of Alastair MacIntyre on the internal goods of practices, although my conception of internal goods may differ from his. See his *After Virtue* (South Bend, IN: University of Notre Dame Press, 1984).

29. See Dixon, "On Winning and Athletic Superiority," 10–26; Torres and Hager, "The Desirability of the Season Long Tournament," 39–59; and Morgan, *Why Sports Morally Matter*, 28.

30. Stephen Finn, "In Defense of the Playoff System," *Journal of the Philosophy of Sport* 36, no. 1 (May 2009): 72.

31. Ibid., 70.

32. Torres and Hager, "The Desirability of the Season Long Tournament," 48.

33. Ibid., 52.

34. Milton Friedman, *Capitalism and Freedom* (Chicago: University of Chicago Press, 1952), 133.

35. Sandel, *What Money Can't Buy*, 88–91.

36. Robert A. Dahl, "A Prelude to Corporate Reform," in *Corporate Social Policy*, ed. Robert L. Heilbroner and Paul London (Reading, MA: Addison-Wesley, 1975), 18–19, quoted by Norman E. Bowie, "Changing the Rules," in *Ethical Theory and Business*, ed. Norman E. Bowie and Tom L. Beauchamp, 2nd ed. (Englewood Cliffs, NJ: Prentice-Hall, 1983), 103.

37. Bowie, "Changing the Rules," 103. An excellent account of stakeholder theory as well as an assessment and defense of it is found in Thomas M. Jones, Andrew C. Wicks, and R. Edward Freeman, "Stakeholder Theory: The State of the Art," in *The Blackwell Guide to Business Ethics*, ed. Norman E. Bowie (Malden, MA: Blackwell, 2002), 19–37.

38. For an important defense of a libertarian view, see Robert Nozick, *Anarchy, State and Utopia* (New York: Basic Books, 1974), esp. ch. 7.

39. For fuller discussion, see Norman E. Bowie and Robert L. Simon, *The Individual and the Political Order* (Lanham, MD: Rowman and Littlefield, 2008), esp. ch. 3.

40. See John Rawls, *A Theory of Justice* (Cambridge, MA: Harvard University Press, 1971), and the many discussions of it, as well as Rawls's later work in the literature. A discussion of different approaches to justice is found in Bowie and Simon, *The Individual and the Political Order*. An analysis of different approaches to the justice of social and economic institutions, including those of Rawls and the libertarians, can be found in Christopher Heath Wellman, "Justice," in *The Blackwell Guide to Social and Political Philosophy*, ed. Robert L. Simon (Malden, MA: Blackwell, 2002), 60–84.

41. For a particularly important treatment of justice as mutual advantage, concluding that such an approach is intellectually inferior to one explicating justice in terms of impartial agreement, see Brian Barry, *Theories of Justice* (Los Angeles: University of California Press, 1989).

42. Gunnar Breivik, "Generosity as a Principle in Elite Sport," paper presented at the annual meeting of the International Association of the Philosophy of Sport, Pennsylvania State University, October 2002.

=8=

Sport, Moral Education,
and Social Responsibility

In previous chapters we have examined whether and under what conditions competition in sport is ethical as well as ethical issues that arise within competition, such as those involving fair play, cheating, and the use of performance-enhancing drugs. In addition, we have looked at issues involving gender equity, intercollegiate athletics, and the commercialization of sport. We will conclude our examination by briefly considering some of the broader social implications of the ethical values that should apply in sport. In particular, we should ask whether sport can and should play a significant role in broader spheres of moral development, especially in education and in our personal lives.

Because claims for the moral import of sport have often been exaggerated, and because of many abuses within the practice of competitive sports, many people regard sport as a reflection of our moral decline rather than a positive moral influence and the ethical issues in sport as symptomatic of that decline. But perhaps such a negative view has been overstated. Does sport have an important positive role to play in our moral lives?

Morality and Sport

The Reductionist Thesis

How are values in sport related to values in the larger society? According to one influential thesis, which we can call reductionism, values in sport are reflections and perhaps reinforcers of values in the broader society. This view is *reductionist* in that it attempts to explain all values in sport as expressions of dominant social values, thereby reducing the values in sport to those of the wider society. This kind of reductionism implies that if a society is intensely competitive and stresses the advancement of individuals over that of the group, sport will reflect and perhaps reinforce adherence to those values. If, in another society, competition is frowned upon and loyalty to the group is held to be more important than individual advancement, there will be less emphasis on the importance of winning and more on teamwork than in the first society. Some reductionists might add that the emphasis on such values in sport may reflect back on the prevailing social values and reinforce commitment to them in the broader culture. Notice that reductionism is closely related to the theory of sport known as externalism, which, as we argued in Chapter 2, maintains that the values sport promotes either express or simply mirror, reflect, or reinforce the values dominant in the wider society.

Reductionism can be understood as an explanatory theory if its claim is that the existence of values in society fully explains the nature of values in sport. It can also be understood as a normative theory if it holds that the worth or justification of values in sports is no different from the worth or justification of more fundamental social values. For example, writer Paul Hoch, a critic of American sport, sees football as reflecting his pessimistic view of American society as militaristic, capitalistic, and egoistic.[1] In his view football reflects and reinforces these values, which he regards as prevalent in our society. Some forms of Marxism also tend to be reductionist not only in their view of values in sport but also about values generally; some Marxists tend to view all social institutions as reflections of the values of the economic structure of society. An emphasis on individual moral rights, according to this kind of Marxist analysis, is not part of a universal, objective morality, but rather characteristic of capitalistic, competitive societies in which individuals compete with one another for success in the market. Individuals "stand on their rights" against others precisely because the free market puts them in cutthroat competition with each other. Thus, claims about equal individual rights might well be unintelligible in a feudal society, where the hierarchical structure emphasizes the morality of one's station and its duties, or in tightly knit communities where the individual, rather than being viewed as an autonomous unit, is in part defined by his or her place in the communal structure.

The reductionist position faces some serious objections if it is extended to cover all ideas and values. If ideas, moral codes, and social practices are mere reflections of underlying and more fundamental economic relations, isn't that true of the reductionist thesis itself? If so, and if reductionism is used to debunk the universalist claims to objectivity and truth, the reductionist thesis cannot claim to be an objective truth applying in all times and places but can itself be dismissed as a parochial belief fostered by a particular economic system.[2]

Of course, reductionism, or even Marxism, need not be based on so crude a form of economic determinism.[3] Moreover, such a criticism does not apply to limited reductionist analyses that apply only to values in sport because such analyses do not claim that all values are mere reflections of a more fundamental underlying basis; rather, their claim is only that values in sport are expressions of dominant social values, not all values everywhere.

Perhaps the major objection to reductionist analyses of the values in sport is that sport often seems to express values that go counter to prevailing moral beliefs. An interesting example is given by Drew A. Hyland, a former Princeton basketball star and now a philosopher. Hyland has suggested that because of the merits and skills of the basketball players on local playground basketball courts, playground basketball games can help—and, in America's past, have helped—participants to overcome racial prejudice and suspicions. When the only way to retain one's place on a crowded neighborhood court is to put together a winning team, whether other persons are good players will tend to count far more than their race, religion, or even gender. "In this situation, the preservation of . . . racism has a clear price, the likelihood that you will lose and have to sit."[4] Indeed, as we have seen in Chapter 6, prominent social scientist James Q. Wilson, in his discussion of the work of Michael Putnam, identified sports teams as one of the few American institutions in which high levels of trust among diverse groups are actually found.

Another interesting example, decidedly more somber than the previous one, refers to violence. For the most part, sport, like society at large, condemns much violence, especially the intentional attempt to harm opponents. However, different forms of violence are either explicitly sanctioned by the rules of some sports or implicitly accepted by a significant proportion of the sporting community. The former include, for example, boxing and mixed martial arts, and the latter, for example, retaliatory violence. Indeed, sport might be one of the few social institutions that sanctions or accepts violence.[5]

Our own discussion throughout this book also indicates that some values internal to sport are not necessarily mere reflections of a prevailing social order. In Chapter 2 we identified this position as the theory of sport known as internalism. For example, if dominant ideologies within a society were to devalue excellence and challenge, the values expressed in good sports contests, conceived of as mutual quests for excellence through challenge, would conflict with rather than reflect dominant social values. If so, sport might be an important source of moral values and even have a significant role to play in moral education, a topic we will explore later in this chapter.

The Inner Morality of Sport

Suppose a person claims to be a serious athlete committed to competitive success but, in spite of having time to practice, virtually never does so. In addition, this person shows no desire to learn about his weaknesses in his sport or to analyze strategies that might be used successfully against opponents. Surely, in the absence of a special explanation, this individual's behavior would undermine his claim to be a dedicated athlete.

This example suggests that certain values, such as discipline and dedication, are central to competitive sports in the sense that an individual or team concerned with competitive success would have strong reason to act upon them. As noted above, in a society in which little emphasis was placed on achievement or hard work, those committed to competitive success in sport would be endorsing and acting upon values that conflicted with the prevailing values of their culture. If such athletes became sufficiently influential, their values might change and even replace the prevailing value system.

Other values also seem closely connected with a desire to compete in sport and athletics. Consider concern for playing by the rules. Although some athletes may be tempted to cheat and may even do so on occasion, no athlete can normally endorse disrespect for the rules as a universal value all athletes should hold. For if cheating became a universal practice, there would be no athletic competitions in the first place. The very idea of a sports competition is that it is an activity governed by appropriate constitutive rules that, at least partially, define the game.

Concern for excellence and recognition of excellent performance are other values intimately connected to competitive sports. Even if a competitor's main concern is winning rather than achieving excellence, such an athlete must intend to play better than the opposition. This presupposes a conception of better and worse play and, therefore, a conception of standards of excellence for evaluating performance.

Some values may be so intimately connected with sports that they are internal to it. As we contended in the previous chapter, goods are internal to a practice or activity when they cannot be understood or enjoyed independently of that practice or activity. For example, the value of being a skilled playmaker cannot even be understood without some understanding of the constitutive rules of basketball and appreciation of its strategies and nuances. In a society in which the majority highly values such external goods as fame and wealth, athletes who value securing the internal goods of sport and attempt to emulate its standards of excellence might exemplify a way of life that conflict with the norms of the majority and, thus, undermine or question them.

Although there are different and competing conceptions about which ethical principles should apply to competitive sport, an ethics of competition can stand apart from and even conflict with moral principles widely accepted in other domains. Thus, the notion of competitive sport as a mutual quest for excellence conflicts with the view that competitive values are bad, wrong, or always to be abjured as well as with the view that defeating others should be the only fundamental goal of the competitive athlete.

These illustrations strongly suggest not only that the reductionist thesis is seriously flawed but also that the practice of competitive sport and athletics is value laden in important ways. Some values, such as concern for excellence, discipline, and dedication, are traits that all competitive athletes have strong reason to commend and act upon themselves. Others, such as respect for the opponents and the rules, are values that all competitive athletes have good reason to maintain; they should be part of the universal set of norms upon which all athletes should act. Still other values, such as the importance of demonstrating excellence in particular sports, are internal goals that all serious players of the sport normally seek to exemplify and that reflect standards for evaluating one's own play and the play of others. Finally, conceptions concerning the ethics of competition, such as the mutual quest for excellence, constitute moral standards purporting to be morally justified.

These different normative features constitute what might be called the inner morality of sport. They may be more or less in harmony with the ethics of some cultures or subgroups within cultures, but they can conflict with the moral codes of others and may promote change in existing moralities.[6] Although there may be different interpretations of the inner morality of sport and perhaps even different and conflicting inner moralities of sport, such a moral code (or codes) seems capable of profoundly influencing social and individual moral development.

This does not mean that an internal morality of sport is unique to the context of sport. For example, achievement in many areas, including medicine, scholarship, and teaching, requires dedication and commitment. An artist may value excellence at least as much as an athlete. Moreover, the internal morality of sport may cohere with major philosophical ethical systems, and its fundamental values may even be derivable from such systems. Kantianism, with its emphasis on respect for persons, as well as "perfectionism," which in some forms emphasizes excellence through achievement, are examples of such systems. The antireductionist claim, then, is not that an internal morality of sport is unique or logically independent of major ethical principles that apply elsewhere but rather that the values found in sport can conflict with those dominant in the wider society and so are not mere reflections of a prevailing social morality.[7]

If athletes can act upon an inner morality (or moralities) of sport that can be expressed through their actions on the field, we can ask what its broad social role might be. Such a question is too broad to deal with exhaustively here, but one issue is worth our special attention. Sport, as some of our earlier discussions have indicated, has long been thought to influence character development. Accordingly, the role sports can play in moral education is well worth further consideration.

Sports and Moral Education: Can Sports Influence Character Development?

Because moral values play a large role in sport, it is not surprising that sport is often thought of as an area where values can and should be taught and transmitted to the next generation. We have seen in Chapter 2 that a traditional defense of athletic competition rests on its allegedly good effects on character. In Chapter 6 we argued that intercollegiate and interscholastic sports can have educational value when conducted properly.

Many people see a decline in values in our society. Random violence seems to be all too common. Drugs, gangs, and urban decay create risks for youngsters that seem to be higher than those children of the previous generation faced. With the rise in the divorce rate and the decline of the nuclear family, many children seem to be receiving less attention at home than previous generations had. The schools increasingly are asked to take on extra responsibilities, such as sex education, which used to be left, however wisely or unwisely, to the home, church, synagogue, or mosque. It is natural to ask, then, whether the schools should provide moral education and direction. Should sports have a role in moral education? If so, what should that role be?

Should schools be involved in teaching values? If so, whose values should be taught? Should there be formal courses in moral instruction? What, if anything, gives public schools and, through them, the state the right to decide upon an "official" morality to be taught to our children?

These questions suggest two important difficulties with the idea that schools should be responsible for moral education. The first might be called the problem of partisanship and the second the problem of indoctrination.[8] According to the first, the public schools have no business teaching values because there is no one set of values that all agree upon. The schools and, through them, the state have no business deciding on a particular set of values and making them the official ideology of the land. Imagine how you would feel, for example, if you were a political and social conservative (or liberal) and the schools taught liberal (or conservative) values as the correct morality. Second, even if we could agree on the values that should be taught, we would be indoctrinating many of our students. Because many students are not yet sufficiently mature to evaluate complex moral systems rationally, we would be imposing a value system upon them without their autonomous consent.

Because of these difficulties, existing programs of moral education often either attempt to help students clarify their own values or teach procedures of moral reasoning, such as trying to see things through the perspective of others, rather than endorsing substantive moral principles. Such views attempt to avoid the charges of partisanship and indoctrination by restricting themselves to the form rather than the content of moral thought and by encouraging the development of autonomy. Even these approaches have been severely criticized on various grounds, including the charge that they express the hidden agenda of an abstract but highly partisan morality. Thus, advocates of such approaches have been accused, in the case of values clarification, of teaching a disguised moral relativism ("It doesn't matter what values you hold as long as you can clearly articulate them and authentically accept them") or, in the case of concern for the form of moral reasoning, of presupposing a "male-oriented" universalist ethic of impartiality (as opposed, for example, to a communitarian, or "female-oriented," ethic of caring).[9]

Regardless of whether these criticisms are justified, our discussion of the inner morality of sport suggests that informal moral education is going on in the schools all the time. For example, coaches of athletic teams normally stress dedication, discipline, teamwork, concern for excellence, and respect for the opponents and the rules. Indeed, it is hard to see how they could avoid teaching such values, because some values are presupposed by the attempt to succeed in competitive sports. Coaches may also teach related values associated with their conception of the ethics of competition, including sportsmanship, fair play, and the principles required by conceiving of sport as the participants' mutual quest for excellence.

Classroom teachers also are involved in informal moral education. Related to the inner morality of sport, one can argue that there is an inner morality of scholarship, which minimally requires civility in the classroom, respect for evidence, willingness to consider the views of others, and respect for them as fellow participants in critical inquiry. Dedication, discipline, and respect for the rules of evidence apply not just to sports but to intellectual inquiry as well. Thus, elementary school teachers who insist on civility and nonviolent behavior in the classroom encourage their pupils to discuss their differences rather than simply allow them to beat up opponents.

Not only do teachers and coaches often stress such values; it seems entirely appropriate that they do so. An emphasis in the classroom on concern for evidence and willingness to listen to other points of view clearly is not neutral in the sense of being value free; rather, it seems to be presupposed by the educational process itself. Similarly, an emphasis on the playing field on teamwork, discipline, striving for excellence, and respect for the opponents and the rules is presupposed by competition in sport and athletics. Accordingly, such values may be neutral in the sense that they would be agreed upon by those concerned for the practices at issue (education and competition in sports). The inner morality of sport (and of scholarship) is neutral rather than partisan not because it is value free but because it concerns values that all committed to the activities in question have good reason to support.

If this last point is justifiable, the inner morality of sport seems to avoid the charge of partisanship directed against the idea of moral education in the public schools. But is it really free of ideological bias? Aren't we trying to have it both ways here? On the one hand, the claim is that there is an inner morality of sport that is relatively independent of and can even conflict with prevailing social values; on the other, it is claimed that such values are nonpartisan and, in some sense, neutral. Are these claims mutually compatible?

Critics of competitive sport agree that there is an ideology of athletics but reject it as overly competitive, egoistic, and conservative. The critics are correct if they are pointing out that sport can be used to transmit messages about values extrinsic to athletic competition. For example, a coach can call for blind loyalty to the team regardless of the players' behavior and equate that with the sentiment of "My country, right or wrong."

Although such values as discipline and respect for the rules might be central to an inner morality of sport, it can be argued that blind loyalty is not. The difference is that the practice of competitive sports presupposes the former values but not the latter. Discipline, unlike blind loyalty to a team, is a value that anyone interested in competing well in sport has reason to pursue, regardless of ideology. Similarly, respect for the rules cannot be equated with blind loyalty to the status quo; rather, respect for the rules is a way of recognizing others' equal moral standing by abiding by the public conditions for competition that every competitor is entitled to believe will apply. Respect for others' equal moral standing is not value free because it is incompatible with viewing the interests of others as of less moral significance than one's own, but it does seem to be presupposed by the idea of fair and meaningful competition.

Similarly, the classroom teacher who insists that students discuss differences rationally rather than forcing their opinions on others through violence is rejecting some values, such as belief in the use of intimidation or retaliation as means of settling disagreements, in favor of others, such as belief in settling agreements rationally and in fostering respect for others as participants in the discussion; however, in this case the favored values are central to education in a way that the rejected values are not. Thus, we can argue plausibly that in applying the inner morality of sport and the inner morality of scholarship, the schools are not imposing an "official" or partisan ideology upon pupils but instead teaching values that activities properly included in the educational curriculum presuppose.

What about the charge of indoctrination? Many coaches and teachers do not explicitly discuss the core moralities they are acting upon but simply impose them on students, many of whom are themselves too young or immature to make competent and autonomous decisions about morality. Teachers who insist that the bigger children in their elementary school classes do not beat up smaller ones are not offering a philosophical defense of civility but simply commanding their pupils to be civil. Similarly, by disciplining young athletes who loaf in practice, coaches normally are not engaging in Socratic dialogue about the value of commitment and dedication but rather insisting that their players show discipline and commitment. If this isn't indoctrination, what is? In particular, what gives athletic coaches the right to impose such values on players?

In assessing this point, we need to ask whether what is going on is indoctrination in a pejorative sense of that term. In particular, as some writers have suggested, perhaps not all values can be autonomously adopted; rather, some may be presupposed by the practice of autonomous reflection.[10] For example, before one can autonomously evaluate the justifiability of conflicting points of view, one must acquire the disposition to evaluate evidence and consider arguments rather than merely going along with one's friends or popular opinion. The acquisition of such a disposition cannot itself be the result of critical inquiry and autonomous reflection because one must already have the disposition needed to engage in critical inquiry and autonomous reflection in the first place. Training that helps immature and not-yet-competent individuals develop such traits is not harmful indoctrination that subordinates critical thinking but instead part of a social process that develops critical thinkers and autonomous persons.

Similarly, the inner morality of sport, insofar as it forms part of a defensible practice of moral education, does not place athletes in intellectual blinders. Values such as commitment, discipline, respect for the standing of others and for the rules, and appreciation of excellence are also presuppositions of moral and rational development.

If this position can successfully withstand critical examination, what are its implications for educational policy? In particular, the idea that there is a defensible inner morality of sport as well as of scholarship suggests that moral education of a limited sort is properly the function of our schools and that organized athletics can and should be part of it. Moral education of the kind at issue is limited to promoting those dispositions of mind and of character that can reasonably be regarded as prerequisites of the capacity to engage in autonomous critical inquiry with others. Just which values are to be cultivated will often be controversial, but a strong argument can be made for those core values constituting the heart of what we have called the inner morality of scholarship and sport.

This approach provides an important reason for athletic programs to be considered a significant part of the curriculum of public education and not just a "frill" to be done away with as soon as school taxes get too high. By reinforcing values taught in the classroom and bringing together people from diverse backgrounds and perspectives so they might engage in a common quest for excellence, sport can help promote and illustrate values that all people who are committed to fostering autonomy and critical thinking, in both public and private life, have reason to support.

This discussion further strengthens the defense of intercollegiate athletics we presented in Chapter 6. The values residing at the core of the inner morality of sport are not only compatible with academic values but may also enhance and reinforce them. In other words, the inner morality of sport can be educational in its own right. Drew A. Hyland summarized this view forcefully when responding to the charges against intercollegiate athletics. He argued that it is a scandal that the country has "so woefully neglected the educational potential of athletics."[11] After all, he continued, as the ancient Greeks knew, *gymnastike* and athletics, its contemporary manifestation, is a fundamental discipline for education to full humanity. By embodying and fostering the core values of the inner morality of sport, college athletes could be said to be embarked in and exemplify a more complete and richer form of education.[12]

Sports and Moral Responsibility

If sport can play an important moral role in society, does it follow that individuals involved in sport have special moral responsibilities to the rest of us? What about the duties of leaders in the world of sport or of highly visible elite athletes? Let us consider the role of the coach in interscholastic and college athletics as well as youth sport.

Coaching and Its Duties

Coaching can take different forms at different levels of sport or different areas of competition. In individual sports such as golf and tennis, the coach can be virtually an independent contractor the athlete hires to provide technical advice on mechanics or, like a sports psychologist, to work on improving mental aspects of the game. Thus, Tiger Woods hired famous golf instructors Butch Harmon, Hank Haney, and, more recently, Sean Foley to bring his game to an even higher level. Foley's relation to Woods is different from that of, say, the coach of a high school team to her players because, for one thing, the contract between Foley and Woods can presumably be dissolved by either party. The high school coach, in contrast, may have to be a team leader in a way that Foley is not, is responsible for team behavior to some extent, sets practice schedules, and performs many duties in addition to teaching mechanics or form. Although an individual coach also may perform some of these duties at the highest levels of elite individual sports, and the difference, therefore, is one of degree, there surely is a substantial distinction between coaches of team sports at the high school and college level, on the one hand, and the golf or tennis professional, on the other.

Coaches of teams may be asked to perform many duties and be evaluated on various factors. Often, in American sports at least, coaches are judged primarily by their wins and losses. At the level of elite intercollegiate sport, coaches in high-profile sports with losing records may not bring in sufficient revenue or create sufficient visibility for the institutions that employ them. At the professional level winning may relate to profits even more. Coaches also are often expected to promote their program to the general public, to be great recruiters, and, at the same time, to keep their players in good academic standing and out of trouble.

Many of these functions are legitimate and important, but they can also conflict with each other. Perhaps the college coach can improve the team's competitive record by recruiting students who are marginal academically or by not enforcing disciplinary codes when star athletes misbehave. At the extreme, as happened at the University of Minnesota (discussed in Chapter 6), the coach might tolerate academic fraud in order to keep players eligible and make sure the team has the best possible chance of winning. In other words, if the main function of the coach is to make sure the team wins games, then important values may have to be ignored and basic ethical principles violated when necessary to achieve that goal.

Perhaps the coach's goal should be to win, but only when appropriate ethical constraints limit the pursuit of victory. Our suggestion is that the constraints that the basic argument of this book proposes are sufficiently stringent that although coaches should surely strive for competitive success, they should be regarded primarily as educators and evaluated as such as well as on their record of wins and losses.

Indeed, at the level of youth sports, coaches should respect youths' interests and needs, which center on developing the capacity to authoritatively rule over themselves, and place competition at the service of these interests and needs. This recommends that coaches be not primarily concerned with competitive success but rather with helping youth flourish through competition. In this regard, Cesar R. Torres and Peter F. Hager have claimed that it is "reasonable to conceive of youth sports coaches as individuals who open a path to a good life."[13] Coaches at the youth level play a role of paramount importance in the lives of youths, "as they are not simply technicians who facilitate skill acquisition and mastery, but rather individuals who introduce and mentor young athletes into a social practice with internal goods and standards of excellence."[14]

In particular, if competition in athletics is best regarded as a mutual quest for excellence through challenge, and the experience of meeting challenges is one in which we learn about ourselves and others, then coaches should, as part of their role, facilitate this experience and assist the youth in developing and understanding what is required from them when competition is conceived mutualistically.

This task involves not only teaching the skills needed to play competently as well as clarifying the principles behind strategies but also setting guidelines about the commitments and responsibilities inherent to the competitive process. The lure of winning should override neither the moral nor the aesthetic obligations young "athletes have within their sports if those athletes learn to adopt a mutualist perspective that will, in turn, help them to prioritize the internal goods and the standards of excellence of their sports and their supporting values over the external goods that can come with winning."[15]

Notice that conceiving the responsibilities of youth coaches in this way is compatible with promoting enjoyment, socialization, and health goals, all typically highlighted in youth sport. Notice also that we think it is reasonable to acknowledge that, as athletes mature and become more skilled, concerns for competitive success may be assigned a higher priority, but always keeping in mind that the overall goal of youth coaches should be the moral growth of their young charges and the provision of opportunities to develop their potential through meaningful participation in sport. Coaches, therefore, should be evaluated primarily on how well they facilitate this process and on how well they promote understanding and love of the sport. Indeed, as our argument in Chapter 6 suggests, in educational institutions, coaches can play an important academic role in integrating academic and athletic values and in ensuring student athletes' success in both areas.

Thus, a coach can be successful as a teacher even if he or she does not have a winning record, although it is sadly true that, at many levels of intercollegiate and even interscholastic sports, losing coaches may have trouble keep-ing their jobs. Sometimes, of course, a continual run of losses or losing seasons may suggest the coach is a bad teacher, but that is not always so.

Even if we do regard the coach primarily as an educator, many ethical issues arise in coaching. Should a coach always play the best players or always aim at winning, even if it means some players always ride the bench? How is participation to be balanced against excellence? Should a college or high school coach play a talented freshman over a senior who is less talented but has been loyal to the program for years? Ethical issues that arise within coaching are extensive and deserve thorough treatment of their own.[16]

Perhaps the supreme imperative for a coach, however, is to treat the play-ers with concern and respect and not regard them as mere means either for self-promotion or for pursuit of revenue or visibility for an institution. Win-ning, of course, is not unimportant. For example, as argued earlier, the record of wins and losses usually indicates how well a team has met the challenges of competition. As the level of competition gets higher, greater emphasis appro-priately is placed on competitive success.

But athletes are not just means for achieving victory, either; they are per-sons in their own right. Constraints on the coach that arise from the status of the players limit the pursuit of victory at all levels of sport, although they may apply differently to youths and children from those at elite levels. Thus, em-phasizing participation may be highly desirable in youth sports when players are still in the early stages of developing skills and understanding strategies; indeed, young players cannot learn about the nuances of play and how to meet the challenges of the game without substantive participation and meaningful experience in the game. At the level of elite sports, however, which athletes freely engage in precisely because of the challenge and the desire for compet-itive success, a coach normally has good reason to put his or her best players on the field in key situations.

As an aid to developing a broader theory of the rights and responsibil-ities of coaches and athletes, we might ask what coaches and athletes would expect from one another if they considered the roles impartially, perhaps by employing Rawls's veil of ignorance and asking what principles they would endorse without knowledge of which role they actually would play. Although it is unclear what a full hypothetical social contract between players and coaches would look like, surely there are some fundamentals that neither party could reasonably reject. Thus, it is reasonable for coaches, like other teachers, to ex-pect their athletes to be dedicated, committed to learning, and willing to abide by appropriate team policies. Athletes, for their part, reasonably should be able to expect the coach to be focused on their development, have knowledge of the game and appropriate teaching skills, and treat them as persons, not simply as resources to be used in the pursuit of victory. How these guidelines play out in specific contexts will often be debatable, but perhaps such an account can provide an ethical framework that can be brought to bear on specific controversies.

Spectating and Its Duties

Although they are not the locus of much analysis, spectators might also have moral responsibilities if athletics are understood as a mutual quest for excellence through challenge. Whether partisan or purist, it seems that, as Nicholas Dixon argues, spectators should display respect for all contestants.[17] We could extend such respect to coaches, referees, and fellow spectators. In light of accepted fan behavior, "including attempts to distract or otherwise interfere with opponents through jeering, catcalls, waving distracting banners, drowning out signals, trying to intimidate referees[,] etc."[18] it is important to highlight this basic spectator obligation. After all, fulfilling it encourages and facilitates meeting the goal of athletic competition.

Spectators should also "desire fair, skillful play from all participants"[19] as well as exciting and excellent games. This means that spectators have a duty to recognize, if not celebrate, athletic excellence. Consequently, they should criticize poor performance and desist from embracing or endorsing a win-at-all-cost mentality. None of this implies that spectators should take a purist approach to spectating sport, which supports the player or team that best "exemplifies the highest virtues of the game."[20] In fact, regardless of whether fans are purists or moderate partisans, from a mutualist conception of athletic competition all spectators should primarily focus on the internal goods and standards of excellence of their sport. This could be done even while spectators are loyal supporters of a particular player or team.

This discussion indicates that discerning and responsible spectators might be obliged to criticize their team if it engages "in such indefensible practices as violent play or other forms of cheating, or even if it starts to use cynical, negative tactics, which may be within the letter of the law of the game, while violating its spirit."[21] Blind loyalty or the acceptance of anything our favorite teams and players do simply because they are our favorite teams and players are in stark contrast with the vision of athletic competition as a mutual quest for excellence through challenge. A discerning spectator recognizes excellence regardless of who achieves it and possesses a critical attitude that distinguishes the strengths and weaknesses of all contestants.

In short, spectators have a duty to exercise moral regard for contestants, coaches, referees, and fellow spectators. They also have a duty to at least recognize the competent display of the internal goods of their sport as well as of athletic excellence irrespective of who achieves it. It seems, then, that the basic requirements of spectators are those of moral regard for others and respect for fair play and for the aesthetics of the game, which is encapsulated in its best interpretation. If sport has a morally and aesthetically educative role, this certainly places responsibilities on spectators as much as it does on coaches and athletes.

Should Athletes Be Role Models?

In considering athletes' moral responsibilities, Pete Rose comes immediately to the minds of many observers of sport. Rose, formerly a star Major League Baseball player for the Cincinnati Reds, became known as "Charlie Hustle" because, through hard work and effort, he was able to turn what many regarded as less-than-extraordinary athletic ability into a distinguished major league career. Rose ended his career having recorded more base hits than anyone else who had ever played the game. His place in the Baseball Hall of Fame seemed assured. To many, Rose was not only a star player but also a symbol of what dedication and commitment to excellence could accomplish.

Following an investigation of charges alleging that Rose, then manager of the Reds, had gambled extensively on baseball games, he was banned from baseball for life in 1989 (although the lifetime ban might now be reconsidered if Rose acknowledged the extent of his involvement in gambling). Not only was Rose accused of being a compulsive gambler; he was also convicted of felonies involving tax evasion, presumably committed to support his gambling habit, and served a jail sentence in 1990. In addition, Rose was precluded from election to the Hall of Fame.

Did Pete Rose, as a star athlete and presumably a hero and role model to many youngsters, have a special obligation to behave ethically because of his participation in sport? Do athletes in general have special responsibilities to be good role models for the rest of us, particularly for the children who look up to them as heroes? Or are athletes simply ordinary people with special skills who have the same legal and moral responsibilities as anyone else but have no special obligation to be models for the rest of society? (Note that similar questions could be raised about Tiger Woods, whose dedication to excellence in golf is admirable but whose status as a moral role model for others was severely undermined by a scandal involving reported marital infidelities that erupted in 2009.)

What does it mean to claim that athletes have special moral obligations to the rest of us to behave ethically? Although it is not always clear what proponents of such a view might be claiming, they might mean that there are reasons over and above those that apply to us all for athletes to behave ethically.

A second thing they might mean is that if an athlete behaves unethically, it is somehow more seriously wrong perhaps because it is more harmful than if someone else who is out of the public eye commits the same unethical act. These might not be the only interpretations of what is meant, but we can work with them in exploring the scope of athletes' moral responsibilities.

Why should we believe that athletes have special moral responsibilities? Athletes, it might be argued, are just people who have particular skills but in other respects are the same as the rest of us. All of us have obligations not to wrong others, so why should the possession of a special talent, such as athletic skill, carry with it an additional moral obligation to be a moral exemplar for others? Athletes may indeed have special moral obligations within competition to, say, follow the rules and play hard, so as to provide a challenge for opponents, but it is quite another thing to say they have a special responsibility to be ethical generally. Surely, from the premise that certain individuals have unusual athletic talents, it doesn't logically follow that they have special moral obligations outside of competition as well.

It can be argued, however, that athletes occupy a special place in our society. Children and young people often regard them as heroes. To many disadvantaged youth, particularly minorities, many star athletes may illustrate that escape from deprivation can be achieved through success in competitive sport. Because a large portion of the population reveres athletes, many people in fact regard them as models to be emulated. Therefore, they have a special reason to behave morally: the unusually great influence they can have on others arguably generates responsibility and obligation. When they behave immorally, they can do more harm through their influence on others than the ordinary person can. Thus, athletes who use addictive drugs, for example, may, however unintentionally, convey the message that it is "cool" to take drugs and, thus, induce their fans to become "copycat" users.

This sort of argument is open to many objections. Instead of expecting athletes to live up to the perhaps unreasonable expectations of many of their fans, perhaps the fans ought to become more realistic. Indeed, the hero worship of athletes can be harmful, especially when it leads youngsters to try to develop athletic rather than academic skills in the grossly unrealistic hope of becoming professional athletes. In any event, why should fans, particularly youngsters, regard athletes rather than physicians, nurses, teachers, scientists, or their parents as their heroes? From the perspective of the athletes, why should they have any more responsibilities to be moral exemplars than other entertainers, such as movie or rock stars, who often not only fail to be desirable role models for young people but also are not usually assigned any special moral blame for their derelictions?

These points surely are worth our consideration. But are they decisive? It can be argued that sport not only does but should play a central place in our society because of its concern with excellence and because appreciating sport does not require the special training or background often needed to appreciate excellence in such fields as medicine, science, mathematics, and even the fine arts. Sport, by its very nature, is accessible to large and diverse portions of the population, yet it expresses and illustrates a concern for excellence. Given the attention the media pay to sport and the love that many people, particularly the young, have for sport, it is doubtful that fans will suddenly become "realistic"; it is far more likely that they will continue to have special regard for national sports figures as well as local athletes.

What does this have to do with athletes' moral obligations off the field? Arguably, because of the special connection between competitive sport and the quest for excellence as well as the broad accessibility of sport it is not unreasonable for many segments of the population, particularly children and young people, to hold athletes in high regard and seek to emulate them. Top athletes profit from this emulation and are often represented to the public as having exhibited special virtues on the field. For example, Pete Rose was known for his dedication and hustle, Michael Jordan was loved for his enthusiasm for the joy of competition, and Tiger Woods was known for his ability to perform his best under the greatest pressure. Michael Phelps rose to prominence because of his extraordinary success under pressure in Olympic competition. Indeed, our own discussion of an inner morality of sport and of the function of sport in expressing values suggests there is an unusually intimate relationship between participation in athletics and ethics.

If so, and if it is, therefore, not unreasonable for the general public, particularly youngsters, to regard top athletes as heroic figures, and given that many top athletes accept and welcome the benefits of their position resulting from the way they are regarded, then perhaps it is not unreasonable to conclude that they have special reasons for at least avoiding the kind of immoral behavior, such as drug and alcohol abuse, cheating, and lawbreaking, that impressionable young people are likely to emulate. If athletes are regarded as role models in part because of the values expressed through their play, they can do unusual harm if their misbehavior leads their fans either to emulate their misdeeds or to become skeptical of the original values the athletes were thought to stand for.

Perhaps a more important reason for thinking athletes have special moral obligations rests not upon controversial empirical claims about their effect as role models but rather on the special place values have in sport. If there is an inner morality of sport in which such values as dedication, concern for excellence, and fair play are central, then athletes express such values through their play and benefit from other competitors' adherence to these norms. Without such commitment, we couldn't have the good sports contest and the basic, scarce, and internal benefits it provides. To express such values and benefit from them in a central area of one's life and then undermine them elsewhere seems wrong or, if not outright wrong, at least morally undesirable. Similarly, it is wrong, or at least open to moral criticism, for a professor to claim to value intellectual integrity in scholarship and yet fail to do so outside the classroom by, for example, ignoring evidence in political debate.

Thus, it is not just that sports fans often do look up to and emulate star athletes that underlies the claim that athletes have special reasons to be role models; it is also that the athletes owe much of their fame and fortune to the esteem in which they are held. This esteem arises in significant part not just from their athletic performance but also from the way it expresses an inner morality of sport encompassing such virtues as dedication, commitment, excellence, coolness under pressure, and respect for the game and its challenges. If athletes willingly benefit from their exhibition of such virtues, which are part of their performance as athletes, it is not unreasonable to expect them to respect other often similar virtues off the field as well.[22] This does not mean that athletes must be saints, but it does suggest that they have special reasons to avoid morally immature behavior, to say nothing of criminal actions or the abusive treatment of others; such behavior not only can have harmful effects on young fans but is also arguably hypocritical.

Although these suggestions need fuller support than has been presented here and are intended as invitations to reflection rather than as decisive argument, they may have sufficient force to show that the claim that athletes have special moral responsibilities is worth taking seriously. Again, the point is not that athletes should have to meet some unusual moral standard that most people cannot attain but that they have special reason not to violate minimal standards of good behavior or to discredit values central to the inner morality of sport. Although we could take the opposite tack and argue that athletes should not be our heroes[23] and should be respected only for their physical skills, the role of athletes in illustrating and expressing important values through their play suggests that sport tends to thrust them into the spotlight in a way that carries some moral obligation. Even those who believe athletes should not be role models accept that people can learn from athletes "and how they deal with the trials of their lives."[24]

Perhaps, then, we need to seriously reflect on the values embedded in the practice of athletic competition. What specific implications this might have for our actual practices, especially within educational institutions, needs further consideration, but at least two possibilities are worth mentioning. First, our discussion suggests that coaches in educational institutions ought to be evaluated more for their teaching than for their record of wins and losses. If appropriate standards of competitive sport have implications for life outside the playing field as well as on it, we need to reward instructors who can teach young athletes to play according to a plausible version of an inner morality of sport rather than fostering an amoral indifference to ethics in the pursuit of victory. For example, coaches in colleges and universities might be accorded faculty status and be judged for retention and promotion by applying criteria that are similar to those used to evaluate other faculty members' performance. Second, we should expect athletes in our schools not simply to satisfy minimal standards of behavior and academic progress but to be good citizens and committed students as well. Although such specific suggestions may or may not have merit, an emphasis on the inner morality of sport and the lessons it can teach may have a role to play in moral education and, more broadly, in our moral life.

Sport, Violence, and Respect for Fellow Competitors

Although sport may illustrate or express values such as dedication, commitment, and respect for others and fair play, we also can find examples of cheating, bad sportsmanship, racism, and violence in sport. Even more, given their structure, are some sports the collective or institutional equivalent of bad role models for society?

Although it is arguable that indefensible values are not central to sport but can be separated from sport as it should be played, what of the claim that some sports, by their very nature, are ethically suspect? This claim often is expressed about what many would regard as inherently violent sports, such as boxing, mixed martial arts, and, perhaps, football. How are such claims about so-called violent sports to be assessed? In particular, when is a sport violent? And are violent sports unethical?

We should begin by considering what counts as violence. Clearly, a physical assault is violent. But is a hard tackle in football violent? What about a brushback pitch in baseball, in which a pitcher throws just inside home plate in order to intimidate the batter and get him to move further away from the plate into a strategically less advantageous position? Or what if a tennis player intentionally hits a hard slam directly at her opponent, who has come up close to play the net?

An important distinction can be made between the use of physical force to achieve a strategic advantage within the confines of a sport's rules and the use of such force designed to injure or harm an opponent. Although the term *violence* can be applied to both, violence in the former sense generally is ethically unproblematic, as when a golfer uses physical force to hit a 280-yard drive. An observer might say that the golfer "killed" the ball or speak of the "violence" of the swing, but surely nothing the golfer did was unethical. Accordingly, in our discussion the use of the word *violence* will be reserved for the use of physical force designed to harm others, keeping in mind that sometimes the use of physical force in itself may be ethically questionable, even if there was no intent to harm (for example, the brushback pitch in baseball) and that it sometimes may be appropriate to speak of psychological as well as physical violence.

Applying this distinction, we may well conclude that boxing is a violent sport. Boxers often suffer extensive brain damage, as seems to have been the case with one of the greatest boxers of all time, Muhammad Ali. In addition, hundreds of participants in the sport have been killed or permanently impaired as a result of their boxing injuries. Arguably, boxing requires contestants to harm their opponents. As accomplished writer Joyce Carol Oates put it, boxing's ultimate aim is "to attack another and to force him into absolute submission."[25] Moreover, she argued that "boxing is the only sport in which the objective is to cause injury: the brain is the target, the knockout the goal."[26] Even though boxing may have many virtues, including demonstrating great courage in the face of physical adversity and danger, and although many would argue that boxers consent to the risks of their sport, boxing surely is ethically problematic.[27]

Violence and Contact Sports

Can arguments concerning violence in boxing be carried over to contact sports? For example, if it can be successfully argued that boxing, because it is inherently violent, is morally problematic and perhaps ought to be eliminated or reformed, then shouldn't the same conclusion be drawn about football? This question seems to be especially apt given the controversy and concern regarding the health effects of concussions on football players.[28] Even President Barack Obama participated in this discussion, saying that "I'm a big football fan, but I have to tell you if I had a son, I'd have to think long and hard before I let him play football. And I think that those of us who love the sport are going to have to wrestle with the fact that it will probably change gradually to try to reduce some of the violence."[29]

Critics of football maintain that it is indeed a violent sport. Coaches and fans sometimes urge players to "smash," "smear," or "bury" the opposition. We mentioned in the last chapter the bounty system that the New Orleans Saints had in place for a while, in which some of its defensive players were paid bonuses out of a slush fund for deliberately injuring opponents. The critics see football as a miniaturized version of war. Even players who claim to compete within the rules acknowledge that physical intimidation is part of the game. As former Oakland Raider safety Jack Tatum put it in his perhaps aptly named book, *They Call Me Assassin*, "My idea of a good hit is when the victim wakes up on the sidelines with the train whistles blowing in his head and wondering who he is and what ran him over."[30] Tragically, one of Tatum's hits in a 1978 game against the New England Patriots resulted in the permanent paralysis of Patriots receiver Darryl Stingley.

Tatum claimed that although he hit hard when he tackled, he played within the rules and did not take illegal "cheap shots" at opponents. (The kind of tackle made by Tatum on Stingley was not against NFL rules at the time, and no penalty was called on the play.) His view was that, as a professional, he was paid to make sure that pass receivers didn't make catches in his territory. A good way to achieve this goal was to make receivers aware that they would get hit hard when running pass patterns. Then, the next time a pass was thrown, the receivers would think more about getting hit and concentrate less on doing their job and catching the ball. As Tatum put it, "Do I let the receiver have the edge and give him the chance to make catches around me because I'm a sensitive guy or do I do what I am paid to do?"[31]

It is understandable why critics of football would say that it glorifies violence, encourages militaristic attitudes, and amounts to a public celebration of many of our worst values. In effect, these critics claim that football is to our society what bloody gladiatorial contests were to Rome: a distraction for the masses through the presentation of violence as entertainment. Thus, Paul Hoch, author of *Rip Off the Big Game*, a highly ideological critique of American sports, suggested that because violence in football is rule governed, it "provides powerful ideological support for the officially sanctioned, rule-governed violence in society, in which judges have the final say. In short, the fans are supposed to identify with the distorted framework of law and order, both on the football field and in society, irrespective of what that law and order is supposed to protect."[32]

All of these charges against football can be understood in numerous ways, but two sorts of claims seem especially worth discussing. First, football is held to be a violent sport. Second, football is thought to express or encourage acceptance of officially sanctioned violence while discouraging external criticism or struggle against the official rules themselves. Thus, football, in our society at least, is not ideologically neutral but expresses a conservative bias against social change.

Are these charges justified? In considering them, we need to keep some distinctions in mind. The first concerns an internalist approach to establish whether violence is necessary to football or merely contingently attached to it. The second is the distinction noted earlier between violence and the use of physical force.

Violence in the sense of physical force intended to harm an opponent is normally as indefensible in sports as it is elsewhere. Such violence treats the opponent as a mere thing to be used for one's satisfaction or gratification; thus, it violates the morality of respect for persons that is expressed in the ethic of competition as a mutual quest for excellence. But is violence in this strong sense necessarily part of football in the first place as it is part of boxing?

Football is a contact sport requiring the use of bodily force against opponents, but it does not follow that football is necessarily violent. The use of physical force is quite distinct from violence, because only the latter covers the intent to harm others. In particular games or on particular teams players may indeed act violently toward opponents, but it does not follow that football itself is a violent game, because players who use physical force need not intend to injure the opposition. (A question we cannot explore here but is well worth considering is whether there always is a morally significant distinction between intending to do violence and intending only to use physical force when one knows it is highly probable or even certain that such use of force might result in unintended injury to an opponent.) This, of course, does not mean that football is not a very dangerous sport.

How is the line between violence and the use of physical force to be drawn? When Jack Tatum attempts to intimidate an opponent through hard hits, is he being violent, or is he merely using physical force efficiently? Tatum could say that because it is not his intent to injure his opponent, he is using physical force but not ethically indefensible violence. How is this claim to be evaluated?

To begin, it is clear that many sports often involve the use of physical force applied to opponents to achieve strategic goals. The use of the brushback pitch in baseball, the hard smash directly at the opponent in tennis, and the hard drive to the hoop in basketball can all involve the use of physical force against opponents. Not infrequently this use of physical force carries some risk of injury. Presumably, participation requires players to bear the risk willingly. The key ethical question in fair competition may be whether the use of physical force takes advantage of an opponent's physical vulnerability. Thus, Major League batters are supposed to have the reflexes to avoid a brushback pitch. The same pitch may be ethically permissible in Major League Baseball but indefensible when thrown against an out-of-shape older recreational player who hasn't played ball in years.

If this suggestion has force, it supports what might be called the Vulnerability Principle, or VP. According to the VP, for the use of physical force against an opponent in an athletic contest to be ethically defensible, the opponent must be in a position and condition such that a strategic response is possible and injury is unlikely to ensue. Thus, attempting to block a shot from the front of an opponent in basketball conforms to the VP, but "undercutting" an opponent already in the air from behind does not.

Normal play in football conforms to the VP as long as opponents, using basic skills common among players, can be expected to be able to respond with strategic countermoves. A tackle from the receiver's blind side when the receiver is in a position of vulnerability is ethically dubious. Indeed, when defensive backs recommended the rules be redesigned to give more protection to receivers, such protections were added. Recently the NFL has renewed its efforts to promote player safety.[33]

Our discussion so far suggests that football can be (although not always is) played without players intending to harm opponents. It is often difficult to draw the line between the defensible and indefensible uses of physical force in contact sports, although the VP may represent a useful first step in that direction. Perhaps football can be criticized because violence is too prevalent in the sport or because the use of physical force creates too much risk of injury for the players, but it does seem to be true that unlike boxing, the nature of football is not violent.

Concluding Comments

We have seen that sport raises a host of significant ethical issues. At its best, sport is a stimulating challenge to mind and body; at its worst, it can be a joyless endeavor in which losing is equated with being a failure as a person and winning becomes just a means to egoistic self-posturing over others.

But our discussion also suggests that some values are so intimately connected with a desire to compete in sport that they form an inner morality. We can learn to value activities for their own sake, apart from any extrinsic reward they provide, and learn to appreciate the contributions of others, even when we are on opposing sides. We can also learn to overcome adversity, apply ourselves, and appreciate excellence and the relevance of internal goods. Through sport we can develop and express moral virtues and demonstrate the importance of dedication, integrity, fairness, and courage. Undoubtedly, the values at the core of the inner morality of sport as well as other values that sport typically illustrates and perhaps reinforces are of enduring human significance.

Consequently, sport presupposes the importance of standards, including standards of excellent play and standards of appropriate conduct. Whether or not we accept some version of the ethic of the mutual quest for excellence, some moral standard is needed to distinguish sport as it should be conducted from degradations of the sporting ethic. These standards can be arrived at and examined only through the kind of critical reflection that is characteristic of philosophic inquiry.

Moreover, if there are justified standards that really do distinguish aesthetically excellent from poor play as well as ethical from unethical behavior in sport, they provide reason for questioning many theorists' claim that all standards are merely subjective and arbitrary preferences simply reflecting our race, gender, socioeconomic status, religion, or cultural upbringing. Although what we learn surely arises from the particular social and historical perspective in which we find ourselves, whether our beliefs are justified is another question. Our discussion about sport suggests that the search for justified standards is not necessarily fruitless. Our particular positions at a given time may always be fallible and subject to criticism, but the claim that there are justified standards of excellence in play and in the ethics of playing indicates that the search for justifiable standards need not always be in vain.

We could do worse, then, than to conclude with the remarks of Socrates in Plato's *Republic*. Though he was talking about music and gymnastics, his comments may apply equally to creative activity in general and especially to sport: "There are two arts which I would say some god gave to mankind, music and gymnastics for . . . the love of knowledge in them—not for the soul and body incidentally, but for their harmonious adjustment."[34]

QUESTIONS FOR REVIEW

1. What does it mean that sport has an inner morality?
2. Can sport positively influence character development? Why?
3. What are the differences between the duties of coaches and those of spectators?
4. Should athletes and coaches be role models?
5. Why is boxing, unlike football, a violent sport? Do you agree that football is not necessarily a violent sport? In your view, are violent sports unethical?

Notes

1. Paul Hoch, *Rip Off the Big Game: The Exploitation of Sports by the Power Elite* (Garden City, NY: Doubleday, 1972), 22.

2. Not all philosophers find such appeal to versions of the so-called Paradox of Relativism convincing or conclusive. According to the paradox, relativists who assert that "there are no truths, only claims which hold within localized cultural, religious, or socioeconomic perspectives" are themselves making a claim, which is either true (thereby contradicting relativism) or itself relative to some particular perspective and, therefore, others need not accept it. But Marxists, for example, might seek to avoid the paradox by claiming that the

socioeconomic perspective from which they make their own claims is more developed and comprehensive than earlier, more parochial perspectives, that they have reached the point in history that comes closer to objectivity than ever before. But doesn't this strategy itself involve universal claims about which views are more comprehensive and developed than others that presuppose the possibility by comparing perspectives and making a judgment about them that purports to be objective?

Other thinkers might embrace the claim that their own assertions are themselves relative and context dependent but also claim that they make the best sense of the values inherent in that particular social setting; although critics might respond that such a claim, which purports to be an objective truth, goes well beyond what relativism allows. For an excellent discussion, see Simon Blackburn, *Truth: A Guide* (New York: Oxford University Press, 2005).

3. Many contemporary writers who try to retrieve ideas of worth from the general body of Marx's work need not be reductionists or relativists at all or accept the cruder deterministic aspects of some Marxist thought. For an example of such retrieval, see Richard Miller, "Marx's Legacy," in *The Blackwell Guide to Social and Political Philosophy*, ed. Robert L. Simon (Malden, MA: Blackwell, 2002), 131–153.

4. Drew A. Hyland, *Philosophy of Sport* (New York: Paragon House, 1990), 12.

5. See, for example, Nicholas Dixon, "A Critique of Violent Retaliation in Sport," *Journal of the Philosophy of Sport* 37, no. 1 (May 2010): 1–10.

6. Of course, various versions of utilitarianism or Kantian ethics based on respect for persons also can conflict with prevailing moral beliefs, such as, for example, in a tyranny or repressive theocracy. The internal morality of sport overlaps with elements of many philosophical ethical systems as well as ordinary moral thought. The notion of respect for the opponent, for example, expresses a form of the Kantian injunction never to treat other persons merely as means to one's own goals.

7. As we also pointed out in a note to Chapter 4, this corrects earlier remarks of Robert L. Simon that might have suggested that he thought the internal morality of sport was unique to sport. John Russell offered useful criticism of my earlier confusion in "Broad Internalism and the Moral Foundations of Sport," in *Ethics in Sport*, 2nd ed., ed. William Morgan (Champaign, IL: Human Kinetics Press, 2007), 51–66.

Perhaps, however, if we give up the uniqueness claim, we run into the problem of triviality. As Mark Andrew Holowchak acutely pointed out in "Review of *Fair Play, The Ethics of Sport*, 2nd ed.," *Journal of the Philosophy of Sport* 31 (2004): 247, "the internal morality of sport is just the inner morality of all properly run social practices." Although we do not have space for a full response here, we would note that because of its visibility, accessibility, and emphasis on fair play, excellence, and challenge, the inner morality of sport, although not unique, pragmatically is, at least potentially, of special social and educational significance.

8. For a discussion of the obligation of educational institutions to be neutral and nonpartisan, see Robert L. Simon, *Neutrality and the Academic Ethic* (Lanham, MD: Rowman and Littlefield, 1994).

9. Thus, Carol Gilligan, in her book *In a Different Voice: Psychological Theory and Women's Development* (Cambridge, MA: Harvard University Press, 1982), argued that emphasis on impartiality and universality in ethics expresses a moral perspective more associated with males than with females in our society. The implications of a female-oriented approach to ethics is usefully explored by Virginia Held in her "Non-Contractual Society: A Feminist View," *Canadian Journal of Philosophy*, supplementary 13 (1987): 111–137, and more recently in her "Feminism and Political Theory," in *The Blackwell Guide to Social and Political Philosophy*, ed. Robert L. Simon (Malden, MA: Blackwell, 2002), 154–176.

10. For a defense of a "core values" approach to moral education along these lines, see William J. Bennett and George Sher, "Moral Education and Indoctrination," *Journal of Philosophy* 79, no. 11 (November 1982): 665–677.

11. Drew A. Hyland, "*Paidia* and *Paideia*: The Educational Power of Athletics," *Journal of Intercollegiate Sport* 1 (2008): 66.

12. Ibid., 66–71.

13. Cesar R. Torres and Peter F. Hager, "Competition, Ethics, and Coaching Youth," in *The Ethics of Coaching Sports: Moral, Social, and Legal Issues*, ed. Robert L. Simon (Boulder, CO: Westview Press, 2013), 179.

14. Ibid.

15. Ibid., 181.

16. For a variety of perspectives on ethical issues that arise in coaching, see Simon, *The Ethics of Coaching Sports*. A very useful discussion of ethical dilemmas that may arise in coaching is found in Jeffrey P. Fry, "Coaching a Kingdom of Ends," *Journal of the Philosophy of Sport* 27, no. 1 (May 2000): 51–62.

17. See Nicholas Dixon, "The Ethics of Supporting Sports Teams," *Journal of Applied Philosophy* 18, no. 2 (2001): 149–158.

18. J. S. Russell, "The Ideal Fan or Good Fans?" *Sport, Ethics and Philosophy* 6, no. 1 (February 2012): 28.

19. Ibid., 27.

20. Dixon, "The Ethics of Supporting Sports Teams," 149.

21. Ibid., 153.

22. Must athletes *willingly* accept such benefits? What if an athlete does not want to be regarded as exhibiting moral virtues? Our own view is that because good sport has an inner morality of its own, athletes who consent to participate and who try to be good competitors are freely committing to the virtues outlined in the text.

23. For this view, see, for example, Stephen Mumford, *Watching Sport: Aesthetics, Ethics and Emotion* (London: Routledge, 2012), 99–109.

24. Ibid., 109.

25. Joyce Carol Oates, *On Boxing* (Garden City, NY: Dolphin/Doubleday, 1987), 49.

26. Ibid., 93.

27. For further discussion, see Paul Davis, "Ethical Issues in Boxing," *Journal of the Philosophy of Sport* 20–21 (1993–1994): 51.

28. The *New York Times* has an online section on "Head Injuries in Football" with news, commentaries, and archival articles. See http://topics.nytimes.com/top/reference/timestopics/subjects/f/football/head_injuries/index.html.

29. Franklin Foer and Chris Hughes, "Barack Obama Is Not Pleased: The President on His Enemies, the Media, and the Future of Football," *New Republic*, January 27, 2013, www.newrepublic.com/article/112190/obama-interview-2013-sit-down-president.

30. Jack Tatum, with Bill Kushner, *They Call Me Assassin* (New York: Everest House, 1979), 12.

31. Ibid., 176.

32. Hoch, *Rip Off the Big Game*, 22.

33. See, for example, Sam Farmer, "NFL Rules Changes Take Effect, with Greater Player Safety a Goal," *Los Angeles Times*, September 4, 2013, http://articles.latimes.com/2013/sep/04/sports/la-sp-nfl-rule-changes-20130905.

34. Plato, *Republic*, Bk. 3, l. 412.

Index